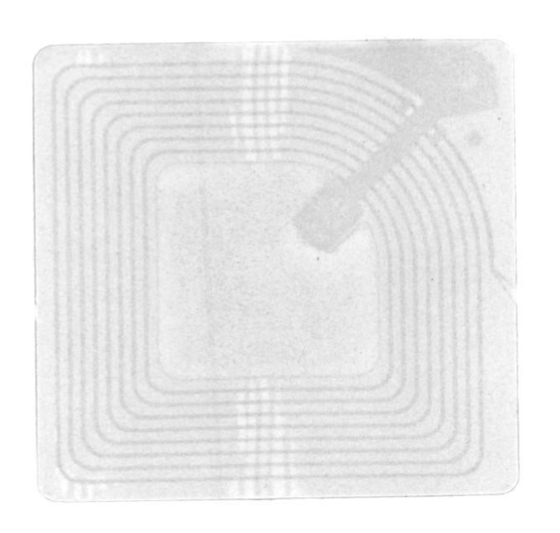

GWEITHIAU MORGAN LLWYD O WYNEDD

Cyfrol III

Deare friend 11.438 147 12th m. 58.

you write no Hebrew to mee (as you say you do)
nor shall this bee Arabick to you. you writt
lately to mee when I was not able to crawle in
the streets for many weeks nor go a bow shoot
off my bed (I shall not now tell the cause of
that bodily weaknesse lest some canot beare it)
I say then you writt to mee that it was a venerable
thing for mee to come to southwales, where I
would haue come (had I beene able) to visit that
my one owne friend as if my other alien friends
had all mett in one. But though you (it seemes) &
others bee not satisfyed, every one shall haue
praise of God when all is cleared vp. In the
while If any bite behind ones back, its seasonable
to thinke that our lord is no blind or deafe lord
Hee knoweth all. our consciences know a little, &
I doubt my great old friend knowes little of my present
condition. for you list to looke on mee through
a false glasse. If it were otherwise, you would
find mee one line at least of some particular
vnsoundnesse in my doctrine or books which you
call volumes, though they all will not amount
to the bulke of an ordinary booke. & so they may
bee accounted of: And if no particulars bee mentioned but generalls (& dolus in vniversalibus)
it may prove Gospell-grace to leave off the
backbiting in letters to others, or otherwise
in discourses to traduce any. I will as willingly
recant an error as publikely as euer I
deliuered it, if first it bee an error indeed &
so proued to mee. I could but note your change
of Doctrine. One while (the first blessed while
to mee & many more, for which I euer praise God
& honour you in him) the doctrine of the new
birth from phil 2.12. Joh. 3.3. Another while to
Antinomy in your house which relieued Sinners
out of Deut 8. And for my changes in opinion

Llythyr 80 yn y gyfrol hon. (NLW 11438D, f. 1)
(Trwy garedigrwydd Llyfrgell Genedlaethol Cymru)

GWEITHIAU MORGAN LLWYD O WYNEDD

Cyfrol III

golygwyd gan

J. GRAHAM JONES

a

GORONWY WYN OWEN

ynghyd â
Nodiadau a Rhagymadrodd
gan

R. TUDUR JONES

CAERDYDD
GWASG PRIFYSGOL CYMRU
1994

ISBN 0–7083–1136–9

Mae cofnod catalogio'r gyfrol hon ar gael gan y Llyfrgell Brydeinig

Cyhoeddwyd ar ran Bwrdd Gwybodau Celtaidd, Prifysgol Cymru

Cysodwyd ac argraffwyd yng Nghymru gan Uned Argraffu Llyfrgell Genedlaethol Cymru

Cynnwys

		Tud.
RHAGYMADRODD		ix
BARDDONIAETH		
1	Salm 19	2
2	Salm 37	3
3	Salm 44	6
4	Salm 45	7
5	Salm 46	8
6	Salm 120	10
7	Salm 121	11
8	Salm 122	12
9	Salm 126	13
10	Salm 103	15
11	Emyn Saesneg yn ôl Caniad Solomon 2	16
12	Emyn Saesneg yn ôl Eseia 53	18
13	Penillion Saesneg, 'The Lord hath scattered . . . '	19
14	Penillion Saesneg, 'Lamentations on the 9th month 1655'	20
RHYDDIAITH GYMRAEG		23
15	Ymddiddan rhwng Henwr a Phlentyn	24
16	Y Llyfr Bychan	27
17	Dim iw henw y Llyfr	31
Y BYWYD CYHOEDDUS		33
18	Llythyr at Syr Thomas Myddleton	34
19	Brwydr Maidstone	36
20	Cyfiawnhau'r Fyddin a'r Senedd	38
21	Dychanu Gwŷr y Senedd	45
22	Annerch Saint Caer	47
23	Llywodraeth Cromwell	53
24	Word for God	57
25	Nodiadau ar y Word for God	66

26 The Humble Representation and Address . . . 69
27 Sylwadau ar The Humble Representation and Address gan Vavasor Powell a'i gyfeillion 78
28 Gwŷr y Bumed Frenhiniaeth 80

BRIWSION CYMRAEG A SAESNEG 83

29 Dirgelion y Galon 84
30 Sylwadau Beiblaidd 86
31 Ysbrydion yn Abertawe 90
32 Esgyrn Pregeth 91
33 Cyfarwyddiadau i Argraffydd 93
34 Trefn Llywodraeth 94
35 Rhai Cyfeiriadau 95

LLYTHYRAU 97

36 Ri[chard] Baxter at Morgan Llwyd, 10 Gorffennaf 1656 98
37 Ri[chard] Baxter at Morgan Llwyd, 31 Mawrth 1657 101
38 Hugh Courtney at Morgan Llwyd, 3 Ebrill 1649 106
39 William Erbery at Morgan Llwyd, heb ddyddiad 108
40 William Erbery at Eglwys Gynnull Wrecsam, heb ddyddiad 112
41 William Erbery at Morgan Llwyd, heb ddyddiad 113
42 William Erbery at Morgan Llwyd, Mai 1653 118
43 Philip Eyton at Morgan Llwyd, 22 Hydref 1656 121
44 Robert Hughes, o Westminster, at dderbynnydd dienw, 15 Mawrth 1659 123
45 Samuel Hughes, Abertawe, at dderbynnydd dienw, 3 Hydref 1656 124
46 Eglwys Henry Jessey yn Llundain at Morgan Llwyd, 10 Awst 1656 126
47 Henry Jones, Dulyn, at Morgan Llwyd, 23 Mai 1655 129
48 Cyrnol John Jones, Dulyn, at Morgan Llwyd, 9 Hydref 1651 131
49 Cyrnol John Jones, Dulyn, at Morgan Llwyd, 20 Mawrth 1652 134

50	Cyrnol John Jones, Dulyn, at Morgan Llwyd, 1 Mawrth 1652/3	136
51	Cyrnol John Jones, Dulyn, at Morgan Llwyd, 30 Awst 1653	138
52	Esther Jones at Morgan Llwyd, 19 Hydref 1655	140
53	[Esther Jones] at Morgan Llwyd yn Nyffryn Ardudwy, 25 Medi 1655	141
54	Holiadau i Gredinwyr Wrecsam gan James Parke	144
55	Vavasor Powell at Morgan Llwyd, 23 Ebrill 1657	146
56	Vavasor Powell at [Morgan Llwyd], 27 Mehefin 1659	148
57	Hugh Prichard at Morgan Llwyd, 1 Rhagfyr 1651	149
58	Hugh Prichard at Morgan Llwyd, 18 Rhagfyr 1651	151
59	Hugh Prichard at Morgan Llwyd, 17 Ionawr 1651/2	153
60	Hugh Prichard at Morgan Llwyd, heb ddyddiad	155
61	Hugh Prichard at Morgan Llwyd, 28 Rhagfyr 1652	158
62	Hugh Prichard at Morgan Llwyd, 1653	159
63	H[ugh] P[richard] at dderbynnydd dienw, 23 Mehefin 1654	160
64	P[hillip] Rogers at Morgan Llwyd, 23 Chwefror 1653/4	161
65	Phill[ip] Rogers at Morgan Llwyd, 24 Mawrth 1653/4	163
66	P[hillip] Rogers at Morgan Llwyd, 4 Mawrth 1654/5	164
67	P[eter] Sterry at Morgan Llwyd, Mehefin 1651	166
68	P[eter] S[terry] at Morgan Llwyd, 14 Ionawr 1651/2	167
69	[Peter Sterry] at Morgan Llwyd, 4 Gorffennaf 1652	170
70	Peter Sterry at Morgan Llwyd, 23 Gorffennaf 1654	173
71	Peter Sterry at Morgan Llwyd, 27 Medi 1656	175
72	[Peter Sterry] at Morgan Llwyd, heb ddyddiad	177
73	W[illiam] Rider a Walter Thimelton at Morgan Llwyd, 1 Chwefror 1652/3	181
74	Wal[ter] Thimelton a Will[iam] Rider at Morgan Llwyd, 16 Chwefror 1652/3	184
75	Wal[ter] Thimelton a W[illiam] R[ider] at Morgan Llwyd, 9 Mawrth 1653/4	186
76	W. T. o Chapellizard at Morgan Llwyd, 5 Hydref 1653	188
77	Morgan Llwyd at H[enry] Jessey, Gorffennaf 1656	189

78 Mor[gan] Lloyd [Llwyd] at Samuel Hartlib, 30 Hydref—Rhagfyr 1652 191
79 [Morgan Llwyd] at ohebydd dienw, heb ddyddiad 193
80 [Morgan Llwyd] at gyfaill dienw, heb ddyddiad 194
81 Morgan Llwyd at dderbynnydd dienw, heb ddyddiad 196
82 Cyrnol John Jones, Dulyn, at Mrs Lloyd, 24 Mawrth 1652/3 198
83 Cyrnol John Jones, Llundain, at [Mrs Lloyd], 28 Mai 1656 200
84 E. Herbert at [Mrs Morgan Lloyd?], 5 Mawrth 1658/9 201

ATODIAD A 203

Manion Barddonol a Nodiadau 204

ATODIAD B 211

Cerddi Dienw 212

MYNEGAI 217

Rhagymadrodd

Cyhoeddwyd y rhan gyntaf o gynhyrchion Morgan Llwyd yn *Gweithiau Morgan Llwyd o Wynedd* (Bangor, 1899), o dan olygyddiaeth Thomas E. Ellis. Golygwyd yr ail gyfrol gan J. H. Davies, gyda rhagymadrodd sylweddol, a'i chyhoeddi ym Mangor yn 1908. Fel y digwyddodd, nid oedd y gyfrol gyntaf yn cynnwys popeth a geid yn y llawysgrif a ddefnyddiai T. E. Ellis. Fe'u ceir, fodd bynnag yn llyfr E. Lewis Evans, *Morgan Llwyd* (Lerpwl, 1930), 4–5, 176–83, ond nid yn fanwl gywir fel y maent yn y llawysgrif. Ceir y llawysgrif honno yn Llyfrgell Tref Caerdydd, Llsgr. 1.6. Cyfrol nodiadau ydyw. Daeth i ddechrau o lyfrgell Syr Thomas Phillips (1792–1872), gŵr cefnog a roesai ei fryd ar gasglu llawysgrifau nes bod ganddo yn y diwedd tros 60,000 o eitemau. Yn 1895 prynwyd y llawysgrifau a oedd o ddiddordeb Cymreig gan Lyfrgell Tref Caerdydd ac yn eu plith yr oedd y gyfrol fechan hon o eiddo Morgan Llwyd. Daeth cyfle'n awr i gyhoeddi'r darnau nas ceir yn *Gweithiau Morgan Llwyd I.*

Ond daw'r rhan helaethaf o'r defnyddiau yr ydym yn eu cyhoeddi yma o gasgliad Plas Yolyn, Duddleston, Sir Amwythig, a sicrhawyd gan Lyfrgell Genedlaethol Cymru yn 1937. Cysylltiad teulu Cilhendre a Phlas Yolyn â John Jones, Maesygarnedd, a ddaeth â phethau Morgan Llwyd i'w meddiant. Yr oedd gan John Jones fab, yntau hefyd o'r enw John, a oroesodd ei dad. Ar aelwyd Morgan Llwyd ym Mrynyffynnon, Wrecsam, y magwyd y mab hwn ar ôl marwolaeth ei fam, Margaret, merch John Edwards, Stantsy, ar 19 Tachwedd 1651. Yr oedd cyfnither iddo'n briod â Thomas Edwards, Cilhendre, meddyg a fu farw yn 1668. Cymerai John Jones ddiddordeb hael ynddi a chymerodd brydles ar y tŷ ac yno y bu farw tua 1717. Ar ôl priodi John Morall, Plas Yolyn, aeth Judith, merch ac aeres Thomas Edwards, i'r plas i fyw a chwalwyd Cilhendre yn 1794. A thrwy'r cysylltiadau hyn y treiglodd y defnyddiau sydd â pherthynas â Morgan Llwyd i lyfrgell Plas Yolyn.

Casglwyd y defnyddiau hyn at ei gilydd ddeugain mlynedd yn ôl gan E. Lewis Evans gyda'r gobaith y gellid eu cyhoeddi fel trydedd gyfrol gweithiau Llwyd. Ceir copi o'r deipysgrif yn Llyfrgell Coleg Prifysgol Bangor – Llsgr. 3135. Methwyd â chael y moddion i'w hargraffu ar y pryd ac yn awr daeth cyfle i gywiro'r copi hwnnw yng ngoleuni'r llawysgrifau ac i wneud y defnyddiau'n fwy hwylus i ymchwilwyr.

Paratowyd y deunydd sydd yn y llawysgrifau gan Dr Goronwy Wyn Owen, Bethesda, a gynhwysodd y rhan fwyaf ohono fel atodiad i'w draethawd ymchwil, 'Astudiaeth Hanesyddol a Beirniadol o Weithiau Morgan Llwyd o Wynedd (1619–1659)' ar gyfer gradd Ph.D. Prifysgol Cymru, 1981, a chan J. Graham Jones, y Llyfrgell Genedlaethol.

Yr Athro Emeritws R. Geraint Gruffydd a minnau sy'n gyfrifol am y nodiadau. Diben y nodiadau yw arbed darllenwyr rhag y mân ymchwiliadau ynglŷn â phobl, lleoedd a digwyddiadau, a allai beri rhwystrau wrth ddarllen. Fel y gwelir oddi wrth absenoldeb nodiadau yma ac acw nid ydym wedi llwyddo bob tro i roi gwybodaeth am bobl y cyfeirir atynt. Bydd hynny'n gyfle i ymchwilwyr eraill gyfoethogi ein gwybodaeth. Yr ydym yn ddiolchgar i Dr Geoffrey F. Nuttall, ac i Archifydd Sir Amwythig, Archifydd Dinas Caer, Dirprwy Lyfrgellydd Prifysgol Sheffield, Llyfrgellydd Llyfrgell Dr Williams a Tom Roberts, Llyfrgell Coleg Bangor, am ein cynorthwyo. Cawsom oleuni gwerthfawr ar gysylltiadau Llwyd â Richard Baxter gan Dr Neil Keeble o Brifysgol Stirling a diolchwn iddo yntau.

Rhaid cydnabod fod y defnyddiau sydd yn y gyfrol hon yn amrywio'n fawr yn eu gwerth. Nid yw rhai pethau ond sgribliadau digon anodd i'w hesbonio. Ein tyb oedd fod Morgan Llwyd y fath o ddyn y mae pob dim a drawodd ar bapur yn werth ei ddiogelu. Dichon y bydd darganfyddiadau pellach yn y dyfodol yn bwrw goleuni hyd yn oed ar y briwsion hyn. Ar y llaw arall, y mae dogfennau yma sy'n mynd â ni yn agos at galon y gŵr. Mae hynny'n arbennig o wir am y llythyrau. Dangosant yn glir iawn pa mor gwmpasog oedd cylch ei gydnabod ac fel yr oedd yn ŵr hysbys i gynifer o bwysigion cyfnod yr oruchafiaeth Biwritanaidd. Gellir gweld pa mor wresog oedd ei ddiddordeb mewn llyfrau ac yn neilltuol gynhyrchion yr ysgrifenwyr 'ysbrydol', fel y gelwir hwy. Ceir aml fflach hefyd ar ei gyfrinachau personol. Er enghraifft, gellir ymdeimlo â'r digalondid hwnnw a'i blinai at ddiwedd ei yrfa, pwnc y mae J. H. Davies yn ei grybwyll at ddiwedd ei ragymadrodd i'r ail gyfrol o'i weithiau. Nid ydym yn ein nodiadau wedi cyffwrdd ag arwyddocâd y dogfennau fel cyfraniad at ddeall troeon a datblygiad syniadau Llwyd. Gadawn hynny i'w drafod gan bobl sy'n gyfarwydd â'r maes.

Dyma felly *Gweithiau Morgan Llwyd o Wynedd III.*

R. Tudur Jones

Barddoniaeth

1

Salm 19

(LLGC 11433B, f. 18)

Ps. 19

Y nefoedd uchel traethu wnant
   ogoniant Duw ir hollfyd
Datcuddio mae'r ffurfafen draw
— siwr waith ei ddwylaw hefyd.

Mynegi y mae dydd i ddydd
   ryw newydd oi ragluniaeth
Yr un wedd hefyd nos i nos
— Sy'n dangos oi wybodaeth.

Nid oes dan haul na mor na thir
   nas clywir ei hymadrodd
ei llais drwy'r byd yn myned sydd
— ai swn drwy'r gwledydd cerddodd.

2

Salm 37

(LLGC 11433B, ff. 17ᵛ—17)

Ond Duw a drŷ ei cleddyf nhwy
  i fyned drwy ei calon
fe ddryllia hefyd ei bwâu
— ai gwaedlyd arfau creulon.

gwell iw'r ychydig o dda'r byd
  sydd gan ddyn diwyd duwiol
na chyfoeth mawr y ddayar hon
— sy'n eiddo dynion bydol.

Caiff nerth y dynion drwg wanhau
  ei breichiau oll a dorrir
ond drwy yr arglwydd mawr ai waith
— y perffaith a gynhelir.

Mae Duw'n adnabod yn dda iawn
  holl ddyddiau unïawn ufydd
ai hetifeddiaeth hyfryd frŷ
— a berŷ yn dragywydd.

Pan fytho adfyd yn y tir
  fe gedwir y ffyddloniaid
yn amser newyn nhwy gant fyw
— fe bortha Duw ei henaid.

Ond Duw a gospa gar ei fron
  ei holl elynion diffaith
fel brasder wŷn diflannu wnant
— fel mwg nhwy ddiangant ymaith.

dwyn echwyn byth heb dalu'n ol
  a wna'r anuwiol diflas
ond llawn trugaredd yw'r gwr da
— yn rhwydd fe wna gymwynas.

Y rhai sy'n derbyn bendith Duw
  mewn hedd cant fyw a llwyddo
ond llei bo melldith Duw ai gas
— mae anras iw diwreiddio.

Dyn da sy'n cael gan dduw bob tro
ei fforddio ar y gorau
a da iawn gan yr Arglwydd nef
— i ganfod ef ai lwybrau.

Os digwydd iddo ar un pryd
i fai neu adfyd gwympo
Codi a wna er mynd yn ol
— mae'r brauch tragwyddol dano.

Ieuangc a fum r'wyf hen mewn oed
erioed ni welais etto
mo dduw yn gadel un gwr da
— nai blant am fara'n begio.

trugarog iw fo rhyd y dydd a thosturiol fydd
— yn rhwydd fe rydd fenthygion
ir rhai anghenus rhyd y wlad
— a bydd iw hâd fendithion.

Ymad ar drwg edifarha
daioni gwna or diwedd
ag di gei lwyddiant ddydd a nos
— ag aros mewn tangnefedd.

Am fod Duw'n caru barn a gwir
fe gedwir byth ei seinctiau
Ni ad ef monynt, nhwy gant fyw
— er amled yw ei beiau.

Ond hâd gweithredwyr drwg o'r tir
destrywir gidai tadau
ar cyfiawn a feddianna'r wlad
— hwynthwy ai had y piau.

Tafod y cyfiawn peraidd da
a draetha yr uniondeb
Oi enau fel o ffynnon bur
— daw cysur a doethineb.

Cyfraith ei dduw sydd ddydd a nos
yn aros yn ei galon
Ni lithra byth moi gamrau chwaith
— or llwybrau perffaith union.

Y gwr anuwiol gwilio wna
i ddifa y dyn cyfion
odfa iw ladd a gair bob pryd
— mor waedlyd iw ei galon.

Ni rydd yr Arglwydd byth moi blant
iw feddiant iw dinistrio
er barnu'r gwirion gwan yn rhwydd
— fe ddadleu'r Arglwydd drosto.

Ymddiried i dduw byth drwy ffydd
ai lwybrau bydd iw canlyn
cei feddiant teg mewn clod a hedd
— cei weled diwedd drygddyn.

Mi welais ddrygddyn o flaen barn
yn gadarn yn ei wreiddiau
yn frigog ag yn uchel iawn
— fel lawryf llawn canghennau.

Er hyn i gid diflannu wnaeth
yn ebrwydd f'aeth oddiyno
Nid oedd ef mwy o fewn y byd
— er ym i ddiwyd geisio.

Ond edrych ar wr perffaith da
ystyria'r uniawn hefyd
canys iw heppil fe fydd hedd
— caiff yntau ddiwedd hyfryd.

Ond gwyr anuwiol cyn bo hir
ddestrywir gidai gilydd
ac heppil ar ei hol ni bydd
— ei diwedd fydd anedwydd.

Mae'r iechydwriaeth oddiwrth dduw
ir rhai sy'n byw yn gyfion
fe iw ei nerth oi blaen ai hol
— ynghanol eu trallodion.

A Duw a weryd dynion da
ai cadw wna rhag niwed
fe ai hamddiffyn ar bob tro
— am iddynt iddo 'mddiried.

3

Salm 44

(LLGC 11433B, f. 18[v])

Duw clywsom son am danat ti
ein tadau ni an dysgent
gan adrodd dy holl wrthiau gynt
— iw plant ei hynt a draethent.

Cans nid ei nerth ai brauch ei hun
nid cleddau'r un o honynt
a roes y wlad ir rhain yn rhodd
— ag ai henillodd iddynt.

4

Salm 45

(LLGC 11433B, f. 20v)

Ps. 45

Fy-nghalon sydd yn gwneuthur can
  ir brenin glan mawr hynod
berwi yr wyf am tafod sydd
— fel pin sgrifennydd parod.

tecach na holl blant Adda wyd
  gras a dywalldwyd arnat
am hyn Duw ith fendithio sydd
— ai wyneb fydd tuag attat.

gwisg ar dy glun dy gleddyf barn
ryfelwr cadarn

5

Salm 46

(LLGC 11433B, f. 20)

Ps. 46

Duw iw ein noddfa ni an nerth
   an cymorth prydferth parod
mae'n hawdd ei gael mewn diwrnod du
— in helpu yn ein trallod.

am hyn be siglai'r ddayar gron
   nid ofnai nghalon ronyn
er symud bryniau mawr ir mor
— nid rhagor fydd fy nychryn.

er bygwth or mor foddi'r wlad
   er maint iw rhuad dyfroedd
er ir mynyddoedd mawr wanhau
— rhag ofn holl donnau'r moroedd.

mae afon wych yn ninas duw
   purloyw yw hon ag araf
ai dyfroedd sydd yn llawnhau
— holl demlau y Goruchaf.

yr Arglwydd yn ei chanol sydd
   ei ddinas fydd ddiysgog
Feddaw iw helpu ar y wawr
— a chymorth mawr galluog.

Cenhedloedd yn terfyscu sydd
   a gwledydd a gynhyrfodd
Fe roddodd Duw lef oddifry
— ar ddayar obry boddodd.

Arglwydd y lluoedd byth wrth raid
   sydd ar ein plaid yn taro
Duw Iago i ni sydd dwr da
— a diangfa i ymguddio.

i weled gwrthiau dowch yn rhwydd
   a gwaith yr Arglwydd tirion
y modd y gwnaeth y byd ai medd
— yn anghyfanedd ddigon.

Efe a fyn ddistewi'r floedd
   rhyfeloedd a ostegir
y bwa torrir ar ffon frau
— ar holl gerbydau llosgir.

Am hyn gwybyddwch mai fi'n awr
   iw'r Arglwydd mawr digymar
mi fynnaf foliant ymhob gwlad
— a chodiad ar y ddayar.

Arglwydd y lluoedd byth wrth raid sydd & &

6

Salm 120

(LLGC 11433B, f. 21ᵛ)

gwae fi fy mod yn aros cyd
   ym Mesech enbyd dwyllgar
ag yn presswylio amser maith
— ym mhebyll diffaith Cedar.

gida rhai na fyn hedd oi bodd
   hir iawn y trigodd fy enaid
tra fawn i'n son am heddwch mwy
— rhyfelant hwy yn danbaid.

7

Salm 121

(LLGC 11433B, f. 21v)

Ps. 121

Derchafu wnaf drwy ffydd wrth raid
fy llygaid ir mynyddoedd
or lle i daw im help mewn pryd
— mewn adfyd a blinderoedd.

Fy help mi wn a ddaw yn rhwydd
oddiwrth Yr Arglwydd Hawddgar
yr hwn drwy waith ei ddwylaw ef
a greawdd nef a dayar.

dy droed i lithro byth ni ad
dy geidwad fydd heb huno
ac wele geidwad Israel lan
— heb hun na heppian arno.

Efe ath gynnal tra foch byw
Jehofah yw dy geidwad   achubydd
oi gariad hefyd fe fyn fod
— yn gysgod i ti'n wastad   beunydd

yr haul liw dydd nith dery di
nar nos mo oerni lleuad
ni ddaw yt niwed nos na dydd
— yr Arglwydd fydd dy geidwad.

8

Salm 122

(LLGC 11433B, ff. 21—1v)

Ps. 122

Mi lawenheais yn hyfryd iawn
   pan ddwedent awn i Sion
pan faent yn son am fynd yn rhwydd
— i dy fy Arglwydd tirion.

Ein traed yn awr y rhai fu cyd
   yn tramwy rhyd ffyrdd cystydd
attad Caersal. cyrchu wnant
— oth fewn i safant beynydd.

Caersalem olau ein dinas ni
   ei sail sydd ynddi ei hunan
ai phlant sydd ynddi yn gytun
— a Duw ei hun ai drigfan

Yno i cyrcha'r llwythau'n rhwydd
   daw llwythau'r Arglwydd yno
i roddi diolch i dduw nghyd
— yn unfryd i weddio.

cans gorseddfeingciau yno sydd
   ty Dafydd ein rheolwr
dymunwch heddwch ein tref ni
   gweddiwch drosti'n nerthol
llwyddo a gaiff y sawl ath gar
   Caersalem hawddgar nefol

O fewn dy gaerau heddwch boed
   ith lysoedd doed yr hawddfyd

er mwyn fy mrodyr mae'r arch hon
   am cymdogion nesaf
Er mwyn tŷ Duw sydd ynot ti
— byth dy ddaioni ceisiaf.

9

Salm 126

(LLGC 11433B, f. 21)

Ps. 126

Pan ddygodd Duw yn ol iw gwlad
drachefn gaethgludiad Sion
rhyfeddu wnaem yn llawen iawn
— fel rhai fai'n llawn breuddwydion.

Ni ganwn gan a chalon rwydd
ar galon canem glod yn rhwydd
ir Arglwydd am ei wrthiau
Ein genau oedd yn llawn oi glod
— an tafod oi ganiadau.

yna fe ddwedei gwyr y wlad
wrth siarad gidai gilydd
fe wnaeth duw'r dynion waith mawr
— i ddwyn hwy'n awr oi cystydd.

gwaith mawr yr arglwydd iw'r gwaith hwn
ni allwn ni ond cyffesu
a hyfryd ydym gar ei fron
— mae'n calon yn llawenu.

O dychwel Arglwydd etto'n ol
Yn nerthol ein caethiwed
fel yr afonydd sy'n dyfrhau
— ag yn y dehau'n cerdded.

y rhai mewn dagrau sydd yn hau
yn llawn gofidiau trymion
fe ddaw cynhauaf medi gant
— mewn llawen foliant calon.

y rhai dan wylo aeth or wlad
fel taflu had ir ddayar
a ddont ai yscubau gidan nhwy
— ni welant mwy mor galar.

Byddai'n syndod pe na bai Llwyd yn adleisio *Salmau Cân* Edmwnd Prys gan eu bod ill dau'n mydryddu'r un testun Beiblaidd. Ond ceir mwy nag adleisio yma ac acw. Mae Salm 121, pennill 3, yn atgynhyrchu Prys, ar wahân i ychydig fanion. Yn Salm 122, pennill 3, yr unig gyfnewidiadau gan Llwyd yw rhoi 'olau' yn lle 'lân' Prys, a 'phlant' yn lle 'phobl'. Yn yr un Salm, mae'r geiriau rhwng 'O fewn dy gaerau' a 'cymdogion' yn union fel gan Prys. Mae'r cwpled cyntaf ym mhennill olaf Salm 126 yn dilyn Prys, ond fod Llwyd yn gosod y geiriau 'i'r ddaear' yn lle 'rhŷd gryniau'.

10
Salm 103

(LLGC 11433B, f.11)

The lord is Kind & mercifull
   when sinners do him grieve
the slowest to conceive a wrath
   and readiest to forgive.

He chides us not continually
   though we be full of strife
nor keeps our faults in memory
   for all our sinfull life.

nor yet according to our sins
   the lord doth us regard
and after our iniquityes
   he doth not us reward.

11

Emyn Saesneg yn ôl Caniad Solomon 2

(LLGC 11433B, ff. 13–14)

Some verses of Cant. 2

As in the pleasant Sharon rose
   and lillyes of the fields
So is our lord among his saincts
   and great refreshings yields.

As is the lilly faire and tall
   compared with the thorne
on earth so is the church of christ
   that from above is borne

As is the fruitfull Apple tree
   among the barren trees
so Christ excells all other men
   by thousands of degrees.

Under his shaddow wee sitt downe
   in safety with delight
his fruits are sweet unto our tast
   his words are good and right.

Into his banquett house through grace
   he brought mee lovingly
and over mee his banner spread
   of loving kindnesse high.

Stay mee with flaggons of thy love
   with apples comfort mee
for I am faintly still and weake
   and sicke of love to thee.

Under my head is his left hand
   his right hand mee imbrace
he commeth skipping over hills
   to show my soule his face.

My lord unto my soule Thus spake
Rise up and follow mee
the winter raine and storms are gone
the summer visitts thee.

The flowers appeare the birds they sing
the fig tree doth rejoyce
the vine putt forth their tender grapes
rise love obey my voice.

The foxes take, the foxes small
that spoyle the fruitfull vine
for now the vine hath tender grapes
that yield most pleasant wine.

My Christ (much longed for) is mine
and doubtlesse I am his
hees lovely all there is in him
not any thing amisse.

My love among the lillyes feed
untill the breake of day
when light in stead of Darkn. comes
and shaddowes flee away.

O lord beloved of my soule
turns now about to mee
and like a roe come that my soule
may ever bee with thee.

Mae rhai o'r penillion uchod yn E. Lewis Evans, *Morgan Llwyd* (Lerpwl, 1930), 176–8. Dyma'r drefn y maent ynddo: 3, 4, 6, 8, 9, 1, 2, 7, 10, 13 ac mae 5, 11 a 12 yn absennol. O lawysgrif 'Welsh Poems', 2, yn Llyfrgell Rydd Caerdydd y mae ef wedi codi'r gân. Yn *Gweithiau Morgan Llwyd I* (Bangor, 1899), 10–11 ceir fersiŵn wahanol o bennill 3 a cheir penillion 11 a 12 fel y maent yma. Nid yw penillion 1, 2 a 6 yn *Gweithiau Morgan Llwyd I.*

12

Emyn Saesneg yn ôl Eseia 53

The father of light and love and life
his only son sent downe
The arme of God, that root of sts.,
that plant of great renowne.

A man despised in this world
A man of sorrowes deepe
A man acquainted with our griefe,
that doth us love & keepe.

Our woes & griefs and burdens all,
upon himselfe he tooke
Our peace to make our sores to heale,
he freely undertooke.

Our trespasses mett all on him,
to prison he was cast
and being God as well as man,
hee conquered all at last.

He both delight to see his seed,
for whom he travailed for.
Who with His father do ascend
to raigne for evermore.

His love exceeds, his might is great
his kingd. shall remaine
Our souls to pitty he hath learnt,
he'le visitt us againe.

Our hearts lord quicken thee to love,
& pleasing praise to sing
Our sins destroy, our soules embrace,
& rule us as our king.

Bring downe high things, the meeke exalt,
thy face let sion see
Make way through all for thy renowne
& ever with us bee.

Ar wahân i rai amrywiadau yn y sillafu, ceir yr emyn hwn yn E. Lewis Evans, op.cit, 178–9, wedi ei godi o 'Welsh Poems', 2, Llyfrgell Rydd Caerdydd.

13

Penillion Saesneg, 'The Lord hath scattered . . .'

(LLGC 11433B, f. 12v)

The lord hath scattered wicked men
Stretched out once more his arme
He surely is against those men
that wish his people harme.

Our man of warre, he is not changd
Hee'le ever faithfull bee
He hath deliverd and hee will
and make us fully free.

Men will bee strugling with thy saincts
a greater fall, they'le have
Grant that thy saincts wth valour may
and trueth themselves behave.

Open their eyes yet more & more
thy trueth & love to see
In both unite them, make them strong,
Our God for ever bee.

14

Penillion Saesneg, 'Lamentations on the 9th month 1655'

(LLGC Chirk A4, 31–4)

Morgan Lloyds Lamentations on the 9th month 1655.

1 Soe songs will not attended bee
soe sottish and crafty wise are wee
noe losse of friendes, or change of times
doe make us feel our soules or crimes

2 wee are past verses past reprofe
cold as a stone wee stand aloofe
the saints alive must not reprove
when they are dead wee doe not move

3 natures assertions some put off
and with hard witty hearts they scoffe
wee see our neighbours fall to dust
this doth not mortifie our lust

4 wee stand hard by the gaping grave
yet for the world a mouth wee have
butt for the heaven wee hunger not
what verse or prose can cut this knotte

5 To utter manie wordes are vaine
and to bee silent is not gaine
whether wee speake or silent bee
nothing effects to make us free.

6 Nor life nor death doth better make
impressions doth not us awake
our hearts are gresy slighting all
our spirits feare not sinne nor fall

7 In Babilon wee grope about
as birds in chages gett not out
wee wander in a desart great
backslide wee doe, but not retreat

8 Good men goe downe to graves and rest
our mindes these p.vidences wrest
In graves of earth our hearts remaine
but in our woes wee feele noe paine

9 Why doe I writte or speake or singe?
what good doe these expressions bringe
Surely some good soules will awake
and to the Lord themselves betake

10 Such will abound in love to god
and find his will, and kisse his rod
as Sions stronge as eagles swift
these shall attaine the heavenly gift

11 These doe attaine the spottles loves
the feet of hindes the eyes of Doves
the turtles voyce the blessed call
the — Center of the creatures all

12 But woe is mee I am in paine
I would have Babel heal'd againe
But Babel would not cured bee
Escape her then and let us flee

13 where shall wee flee? Wt shall wee say?
are wee the children of the day
wee walke but know not where wee goe
wee would doe good but evill wee doe

14 wee know wee sin and yett sin on
this our hearts loath to thinke upon
wee dye and yet wee would not dye
wee pray and yett wee cannot crye

15 wee would awake, but still wee sleepe
wee have playne hearts but sadly deepe
wee foes reprove, they are the same
wee friendes rebuke they minde theire fame

16 wee chide our selves to noe effect
wee purpose much, but still neglect
wee would buy time but sell it cheape
wee sow the winde and chaffe wee reape

17 wee read the scriptures yet are blinde
wee seecke the doore, but cannot finde
wee seeke amisse, yet cannot cease
wee are in paine yett still at ease

18 wee talke of newes our hearts are old
wee speake of zeale, but wee are cold
wee presse on love, where is it gone
and life but wee have almost none

19 wee crye out watch, but are secure
wee say bee cleane, but still improve
wee errors hate, but still unsound
wee bee free, yet still are bound

20 wee long for ordinances pure
but of pure hearts wee are not sure
wee censure others cuttingly
but spare our selves most cunningly

21 O Lord what wilt thou with us doe
where but to thee should these soules goe
thy love is deep, thy thoughts are high
in love deale with us woundrously

22 Thou countest things as If they were
thy counts create things everie where
Thou hast of nothing all things made
when thou withdrawest they all fade

23 our ragged righteousnesse wee see
naked, and wretched wormes are wee
Now lord reveale thy glorious sonne
for us, and in us bee it done

24 wee were in paine and brought fourth winde
Now Lord worke thou bringe fourth thy minde
thy hidden minde in hearts of men
for manie crye Lord say Amen

25 Now sonnes of Israel doe not gaze
nor stare in ont anothers face
There is bread in heaven goe downe and buy
ffor Christ our Joseph raignes on high.

Rhyddiaith Gymraeg

15

Ymddiddan rhwng Henwr a Phlentyn

(LLGC 11431B, ff. 1–2)

Hênwr fy anwyl blentyn mae'n dda genif weled dy wyneb di mor iraidd, mor hyddysg, mor hawddgar. Pa fodd yr wyti? Pa sût sydd ar dy gydwybod ath ysbryd di? Pa lewyrch o Dduw sydd yn dy feddwl di? Pa sawl cwlwm sydd yn dy resymau di na fedri di moi dattod dy hunan.

Plentyn Rwi'n diolch i ti fy nhad am hathro am fod yn wiw genit ymofyn am fy iechyd corphorol, a mwy am iechyd fy nghydwybod. Nid oes fawr or bobl yn ymofyn Pa fodd y mae yr enaid ar dyn oddifewn. Ag am gwlwmmau dyrus y meddwl, mae llawer o honynt na fedrafi moi dattod ym mherthen fynghalon fy hun.

Hênwr Pam y gelwi di fi Athro neu Dâd. Un iw dy Dad sef Duw. Un iw dy Athro sef Christ, i ddysgu i ti adnabod dy Dad. Dôd iddo fo yr holl ogoniant. Canys nid da neb o hono ei hunan ond Duw yn unig.

Plentyn Er hyny. Rwyfi yn edrych arnati fel un yn sefyll yn lle fy nhad am hathro nefol, fel ped fait ti yn enau iddo, neu yn udcorn, neu yn bin ysgrifennu rhwng ei fysedd ef ynghanol ei saith ysbryd ef, ond nad fel fo ei hunan. Am hyny rwi'n tybied y dylwn i anrhydeddu fy nhad ysbrydol, yr hwn iw Duw, am mam nefol, yr hon iw caersalem newydd drwy bwy bynnag y danfonont attaf.

Hênwr fy mhlentyn. Gochel addoli'r Creadur yn lle'r Creawdr, rhag i ti ddyfod yn fyrr o fonwes Duw ei hunan. Ag hefyd na ddibrisia mo Dduw mewn un creadur. Mae fo drwy bob peth yn llefaru wrthyti. Ond mae arnafi ofn nad wyti (fymhlentyn) etto yn adnabod yn iawn y Tad ar Fam nefol, er dy fod ti yn medru siarad yn ffraeth, heb nai gwybodaeth (ond odid) yn dy ben di nai parch nhwy chwaith yn dy galon. Ond pa fodd y dyscaist di y ffraethineb yma?

Plentyn Wrth fyfyrio, wrth wrando ag wrth ddarllain. yr wyfi yn ymestyn i gael gwybodaeth or da ar drwg, fel y gallwyf ddewis y da a gwrthod y drwg.

Hênwr Da yr wyti yn gwneuthur trwy na bŷch di yn bwytta o bren gwaharddedig gwybodaeth da a drwg. Ond cyn ymofyn ath di Pa feddyliau yr wyti yn i cnoi a pha fath bregethwyr yr wyti yn i gwrando. Gâd i mi wybod yn gyntaf pa lyfrau yr wyti yn i ddarllain yn y GymruAeg.

Plentyn Y Bibl sanctaidd yn gyntaf, ag yno yr Apocrypha yn nesaf, ar llyfrau mân yn fy iaith fy hun, sef, yr ymroddiad, ar Resolution, ar ymarfer, ar llwybr ar Carwr, ar drŷch ar cordiad, ar ymddiddan ar Deffyniad.
ar llythur ar waedd ar Arwydd.

Hênwr Beth a ddyscaist di or bibl yn benaf ô ddechrau Genesis hyd ddiwedd y Datcuddiad?

Plentyn Mae yn y Bibl ryw bethau anhawdd i deall. A rhyw bethau hefyd hawdd i cippio, ond anhawdd ei cadw ei credu ai canlyn. Nid wyfi yn deall agos ddim. Er bod Biblau yr awron yn aml. Mae, y rhan fwyaf yn darllain i Biblau drwy spectaclau heb wŷdr ynddynt, heb ysbryd y deall ynddynt, (fel y mae tyllau asgwrn pen dyn marw heb lygaid ynddynt). Am hynny mae pob pechadur marw yn deongli yr ysgrythur yn ol ei feddwl ei hun. Ond heb y meddwl nefol ni ellir deall pethau ysbrydol. ô Dangos di i mi Beth iw sŵm yr holl fibl.

Hênwr Sŵm y Bibl iw dangos tri pheth i ddyn, sef Beth iw dyn or cyntaf ir diwaethaf. yn ail Beth iw'r hollfyd yma or dechrau ir diwedd. yn drydydd Beth iw'r Drindod Ryfeddol cyn y dechreuad ag wedi'r diwedd. Dyma sŵm yr holl ysgythurau. Canys yn y Bibl yr wyti yn gweled anfesurol ogoniant Christ ag anfeidrol waeledd dyn hebddo ef. Ag yn canfod un meddwl yn ffrydio i lawer meddwl a llawer afon er hyny yn rhedeg ir un meddwl, ir un môr tragwyddol, a phob enaid dyn yn dychwelyd iw wreiddyn, naill ai drwy'r pechod ir digofaint i ddioddef gloes angau tragwyddol ai drwy'r cyfiawnder ir Cariad i gael bywyd anfarwol. Nid iw dyn yn wastad yn cofio diwedd ei daith, pob Gair, pob ymddygiad, pob gweithred, ie pob meddwl y naill gam ar ol y llall at Dduw neu oddiwrtho. Am am y Diofalwr ar gwatwarwr fe fydd pob pregeth ar a glywo, pob diwrnod ar a wario, pob cerpyn ar a wisgo, pob tŷ ar yr el iddo, pob dyn ar a welo, pob dim ar a ganfyddo, a phob llyfr ar a ddarllenno i gid ynghyd yn tystio yn i erbyn ddydd y farn. A rhag ofn i hyny ddigwydd i ti, fy mhlentyn. Mi fynwn wybod beth a ddyscaist oddiwrth y llyfrau a ddarllenaist.

Y 'llyfrau mân' y cyfeirir atynt gan 'Plentyn' yw:

Morgan Llwyd, *Yr Ymroddiad neu Bapuryn* (1657), gw. *Gweithiau Morgan Llwyd II* (Bangor, 1908), 5–44.

Robert Parsons (cyf. John Davies, Mallwyd), *Llyfr y Resolution* (Llundain, 1632).

Lewis Bayly (cyf. Rowland Vaughan), *Yr Ymarfer o Dduwioldeb* (Llundain, 1630).

Arthur Dent (cyf. Robert Llwyd), *Llwybr hyffordd yn cyfarwyddo yr anghyfarwydd i'r Nefoedd* (Llundain, 1630).

Oliver Thomas, *Car-wr y Cymru* (Llundain, 1630) neu *Car-wr y Cymru* (Llundain, 1631). Am argraffiad diplomatig gw. Merfyn Morgan, *Gweithiau Oliver Thomas ac Evan Roberts* (Caerdydd, 1981).

Oliver Thomas, *Carwr y Cymru. Yn anfon Tri o ddrychau ysprydol i dri math o bobl. . .* (*c.* 1647). Nid oes copi o'r argraffiad cyntaf wedi goroesi ond ceir y gwaith yn Stephen Hughes, *Tryssor i'r Cymru* (1677). Ceir trawsysgrif o'r argraffiad gwreiddiol yn LLGC 527A a chafodd ei adargraffu gan Merfyn Morgan, op. cit., 209–24.

Vavasor Powell, *Cordiad yr Scrythurau* (Llundain, 1653). Nid oes copi wedi goroesi, ond am y manylion gw. Eiluned Rees, *Libri Walliae* (Aberystwyth, 1987), rhif 4058.

Robert Holland, *Ymddiddan Tudur a Gronw* (*c.* 1595). Nid oes copi wedi goroesi, ond am rai manylion am yr ail argraffiad gw. Eiluned Rees, op. cit., rhif 2452.

John Jewel (cyf. Morris Kyffin), *Deffyniad Ffydd Eglwys Loegr* (Llundain, 1594).

Morgan Llwyd, *Llythur ir Cymru Cariadus* (1653?), gw. *Gweithiau Morgan Llwyd o Wynedd I,* 113–23.

Morgan Llwyd, *Gwaedd ynghymru yn wyneb Pob Cydwybod* (1653), gw. *Gweithiau Morgan Llwyd o Wynedd I,* 125–50.

Morgan Llwyd, *Dirgelwch I rai i'w Ddeall Ac i eraill iw Watwar, Sef Tri aderyn yn ymddiddan . . . neu Arwydd i Annerch y Cymru* (Llundain, 1653), gw. *Gweithiau Morgan Llwyd I,* 151–266.

16
Y Llyfr Bychan

(LLGC 11432D, f. 6)

Y llyfr bychan Dan y 6 sel
llais or 4 corn yr allor
rhyddhau 4 angel yn Euphrates
saith daran
mesur y deml
lladd a chodi y tystion
degfed or ddinas fawr yn cwympo
lladd 7000
y lleill yn ofni
Dangos y llyfr bychan yn agored

Phil. 2. 12. 13.
Beth sydd ynot yn gofyn, yn deall yn barnu, nef ag uffern y mhedr.

(LLGC 11432D, ff. 1–2)

1656. mis cyntaf. Ail.

1. Papuryn
y llyfr Bychan. Datcudd. 10 am yr hwn y mae'r papuryn hwn yn sôn mewn papur *ag inc. ond ym meddyliau rhifedi i mae yn agored.*

1: Mae un llyfr bychan, am yr hwn y mae'r yscythurau sanctaidd yn sôn llawer. Ag yn hwnnw y mae pob llyfr a phob peth yn scrifenedig o flaen Duw. yn hwnnw y mae tragwyddoldeb wedi rhoi ar lawr enwau, eneidiau, dynion ai holl feddyliau, ai geiriau ai gweithredoedd, ai dechrau (cyn dechrau'r byd) ai diwedd (ar ol darfod pob peth). yn hwn hefyd y mae'r Tri Trysordâi mawr yn sefyll yn agored, sef y nefoedd ar ddayar, ar môr a phob rhyw o beth ar sydd ynddynt, a naturiaeth pob rhyw Greadur; Mae'r llyfr yma yn llai nag un llyfr arall, a Dim = oll y gelwir ef, ond mae ynddo pob peth. Ni ddichon y RHYWBETH sydd ymmeddwl Dyn moi ddarllain. Canys i hwnnw Diddim iw. Am hyny y gelwir ef yn yr ysgythur sanctaidd, llyfr Bâchigyn. Bibliaridion.

2. Bara'r Bywyd iw'r Gwir DDim ir enaid sydd yn hiraethus am DDuw, Ond gwenwyn ir coegddyn (*doeth ynddo ei hunan*) iw'r ymresymmu

sydd yn canlyn rhwng y Dim ar Rhywbeth. Am hyny, cymer rybudd ymlaen llaw. Ag os wyt ti yn byw yn oferedd dy feddyliau Darllain yn gyntaf lyfr dy gydwybod, a gwêl mor erwin y mae tragwyddoldeb yno yn edrych arnat, cyn myned ymhellach yn y Gair dirgel yma. Onide, Diescus fyddi. Ni pherthyn hyn ir chwyddedig ond ir hwn a ddiddymwyd. Ag onid wyt mewn llawn frŷd ith wadu dy hun i ddilyn mab Duw ni wnei di ond eistedd ynghadair felldigedig y rhai sydd yn gwatwar y Gwirionedd: a serchu bod yn Rhywbeth nes i ti gael dy daflu i lawr i fod *yn waeth na Dim*. Ond os ydiw Duw (drwy ei ysbryd bendigedig) yn dy ddiddymmu di ynot dy hun dan Groes ysbrydol ei fab Iesu Ghrist, Darllen ymlaen y pethau a ysgrifennir mewn dwys feddwl, mewn dwfn olwg. Ag di a gei weled yn eglur Mai fel y gwnaeth Duw bob peth o ddim ynddo ei hunan, felly nad oes neb yn adnabod y Gwir DDuw ond y peth sydd Ddim drwy'r Ailenedigaeth, a bod pob dyn ar y sydd yn ymbalfalu am dano yn y Rhywbeth, (fel y gwna'r dall am y mûr ganol dydd) yn dyfod yn fyrr o orphwysdra y gwir DDuw hollalluog Bendigedig yn dragwyddol.

3. Saith udcorn sydd i seinio or dechrau ir diwedd. Ar llyfr yma sydd yn ymagoryd dan y chweched udcorn: Mae hwn yn felys fel mêl yngenau dealldwriaeth Dyn, ond chwerw iw ir bol ag i lygredigaeth y sawl ai canfyddo ag ai llyngco. Felly melys a chwerw iw. A llawer ai llyngc dan y chweched udcorn. Ag er hyny i gid, ni ddatcuddir mo holl ddirgelwch y Duwdod anfarwol nes ir seithfed Angel udcanu a chyhoeddi dydd y farn olaf.

4. Mae'r oes hon (1655 ag ymlaen) yn byw dan y chweched yr hwn sydd ofnadwy ag enbyd. A pheryglus iw'r tymmor yma, a llithrig iw'r amser, ag ar fôr o wydr tanllyd y rhodia llawer gan ddisgwil wrth DDuw am yr udcorn olaf i gyfodi'r meirw. Hyn sydd hysbys, fod y saith daran yn dangos ei llef yn y ddayaren mewn teyrnasoedd ag eneidiau dynion. Ag ni chlybuwyd mor rhain or blaen, canys nid oeddynt i leisio nes y dele y chweched, (ychydig bach o flaen yr olaf) Ag o flaen y Gair yma, sef Cyngor tragwyddol Duw, nid gwiw i neb geisio myned. ag nid diogel aros ar ei ol, na chamgymeryd chwaith y chweched am y seithfed. A darllenno Dealled. Edrych (o ddyn) yn iawn ar y peth a ysgrifennwyd yn y ddegfed or Datcuddiad; ag di a gei weled mai mawr iw'r peth y sonnir yma amdano.

5 Di elli ddeall a llyngcu y llyfr bychan hwnnw cyn dydd y farn olaf, tra fo'r chweched yn seinio. Ag mae'r saith udcorn yn y byd anweledig, yn eneidiau dynion i seinio mewn trefn ar ol ei gilydd ag ynot tithau. Am hyny Deffro mewn pryd yr awrhon, a deall yr amser ar enaid ynghyd. Nid opiniwn dyn ond cyngor Duw iw hyn. Yn llaw Angel y Cyfamod ar Enfys y mae'r llyfr yma iw gael. Gwaedda yn iawn am dano ag fe ai rhydd i ti. A phan ddarllennych hwn di a gei sicr weled Beth wyti a Christ, a Duw, ith ddiddymiant dy hun ag i foliant y Goruchaf.

6. Eisiau canfod a deall y llyfr hwnnw iw'r achos pam y mae cimaint o chwyddedig lyfrau yn y byd; a chimaint o ymrysonau ag ymddadlau. Cimaint o opiniwnau heresiau ag ymbleidiau. Cimaint o Dywyllwch o Dristwch ag o anwadalwch â helbul crefyddau lawer. Cimaint o ryfeloedd pobloedd a theyrnasoedd. Cimaint o gwyno ag o ymgyfreithio, cimaint o afiechyd cyrph ag aflendid dynion, a chimaint o siarad am dduwioldeb heb i hadnabod. Y cwbl oll sydd, eisiau deall y llyfr bachigyn hwnnw. Ag er a ddywetto dynion, y Drwg a berŷ nes cael y llyfr yma ai lyngcu, ag yno fe fydd hwn fel haul yn y nefoedd ir enaid ai meddianno,

7. Ond meddi di Pwy a ddichon . . .
Duw? Pwy sydd gynghorwr iddo? Wele . . .
a ddywedaist. Ni all meddwl dyn ei ha . . .
chael pethau Duw mwy nar ganwyll ddan . . .
ganol nos. Ond fe a ddichon ysbryd Duw . . .
adnabod y Cyfan. Ie, mae ysbryd Duw mewn
dŷnion . . . canfod Duw ai ogoniant yn ei
ddayar Ef ag yn chwilio dyfnion bethau Duw yn y nefoedd
(medd yr ysgythur) Canwyll Duw iw ysbryd dyn yn chwilio celloedd y bôl, a holl lygredigaeth di(wedd) dyn. A haul dyn iw ysbryd Duw yn chwilio ag yn
mwynhau dirgelwch Duw a thragwyddoldeb yn y . . .
ysbrydol sydd o flaen yr orseddfaingc.

8. Ond meddi eilwaith. Pa beth ydiw . . .
Beth sydd yn y llyfr hwnnw. Pa le y mae fo. Pa
lyfr ydiw fo. Beth a gŷst ef Pa fodd y . . .
i lyngcu fo. Beth a fydd pan agorer ef . . .
ef yn lyfr gan nad iw na phapur ag . . .
ledig ymysg dynion

This begun yt
night D. LL.
was in grave

9. Mi attebaf i ti mewn gwirionedd. Nid y byd nar ysgythur lân nar gydwybod lân . . . (fel y tybia rhai) iw'r llyfr yma. Gair tragwyddol anfesurol anweledig y Duwdod iw. A Drŷch yml . . . mann erioed. A bychan y gelwir ef (er i fod yn fwy) am mai bychan y mae yn cael ei gyfrif ymysg dynion ac yn meddyliau'r bobloedd. Ond y mae'r llyfr bachigyn yma yn fwy nar Gydwybod, yn fwy nar Bibl ag yn fwy nar holl fyd, ag ni chynhwysai'r byd mor geiriau sydd ynddo bei treuthid iddynt. Ie nid y byd nar bibl nar gydwybod iw, er bod rhai o lythrennau y llyfr yn y rhain ag ymhob creadur. Os mynni di fod yn ysgolhaig i Ghrist di elli fodloni Duw er na fedri na darllain nag ysgrifennu fel y byd.

10. Mae llyfr Bywyd ynoti dy hunan. Ag oni agori ef iw ddarllain ag iw ufyddhau, colledig fyddi. Mae'r haul tragwyddol yn disgleirio arnati ag ynoti. Os câr wyt ir Goleuni Darllen dy Hunan. Darllen (meddaf) y tair dalen ynot dy hun. Y ddalen gôch iw angau Christ drosot a thrwot ag ynot. Y ddalen ddû iw dy angau ar uffern sydd raid ith gnawd fynd drwyddynt. Y ddalen wen iw'r bywyd na all dim i frîthio. A Dim iw hyn ir meddwl cnawdol. Ag oni chanfyddi Ghrist yn ysbryd dy galon, ni elli moi weled yn unlle arall.

'yt night D.LL. was in grave'. Yr oedd Daniel Lloyd yn aelod yn Eglwys Annibynnol Wrecsam. Ei enw ef sy'n dod gyntaf ymhlith y rhai o'r fro a lofnododd yr anerchiad yn llongyfarch Oliver Cromwell ar ôl buddugoliaeth Caerwrangon, 3 Medi 1651. Fe'i cyhoeddwyd yn *The Diurnall,* 10 Tachwedd 1651. Yr oedd Lloyd yn un o gomisiynwyr Deddf Taenu'r Efengyl yng Nghymru ac yn drysorydd tros ogledd Cymru. Yr oedd yn un o ohebwyr y Cyrnol John Jones, Maesygarnedd. Yr oedd y beddargraff ar ei garreg fedd gerllaw fferm Pen-y-bryn yn Abenbury yn dweud, 'Here is asleep Daniel Lloyd, Servant of Jesus Christ, interred November 19th, 1655' (A. N. Palmer, *A History of the Older Nonconformity of Wrexham . . .* (Wrecsam, 1888), 30–1). Gan fod y ddogfen uchod wedi ei dyddio 2 Mawrth 1656, rhaid bod Llwyd eisoes wedi treulio tros dri mis yn myfyrio arni.

17

Dim iw Henw y Llyfr

(LLGC 11432D, ff. 3, 5)

(cf Gal. 6^3, 2^6.)

Dim iw henw y llyfr. Neu ymddadleu rhwng dim a rhywbeth. Neu yn hytrach y dim yn gorchfygu y rhwyb. ag yn mynd drwy bob peth.
Beth iw'r Byd ar hyn oedd cyn bod y byd (os gwyddost) a chyn bod ysbryd ag enaid a chorph.

llai na Dim iw'r hollfyd, ar hyn oll a gynhwysir ynddo. A mŵy nar hollfyd iw'r hyn oedd cyn dechreuad amser. Nid Dim ar a welir iw Duw. Nid Dim ar nas gwelir iw'r Byd. Mae Duw ynghûdd yn y byd oddiwrth y Byd. Tragwyddoldeb a greawdd ei ddelw. Mae Dyn yn canfod y ddelw, ond ni ddichon meddwl ddyn ei hun adnabod wyneb Tragwyddoldeb. Nid peth a wêl golwg dyn neu Angel iw Duw. Efe yn unig sydd yn amgyffred ei feddwl ewyllys ei hunan.

Onid allan o ewyllys Duw y gwnaed y byd? Ai Dim iw'r hollfyd! a phob peth sydd ynddo, yn enwedig ai Dim iw enaid ysbryd dyn?

llai na Dim iw'r byd, a Mwy na'r Byd iw ysbryd Dyn, ar cwbl sydd ynddo. Gwreichionen amser iw'r Byd, ond un o fflammiau tragwyddoldeb iw ysbryd dyn, i fod yn y golau tawel, neu yn y tywyllwch tanllyd byth.

Fe ddichon dyn weled yr hyn sydd a Bôd iddo? Ond pwy a welodd y Dim, or hwn y gwnaed yr hollfyd a phob peth ynddo?

Nid iw'r holl fyd yma o flaen Duw ond fel breuddwyd oth flaen di (ynoti) am hyny y mae yn ysgrifenedig. ô Arglwydd *pan ddihunech di* a ddibrisi ei delw hwynt.

Ond mae rheswm yn dangos, *Mai Dim o Ddim a Ddaw,* ag na all Dim wneuthur Dim ond bôd fel ped fai heb fôd.

Er hyny, Gwir iw'r Gair, ag yn haeddu pob derbyniad, wneuthur o DDuw bob peth o Ddim, neu or hyn ni wêl na llygad y cnawd na rheswm y meddwl. Ond mae mewn dyn ysbryd (a chanwyll pan oleuer hi yn y meddwl) a ddichon fyw yn y diddymiad a chanfod pob peth, fel Paul (Dim ydwyf, meddai ef) ag Esay (yr hwn a waeddai fe ddarfu amdanafi) Ag ebr Christ. Oni byddwch blant bychain ni ellwch fyned i mewn i deyrnas nefoedd na gweled ei Goleuni. Canys Rhywbeth tywyll gysgod iw holl naturiaeth a gwybodaeth da a drwg, oni thorrir drwy gwrs natur (yr hwn yw gogr oferedd) ni all dyn weled y goleuni.

Wele. Rhyfedd iawn iw hyn, na all dyn ddyfod i wybod dim yn iawn nes i fod ef iddo ei hunan yn Ddim. A fynnai Duw i ddyn amhwyllo ai anghofio ei hunan ai eiddo ai fatterion dayarol?

Os myn dyn ddyfod iddo ei hunan, rhaid iddo fyned allan o hono ei hunan, ai wadu ei hunan. Os amhwyllo yr wyf (medd Paul) i Dduw yr wyf om côf. Clogwyn iw hwn peryglus ir rhai sydd yn boddi mewn anobaith, ag i lawer myrddiwn o eneidiau sydd yn nythu yn ei rhesymau ei hunain. Ond rhaid iw yscwyd a siglo dyn allan o hono ei hun cyn i sefydlu yn Nuw. Anobaith a laddodd ei mil, a gobaith o anwybodaeth ei dengmil. Rhaid i ddyn ei anghofio ei hun a phob peth sydd ganddo, cyn iddo gofio Duw a gweled yr hyn sydd ynddo Ef; a gwadu'r cwbl, a thrîn y byd ai bethau fel pe bai heb i trin, ond yn farw iddynt.

Yr ymrafael ar ymryson ar ymofyn oedd rhwng Dau. Y Dim ar Diddim. Y Dim iw'r peth na ellir i weled, ar Diddim (neu y Rhywbeth) iw'r peth a ddichon golwg y corph neu lygad meddwl dyn i ganfod. Dyma'r Agoriad i ddatgloi yr hyn sydd yn neshau. Ond os synhwyrol wyti yn barod, na ddarllain air ymhellach, am fod dy Rŷwbeth di yn dy feddwl yn llyngcu dy ysbryd. Ag er bod canwyll yngwaelod dy gŷdwybod (fel rhyw lewŷrch mewn pwll diwaelod) oni ddiengaist oddiwrth sûgn (a nôs) y sêr ni wnei di ond cellwair dy enaid ir tân. Ond os suddaist drwy Groes Christ i wared allan oth feddwl dy hunan (gan wadu dy ewyllys ath synwyr dy hun) di a ddeelli yr hyn a ddywedir yma; a thrwy ddoethineb Duw yngwraidd y Galon di gei fwynhau'r bywyd.

Mae E. D. Jones yn dyddio'r ddogfen, Mawrth-Ebrill 1656, gw. 'The Plas Yolyn Collection of Morgan Llwyd's Papers', *Cylchgrawn Cymdeithas Hanes a Chofnodion Sir Feirionnydd*, III (1957–60), 286.

Y Bywyd Cyhoeddus

18
Llythyr at Syr Thomas Myddleton

(LLGC 11439D, f. 23)

A true copy of the letter sent to Sr. Thomas Myddelton by the Gentlmen that subscribe here under.

Noble Sr.

In pursuance of an order of the house of commons (A copy whereof is herein inclosed) wee have sent for Mr. Ambrose Mostyn and Mr. Morgan Lloyd both of them northwales men, and able to preach in the welch tongue. Of whose piety, zeale to Godlinesse and painfullnesse in the ministery wee have a large and undoubted testimonye. And finding them willing to expose themselves to any exigencies and inconveniences for the furthering of the cause of God and the good of their countrey we have thought fitt to send them to you, being assured (with Gods blessing) that their endeavours will much facilitate the difficult worke you have in hand of reducing that countrey to due obedience. And likewise wee do earnestly recomend them to your care for a competent subsistence respecting not only themselves but their wives and children who must live upon their paines & endeavours. There is an Ordinance prepared for the Houses whereby we hope to send downe more ministers unto you and to enable you with power to provide for them. But these two are all wee can yet find to bee fitt to send downe. Of whom we doubt not but you will have an answerable care. So commending your selfe and your great worke to the blessing of God.

wee rest
your Assured loving friends
to serve you.
John Glynn
Henry Herbert

John Trevor
Symon Thelwall
Stephen Marshall
Joseph Caryll

(1645?)

Am Syr Thomas Myddleton (1586–1667), y cadfridog tros ogledd Cymru ym myddin y Senedd, gw. *Bywg.*

Am John Glyn (1603–66), gw. *Bywg.*, s.n., 'Glyn (Teulu), Penarlag'.

Am Henry Herbert (1617–56), gw. *Bywg.*

Am Syr John Trevor (1626–72), gw. *Bywg.*, s.n., 'Trevor (Teulu), Trefalun'.

Ceir nodiadau bywgraffyddol ar y pedwar uchod hefyd yn W. R. Williams, *The Parliamentary History of the Principality of Wales* (Aberhonddu, 1895).

Am Stephen Marshall (1594?–1655), arweinydd Presbyteraidd, a Joseph Caryl (1602–73), gw. *DNB.* Yr oedd y ddau'n aelodau o Gymanfa Westminster a oedd ar y pryd yn gyfrifol am gymeradwyo pregethwyr. Gw. ymhellach, James Reid, *Memoirs of the Westminster Divines* (Cyfrol I, 1811; Cyfrol II, 1815; adargraffiad Banner of Truth Trust, 1982).

Am Ambrose Mostyn (1610–63), gw. *Cofiadur* (1962), 62–5.

Cyrnol Simon Thelwall, Plas-y-ward (1601–59?), comisiynwr Sir Ddinbych o dan Ddeddf y Gweinidogion Gwaradwyddus, 1642; Dirprwy-lifftenant Sir Ddinbych, 2 Gorffennaf 1646; AS 1640–8, 1654–5. Gw. W. R. Williams, op. cit., 73–4; J. E. Griffith, *Pedigrees of Anglesea and Carnarvonshire Families* (1914 a 1985), 274, lle mae rhyw ddryswch rhwng priodasau Simon a'i daid o'r un enw; Norman Tucker, *Denbighshire Officers in the Civil Wars* (Dinbych, dim dyddiad cyhoeddi), 135–7.

Yr oedd y Tŷ Cyffredin wedi penodi pwyllgor ym Mehefin neu Orffennaf 1644 i geisio pregethwyr Cymraeg eu hiaith i'w hanfon at Myddleton. Ar 20 Gorffennaf 1644 y gorchmynnwyd Mostyn, Llwyd a Vavasor Powell i fynd i Gymru a chadarnhawyd y gorchymyn, 7 Mehefin 1648, a dyna hefyd pryd y ceir y crybwylliad cyntaf am Bwyllgor y Gweinidogion Llwm yn talu iddynt. Am y cyfeiriadau gw. T. Richards, *A History of the Puritan Movement in Wales* (1920), 40, 65.

19

Brwydr Maidstone

(LLGC 11439D, f. 20)

fight at Maydstone

Sr

The ꝑticulars are too many to relate at this time concerning ye last nights engagement wth ye enemie at Maydstone wch in briefe was such as never was since ye war began, ye armie strugle with so much difficultie to overcome a strong & resolute enemie, ye fight began at 7 at night about a mile from Maydestone, & before we could beat ye enemie from hedge to hedge & get in at ye barracades it was nine & after we had enterd ye towne we disputed every street & turninges ye enemy had 8 pieces of ordinance wch discharged about 20 times when 8 men came into ye streetes & by gods mighty helps & assistance we overcame them between 12 & one at night being every minute of an houre firing upon them & they upon us it being extreame wett without during all that time, we took about 700 prisoners & some 400 horses, & or forlorne hope of horse gave the . . . standard of horse as gallant a charge as ever was seene which is said to be Genl Hales troope, ye reason why or army began so soone the traine & Reare being three miles off was the forlorne hope of horse & foot engaged in viewing the towne, the enemy being wth the whole body wthin 2 miles on the top of the hill towardes Porhester all day lying wthin view of or armie about 8000 men who as they perceived we did not dispute the passage at Allyford which would have bin difficult for us to have done they sent in a supply of 1200 men into Maydstone who came in just as we engaged being seamen apprentices & most of the Commanders in ye Kings armye there were in all 200 slaine in & about the towne Capt. Price a gallant honest man & Coll Hewsons Capt: Lt were slaine and about 30 of men most of them fell at the mouth of the Canon & wth Case shott we took 8 peeces of ordnance 6 iron & 2 brasse wth abundance of armes having bin up all night & want of time cannot enlarge only I desire god to let you see how the old quarrell is renewed by the same partie with greater violence than at first you will shortly have royal Earles Lords & others of quality appeared in this busines. his excell: From first minute of engagement to the last could not be drawne from his personall & hazardous attendance in this service & is much impaired in his health

Maydstone June 2 4 . . . 6 in the morning.

Pan ddechreuodd yr ail Ryfel Cartref gyda gwrthryfeloedd yn ne Cymru a Chaint, anfonwyd y Cadfridog Thomas Fairfax i ostegu'r cynnwrf yng Nghaint. Yr oedd y Brenhinwyr wedi crynhoi eu milwyr o amgylch Maidstone, gyda 3,000 yn y dref ei hunan, a rhagor — tua 7,000 ohonynt — yn aros eu cyfle ar y bryniau cyfagos. Cychwynnodd Fairfax ei ymosodiad am saith yn yr hwyr ar 1 Mehefin 1648. Fel y dywed y ddogfen hon, sy'n cytuno â'r adroddiadau swyddogol meddiannwyd Maidstone tua hanner nos. Am y manylion, gw. S. R. Gardiner, *History of the Great Civil War 1642–1649* (Llundain, 1891), III, 382–9.

'Allyford' yw Aylesford lle'r oedd rhyw fil o filwyr y Brenin wedi eu gosod.

'his excell' yw Thomas Fairfax (1612–71), pencadfridog byddin y Senedd. Am ei yrfa, gw. *DNB*.

20
Cyfiawnhau'r Fyddin a'r Senedd

(LLGC 11434B, ff. 1–4)

Among Severall late transactions in England there . . . that offend weake stomakes, and lye undigested in the consciences . . . & inconsiderate, & may proove noisome & dangerous to them. They . . .

1. The late action of the Army upon severall members of Parliament, am . . .
2. The Parliament's prosecutions to the beheadinge of the late Kinge . . . And since both appeare vindicable by Scripture & reason, this unskillfull pen is bold to touch paper in these matters, which though they be past & done yet the offence remaines which every peaceable hand should endeavour to remoove.
   First; It grieves us (say some) to astonishment, to see how the Army hath opposed the ordinaunce of God, which is the supreame lawfull Authority of the land in Parliament. They have forcibly secluded severall members and did keepe out and lett in whom they pleased. Answer: First.

1. The maior part and number in Parliament ought not in all Cases whatsoever to bee accounted the power that is of god. God doth not bind his people in Rom 13:1 to yeeld obedience to the private lusts or wills of one man or 400 in authority; but to that power which is of God. And that Scripture speakes onely of ordinary cases (as then of Submission to Nero and the like) and not of extraordinary, as shal bee prooved after. They yt hold the Contrary must conclude.
1. That the Parliament of England did very factiously sinne in sendinge a letter to encourage the well affected in Scottland to combine against their owne Hambltonian Parliament. In which letter they did over and above teach the upright in England how to deale with the English Parliament in case that Court did fall to the same Scottish vertigo or fallinge sicknesse who were since accordingly attended by the Army, who as they were invited by a melior Part in Parliament to doe what they did, and well encouraged from God in heaven and Saintes on Earth. Soe were they warranted and directed by that notable letter how to use a sicke Parliament in their distracted fitt wherein they enioyed not themselves.
2. Such tenents condemne the Practice of Argiule & the best in Scott Land who when Cromwell came to them (and befoure) were in actuall armes against those who did what they did by vertue and Authority

from that Parliament. and its hoped that some in Scotland will still sticke to their principles of reason and religion and Adore Gods providence with us.

3. That Commaund (follow not amultitude to doe evill) is properly directed to Magistrates Exod. 23:2: And yt they may doe no more in extraordinary cases but enter their dissent one giddy youth in the house may by his superfluous vote undoe a land, Contrary to all sense reason nature, or common rules of Safety.
4. This opinion (now almost up in Armes) among men doth justifye the same . . . power in the entrusted Parliament which they themselves condemned . . . King & cavalierish counsellors, and soe wee face about & retreat to the . . . and strong holes which they could not maintaine by the war . . . ssity (rightly expounded) is a supreame Law. Soe the London ministers . . . (and theareby, they pull downe at once their owne buildinge) . . . apparent necessity not onely the Letter of the law of the land . . . law of god may well bee dispensed with. Its true wee must not . . . that the greatest good may come. But wee must know first what sin is war absolutely unlawfull (unlesse necessity interposed) for David to eat the Show bread (whats: no bread but that to bee had) and yet our Lord Justifyed yt action as also his accused disciples for eateinge the ears of others mens Corne on the Sabboth and an oxe (much more a nation) in the ditch must bee helped out on that holy day. Away then with Pharisaicall glosses upon Scripture. Goe and learne that God will have mercy (as also Justice) & not sacrifice. And who doubts but that if a Generall of an army prooves treacherous (yea and many of his councell too) but that the souldiery may fight it out with the enemy & not suffer themselves to bee trampled on by them. The Souldiery saved worthy Jonathan from Saul his anointed father though he had covenaunted his Death. And shall the Army be blamed for interposeinge to turne off imminent ruine from a good people, or your friends be frowned upon, that seeke to quench the fire that was a Consumeinge your houses.

(O yee Saintes bee not unthankefull)

ob. But who Shall Judge of necessity? Ans. 1. The most part of men are not all ways the most sensible, and they that sitt at sterne see not (perhaps) as much as they that trimme the Sayles. 2 David and Christ Disciples & Sauls Souldiers were then the Sole Judges of that necessity. 3. Devine Providence is the great decider of this point. The wayes in the deepe and great waters are called his wayes. 4. You blesse god and others curse him for that the Army refused to disband by pieecemeales though the Parliament required it. God Intended thereby better things for you than some trustees did. You cannot

forgett how the many Insurrections in Wales, Kent, Essex, London the North etc. were by means of that Army quashed to admiration, & the heeler of those drunken revolters suddenly tript up and the sword of the Lord and of Gideon made terrible. Many of your selves doe thankefully Acknowledge and blesse god that the Army then refused to disband (the finger of god and a divine arme was seene in it) Is yt Action vindicable for which you praise god, then is also this of giveinge a purge to the Parliament by the same rule.
David would have made Keylah good against Saul if the men thereof had Stucke to him. Elisha made them about him to use the Kings messenger . . . chly to resist: Now if oppositions against sudden violence bee . . . lawfull why not against deliberate violence allso?
In this action of the Army they did not resist the power that is of . . . remoove some rotten pillars that endangered the whole building . . .

ob. But they kept out some good and kept in some badd members. Ans: . . . men on earth went in a way to undoe themselves, friends and kingdom. they should be checkt for it, for their sin (being good men) is the more sinfull & their example more winneinge and warrantinge others with their votes to ruine a Kingdome. 2. Some called Independents were a while kept out by the Army, and many Presbiterians were desired to withdraw but for a little while. they might returne if they would. 3. Who can in reason expect that they should in such a straight . . . a haire and doe all things orderly, did they know all? Certainely it is better somethinge bee irregularely done (as to the letter) than all of us undone. In a confused battell though some friends bee wounded by one another (through mistake) and some foes escape cuttinge, yet if the day bee well turnd and the maine Worke done wee count it a mercy. The second grand offence is the beheadinge of the Kinge at which some weepe, some reioyce, some tremble, some praise god, some Curse him, some are astonished, ob: And some much offended in Conscience for (say they) wee have covenaunted with god to preserve his sacred person? Ans: What without any Condition att all, though he should persist in destroyinge England pursue the bloody warre, while he could hurt mens lives in field and garrisons, and though he manifested noe repentance, have you with that mind, Considerately taken that clause in the Covenaunt?

2. You never vowed to preserve his person otherwise than in the preservation of the true religion, which you covenaunt there to doe as also his authority in the defence of the Kingdomes Libertyes & not otherwise.
   Why should the covenaunts wheeles be thus sett one against another or this nationall watch bee put out of order.
3. Though he would not take the covenaunt you would have had him to receive the benefitt of that agreement which he would not himselfe lay

hold on. A: Wee beleeved when the warres began that he was onely seduced by Evill Councellers, and not a seducer himselfe, but the Contrary was of late apparent, hee owned all that was done by the Sons of Belial. Now if god repents of the good he Intended, to a Kinge or Kingdome . . . they are marred on the wheeles Jere. 18. Is it not lawfull . . . Parliament to repent of their Intent of Confirminge the . . . Implacable Enemy.
. . . before god in your Covenaunt that you would bring all delinquents ((without) exception of any) to Condigne punishment. Was not the late King Delinquent in Chiefe? & was not death the Condigne punishment? . . . Either the Parliament or hee deserved to dye the death who caused three hundreds thousands poore soules in three Kingdomes to bee woefully destroyed. The guilt & fault must needs be somewhere and Either or both guilty of a very high treason.

ob. But hee might have prisoner all his lifetime Ans: I Did not you Covenaunt to reinthrone him and to be his loyall subiects and did you of late talke of Imprisoninge him.
2. How Satisfactory would that have beene of God, who sayth he that sheddeth mans bloode by man shall his bloode be shedd, & tooth for tooth must the magistrate require, though private persons are to forgive.
3. how safe would that Imprisonment have beene to the Kingdome, where in are millions of desperate men that would be ever & annon attemptinge a rescue, to the perpetuall care, charge, disturbance, trouble, danger and distraction of you and *the whole* land.

ob. hee was gods anointed, no man ought to have toucht him. Ans. Its true, that a private man should not kill a tyrant. But David was noe magistrate (note that) to execute present Justice on any then, When he spared Saul, but had gathered about him some friends to save him selfe from Cuttthroats. It doth not follow therefore that because a private man may not kill a traytour, the magistrate (that hath the Sword of god) may not doe Justice on him, but Parliaments have as well power over any Individuall Judge or person in the land as they have over Inferiour courts.
2. If hee as King was anointed, why not the Kinge of Fraunce etc. & all others, and then every Kinge may doe what he list and be accountable to none but to god. Then wellcome to the Cavilleers tents and quarters againe.
3. The powers of the Kings of Israel were not soe given and limitted by the people as ours were as appeares by their Coronation oath. (The) power is from god, but how much of that power Shall be putt . . . or men that is of humane Creation and left to the . . . discretion I Peet. 2:13.

ob. But what rule of the word was there for this Execution . . . (as terra incognita) is not searched (as it should) but by tu . . . fields are manured by the husbandman so) the industrious . . . age find out more profittably, the sense of the written word Kings Judges, and Esekiel, you shall find word and warrant enough . . . the blind woman complaine that the house is darke, the fault is in her eyes. See 2 Chron. 23:14:15. Joshua 11 17. Levir. 19. 15. 2 Cron. 25. 27, 2 Kings.
2. Neither monarchicall Aristocraticall, nor democraticall governement is absoultely commaunded of god to bee sett up in all nations, but what rule and regiment nations themselves shall by the light of nature and reason settle and establish, that the lord subscribed to and requires civell obedience.

The lawes of England have provided in this late Case but suppose noe law of the land did warrant this act, the Judgment of the Parliament is above law for it is the ground, and efficient cause of law, & the Cause must bee more substantiall than the effect.

ob. But the Kinge was not permitted to speake. Ans. When did ever any Courts of Justice suffer a prisoner at the barre to dispute their Authority the lawes of reason and nations abhorre it, for then Courts of Judicature should doe nothinge Else but argue their power pro and Con with their prisoners, beinge bound in Conscience & Equity to give satisfaction therein as well to the meanest as to the Chiefest priosners Especially if their lives weree in question.
Ob. But this was not a legall court entrusted by a free Parliament. Ans 1. Was not the Parliament free when they voted no more addresses to the King? how agreeable the proceedings of this Court have been to that vote and Parliament all may see
2. All the commons in Parliament have freely constituted this Court All exceptinge those that would not attend the house, when they might, or stand charged with high treason which treason the Army daily offers punctually to proove against them.

Now to Conclude As wee Cannot forgett the many Aceldamas wee have seene or heard of, the many townes and fields lately drowned with a flood of blood, As Bolton, Liverpoole, Chichester, Edgehill, Yorke, Nazby, Devices & many more Soe wee remember . . . prayed for King Charles, fasted, wrastled wept . . . hoped untill the Lord god himselfe took away that . . . prayer and hope from us.

It is true that Angell reioyce in sinners Just confusion (since god is thereby honoured) but more in their Conversion. And so should wee. Yea wee can appeale to god wee should have been farre more Joyed and Contented with the Kings publique ingenious repentance (if god had been pleased to give it) then with his death and sadd destruction.

Finally, as these matters here mentioned are now past, Soe it is desired that these few lines bee a warninge to all well affected that they stumble not at noone day lest they fall into a snare and bee found fighters against god, or at best indifferent and quiet as the inhabitants of Meroz; neither lett any envy or reproach poore Jael that did the Execution upon Sisera, let not Ephraim fall out with Gilead lest the worst bee yet behind, but since Judgment returnes to righteousness. Lett all the upright in heart follow it with speed and lett them say to god. O how unsearcheable are thy wayes. How Just are thy workes, how dreadfull is thy Justice how well sett are thy designes, how irresistable are thy purposes, how bright is thy soveraignty, how maiestick are thy frownes, how durable is thy raigne, and how happy are thy subiects in thee, Amen.

Si populus vult deci pi de piatur.

1. The law was ever above Kings
   and Christ above the law
   Unhappy Charles provoke the lambe
   to dust hee must withdraw.

2. Not his faire words but all his swords
   enragd by his commaund
   That sheathed themselves in Xtian hearts,
   should make you understand.

3. Looke not too much on few late things
   view all from first to last
   Since James his dayes, and wonder not
   that such a sentence past.

4. Though this pen loathes to touch dead Charles
   it warnes the livinge all
   Lest any stumble at his Courpse
   and breake their necks withall.

5. Make not O Kings your Curbs too sharp
   but truth & Justice seeke
   O land avoyd Kings evill now
   o Parliament bee meeke.

6. Thou Romish Church, that cursed witch
   the mother of our woe
that hast made Kings and Kingdomes too
   thy plagues to undergoe.

7. Shalt thou escape, thou bloody whores
   the ruine of this age
No, no: thy Judge, our lord comes on
   to teare thee in his rage.

8. Lord Jesus Come, and Come in hast
   for men and meanes doe fayle
Show thou thy will and meete thy friends
   and over all prevaile.

Er nad yw'r ddogfen wedi ei dyddio, mae'n perthyn i 1649. Mae'r traethawd a'r farddoniaeth yn yr un llawysgrifen a cheir y penillion hefyd yn *Gweithiau Morgan Llwyd I*, 55–6. Mae'n deg tybio mai Llwyd oedd awdur y traethawd.

21
Dychanu Gwŷr y Senedd

(LLGC 11439D, f. 21)

Ultimo insani Parlamenti

We the Comon Knaves of England asembled together almost . . . minde, for the utter Ruinating of this Church & state, for the . . . of gods ordnances in layinge violent hands on his anoynted & a . . . Episcopasy, but we or selves ordering & ordeyning whatsoever we t . . . Convenient for the mantayning of all sorts of Erors & Heresies, have, (Certaine intelegence) or guilty Consiene asuring us what we must . . . That k: Charles intendith to enter this Kingdome ere the last of this present march wth a Considerable Army for the Recovery of his Kingdome which we have unjustly detained from him, & to be Revenged on us for the most inhumane murder Comitted by us on his father, the aforesd we Traytors . . . of this Kingdome forseing that there is a just & sudden destruction coming upon us like a whirlewinde for the better Regulating or irregular desings, as in other Countrys soe in or (as yet) County of Montgomery & that & all other Countys wthin this Kingdome & in all the world may yett more palpably Convince us of perjury & villany & that all people may know we Concive ourselves lost men we doe order & ordaine both for or owne safety & for the good of all other or Brother Rebels wthin the said County of Mountgomery that all Gallows or Gibbetts be pulled downe by the 10th of this instant March. Further (tolle Capistandi) we doe order & ordayne that all halters ropes slips bedcords, & all flax hempe & hayre be carefully searched for & Burned by the hangman or undershirife by the time afore limeted And that no flax or Hempe be sowed wthin the sd County during or will & pleasure: And whereas it was intended that the great Sesions for the said County should be held the 18th of Aprill next, we doe order that the Sesions be defered untill the 28th of Aprill & or untill the 6 of Mayi & soe forward untill we have better leasure & wheras Capt. Nichols hath Raysed, raysed a Company for Irland we doe order the sayd Capt. to Remaine here in England for to asist us in or great danger & nesesty Quia nos vestigia terrent, omnia tradversi spectantia nulla retrorsu: Last of all we doe order or neere Commanders wth in the sayd Countye: to witt Vaughan of Tyrymuch the spidercacher & Jenkin the poole the shutledriver for to take special heed, that these or orders be carefuly observed desiring them in all ther Conventiles, but especialy when Capt Williams preacheth nere at Poole that they cause to be sung the Lamentation of us Siners.

For ye Knight
E. V. of the shire.

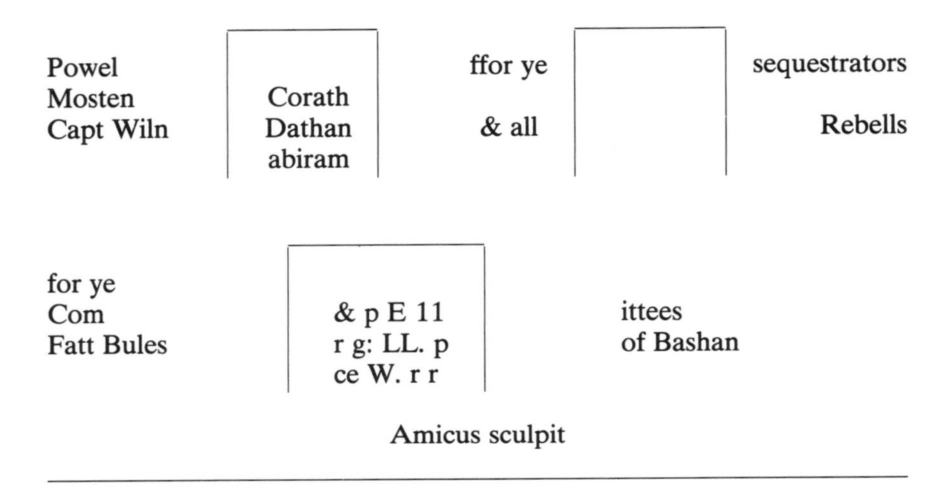

Am wrthryfel Abiram, Corath a Dathan yn erbyn Moses, gw. Numeri 16.

'Powel, Mosten, Capt Wiln' yw Vavasor Powell, Ambrose Mostyn a John Williams.

Am Powell, gw. *Bywg.*, ac R. Tudur Jones, *Vavasor Powell* (1971). Yr oedd John Williams yn un o gomisiynwyr y milisia ym Maesyfed, ac yn un o gomisiynwyr Deddf y Taenu. Clywn amdano'n gadael Sesiwn Chwarter Maesyfed ar un achlysur i wrando 'pregethau peryglus a bradwrus yn erbyn yr Amddiffynnwr' gan Forgan Llwyd (John Thurloe, *State Papers* II, 129). Bu'n pregethu o dan Ddeddf y Taenu; yn aelod o Senedd y Saint, 1653. Yr oedd yn henuriad yng nghynulleidfa Vavasor Powell ym Maesyfed ac un o gefnogwyr mwyaf brwd yr ymgyrch mewn cysylltiad â'r ddeiseb, *Gair Dros Dduw*. Symudodd yn ddiweddarach i Langollen. Bu farw Medi 1681 ac am helynt ei gladdu, gw. Philip Henry, *Diaries*, 305.

Bu Edward Vaughan yn gweithio fel cyfreithiwr o dan Ddeddf y Taenu. Bu'n AS tros Faldwyn, 6 Hydref 1647, ond yr oedd yn un o'r rhai a gollodd ei sedd o ganlyniad i 'Pride's Purge', 1648. Yr oedd yn gapten ym myddin y Senedd ac yn gomisiynydd tros ogledd Cymru fel atafaelwr. Bu'n AS wedyn tros Faldwyn, Ionawr hyd Ebrill 1659, a thrachefn o Ebrill 1661 hyd ei farw'n fuan wedyn. Llwydiarth oedd ei gartref ac yr oedd yn frawd i Syr Robert Vaughan. Gw. W. R. Williams, op. cit., 143.

Cydweithiwr Edward Vaughan oedd Thomas Nicholls, capten yn y fyddin Seneddol ac aelod o Henaduriaeth gyntaf Swydd Amwythig yn 1647.

Yr oedd Vaughan a Nicholls ymhlith y rhai a geisiodd amddiffyn enw da Vavasor Powell yn *Vavasoris Examen, & Purgamen* (1654), 13.

Crocbrenni ar gyfer yr atafaelwyr a'u ffrindiau sydd ar ddiwedd y ddogfen.

22
Annerch Saint Caer

(LLGC 11435D, ff. 1–4)

Wrexham 1651 25th day of the first Month

To the Heaven borne Children, beloved of God, called to bee saints pre-served in Christ, And reserved for perfection, now soiourning In West Chester, Morgan Lloyd wisheth trueth Love & peace wth power.

When I was last present in body with you it was your earnest desire, I might Listen to what was uttered Among you concerning Christ God head, And Accordingly I Attended and also declared Asillable of the truth (Without cunning insinuacōns) out of Micah the Prophett touching the Plurall goings forth of Jesus the Bethlemite. And being through the Grace of gôd unbyassed And sealed (as to my owne soule) In a saveing Assurance of the Mistery of the father And his only begotten son (which you knowe is (certainly) attainable on earth Coll. 2.2.) I am therefore bound and bould to write to yow briefly not knoweing when to see yor faces, the welsh harvest Being Large & our tyme in the shell of the flesh & Wombe of this Earth too short to spin out In thread bare divisions of words, or Quotatons of rusty Impertinent Authors (as some love to doe) But in The sight of the father and of his son & of his Angells I here testifie A word Concerning the being and life of the Glorious lord Jesus Christ.

And first I must reminde you that the roote & raigne of this great ould And yett new Controversye amonge you is As deepe as hell, And as high as heaven, And that teacher where is hee nowe on Earth yt can define describe & declare what the most high God is in himselfe What he was, what he did & what hee purposed (As being the only Inhabitant of Eternity) Surly that Expression now Among you the Most high God, was the best silver, but is Coyned & vended by Satans hands in many marketts, And lest the Dagon of selfe—Confidence gravity & Childish audacity (that sitts as Queene in many) should stand higher then is meet, or lest wee hazard our faith by useing our naturall ratiocinations, and also overcencure others (As if none should Enter into life but through the windowes of some particular narrow Judgmts) My brethren I must first Aske Some Questions: Who knoweth the son besids the father? the father is light love fire & spirit. Who can define him in these foure? How was the first Adam ye son of god? After what manner was his nature taken out of the Earth. After what manner of being had the Creature from eternity in Gods thoughts Who can tell (saith Job) Where wisdome dwelt? or how (God & Christ) wisdome & prudence (as Solomon saith) inhabited Eternally & Coequally together? Christ Was in the forme of god. what profitteth it to inquire into the Image of the forme, or forme of the Image? or to prye into the being of the spirit or spirit of the being,. And where is the Wise, the scribe or schcollerly disputer of this world that can Infallibly & fully define the lower three that beare witnes on Earth, or can demonstrate what bee his owne three, soule body And spirit, the smoake of his owne Chimney.

What man then with Eye of a vulture of a nominall shroller or reall Angell can diserne the three that testifie in from and Above the heavens, or who can bind that ocean in a Coat, or Gather ye Wind in his fist, or as much as take the Behemoth or Leviathan with A hooke. Where wert thou (saith god) When I layd the Earth upon Socketts & numbred the dust thereof, or who hath Asended or descended or is A Learned man indeed Besids the King of Glory. If by sense we understand not things naturall, howe shall wee by reason Containe things spirituall But not withstanding we may, ought, A must grow in the Knowledge & grace of the Lord Jesus, and though in some things our strength is to sitt still, yett must wee soberly walke in the Manifold Chambers & Galleryes of the Scriptures, Churches ordenances tempers, providences, Wheeles And motions of the Eternall spirit of the King of Saints. Who is refiner of reines, And decider of Controversyes. And yong men must not Eat of the shewbread unless their vessells be holly, And new wyne breakes old bottles. Now A word of ye fountaine. Now to the point in hand. The fountaine & father of lights, beings spirits mercies Comforts & glories, should (of right) bee Acknowledged by us & seene feared loved & worshipped as he is the Eternall serching unserchable only substantiall Being unmeasurable & unmixt in ye Universe (As the soule in the body, or pilott in A Shippe he only seeth seeketh subsisteth And Solaceth himselfe In himselfe alone obcerve then whatsoever is in this Ens of God is himselfe for Whatsoever is in this Essence is Infinite (for as is the Essence Soe must the Attributes bee) Now if the being of god be infinit And the wisdome Power & love of god be infinite also, Either Emty man must Corruptly Imagine there are two or more Infinites Which Cannot be because one infinite Concludes all other things or beings finite or Else build all upon this, that the wisdome love power etc. of god is himselfe which is the roote of the matter & indeede the highest & deepest truth, This same is internall Eternall wisdome And because a Word in the begining (as John witneseth) but not from Eternity unless men proove & descrye other worlds before this, for if Christ as the word hath been from Eternity, the worldly Creacōn (fashioned Instantly by the word) had been Eternall also, Which we know was breathed but from the begining though the word was in the /: begining Since which tyme we have in Moses & other Sacred subsequent scriptures the Chiefe mattrs Recorded, which nessesarily Concludes A Period of Created things And yet though or Lord was not eternall as the word, yet as the Liveing internall wisdome he is God coequall, Coessentiall and

Coeternall with the Prime and highest Being (whereof or soules Are the breath, or Grace the seed, As or head is the Essentiall mind And wisdome, which canot without deepe danger be severed from the Everlasting body) Now as the Infinite wisdome became A word hee was then Immediately Cloathed with an unknowne shape, wherein appeared a spirit which to blinded man kinde was a meere stranger. And in that Capacity hee Created all things, And is called ye first borne and begining of all. And though hee passed after through very Many formes & appearances yet hee retaines himselfe in all & all in himselfe & the use of all for & in us, as he is the unchangable Only Potentate & blessed god whome no Eye hath seene or can see in his God head. This eternall wisdome yt. in the begining because Word in the fullnes of tyme became flesh, which mistery what Angell to this day can unclaspe, And soe the Everlasting Graine of wheat must (in a sort) dye to give us a root & rise to bee for him & like him under the sun. But in our nature hee praied. What will god praye to god, yea, God himselfe is often said to advise And discourse with himselfe (and it was Christ duty being then the word as it were in the Sackcloth of the flesh, & now he is made A spirit, that is A body in lightning, searching, Comprizeing Ruleing, quickning & upholding all things, observe therefore the sume is that as WISDOME he is the fathers delight strength and Eternall Beeing As the word hee is his arme Instrumt And Manifestac̄on As manifested in the flesh, he was his Chiefe Ambassador to man kinde & the butt of the wrathfull Arrowes for mans sake (for Christ Crucified is the Large & blessed text) And now hee is A quickning spirit, hee is the wisdome & being of the father as he is the life & head of the Church, And the true understanding of these three (viz Christ mad Word flesh spirit) Is As the Eating the three loaves of life, that are Given to the Inportunate friends of the Bridegroome, Now if any wild asses Colt thinketh himselfe wise rationall or learned or Excellent lett him Answer the former Questions, or Else Acknowledge Christ in god to be the Eternall wisdome and only God. I need not quote to you the scripturall expressions I mention but this I leave As the lyne of them as Concerning Christ who is made word Made flesh, made spirit, but soe made as yt hee (in the great deepe, in the power of god) Made himselfe thus, and soe is God all sufficient. Now as the mistery of the father & the son was ye first Ecclipsed, soe it is the last restored. Those yt are Coheires with Christ in Joye power & glory shall feed thereon in love And liberty as Eagles on the Carcasse, but they beat the aire that houlds Christ as the word to be Eternall, and they allsoe run in vaine yt teach Christ as the wisdome of God to bee Att all a Creature, some know not where they Lead, others Consider not where they keepe the saints, God himselfe hath Layd stumbling blocks before ye feete of many, the Jewes also asigne, the Greekes looke for Learning. The Jewes reiected the King of glory, because their greenish short thoughts were fastned on him only as he was a Nazarite not knowing him as he was ye Bethlemite & (as it were) the Eternall howse of bread.

Diverse of the nominall Christians Crucifie his God head allsoe (to their perill) lookeing on him only (or as first Appearing As first borne) (which yett is as true as yt hee was a Nazarite) but consider not that Christ as the wisdome of God is his being & Inhabited Eternity, The Turke holds yt Moses was the servt Christ the breath & Mohomett the prophett of God, supposing (in their vanity) that Jewes, Christians, & Mohomettans shall At the Great Day be saved under their three banners & thus they Make the Narrowe way broad to their owne phantasines, And as upon the Doctrine of Arius came up the Turke pretending to moderate & unite all opinions of this Nature, so also will the Last Antichrist now flutter upon this point but all in vaine for the Ellect are secured, And oh that god would give us an understanding heart yt soe instead of bounsing the doores to gett in (out of the darke Entry) wee might skillfully use the key of knowledg and light of god & in yt Glass see all the lights and darkneses (the beings and vanityes) of the Creature the trueth as it is in Jessus the lawfull Magick & unlawfull phillosophy, the Anchor of hope, And the ship wracke of all Hymenean hippocrits I am what I am saith the Lord Jesus, hee is not the God of the dead. Hee that is wined to him by his Spirit is one Spirit in the seed & p. taker of the divine nature but not of the divine essence, our Care is not to Condemne in the twilight, what wil be Justified at noone day, But ther Is one plant that I would plucke up, there is one tree (and but one) that I would cutt downe. The roote of it is Atheisme the rine apretended perfection. the body thereof (is Idolized nature, the Juice of it is humane Corrupt reason, the leaves Swelling words, the branches naturall observacōns, the fruits uncleanesses and the End of that tree is burning and the Apostles are yett hewing it downe.

Now finally my Breathren I testifie & Exhort in the Lord. As being a wittnes (though the meanest) that you should not in flesh & bloud be desirious to see all the Chambers of the bottome of this sea (for many ducking downe but never Came up to air of the life againe) allsoe that you should not make your voices heard in the streetes instriveing for the Chaffe of words nor yett in A sinfull Contending about A graine of A trueth (as many now fight like larks) for one Graine of wheat soe as to neglect the blessed heape) The day Spring from on high is at hand, when knowledge shall Cover the Earth as the day light the Aire or waters the seas. When God himselfe shalbe seen as hee Is: when all the saints shalbe like god in Christ in Spirit soule And body And they shall know love & rejoice as they are knowne loved & rejoiced in, when death Sin Selfe hell Satan and Earthly Creation shalbe Swallowed up in victory. When all Natures shalbe Commanded into their severall prop. & Eternall Chambers though now they be mixt & Confounded & therefore they Groane to be in their Center.

But while wee stay for the vision that will not faile though it tarry, lett us take heede wee doe not (in thought) deflowre the Sun, the King &

wisdome of God, of his Eternall Glory. if God be a spirit lett us Converse with him spiritually (as ye spirits of the body doe with the soule) And yett know him more Who is invissible over through & in all, of whome allsoe through whome & to whome are all things, As he is light looke wee on him all wyaes As hee is fire Expect wee that or beloved drosse should bee Consumed by him, & because hee is love (which is In him free full firme Eminent & Eternall) let us alsoe hold fast to the practice of such a love with Calme peace, divine power & inward purity, for Envy strife variance hatred sadnes sournes bitternes & burning are . . . flowers of Satans poosy And death in the Seething pott of any Controversy, but love Joye Meekenes are the heavenly blossomes pleasing to god in the hand of Christ. Lett us mount up with the wings of Joye & Love, for the Spirit of prophecy seldome descended on the sorrowfull or fleshfull sons of the prophetts but on the Joyefull. The head must grow without ricketts When the hart growes sutable to itt, when the hand of faith the Eare of Conscience the breath of spirituall Groanings are exercised, then doth the inward Eye of spirituall understanding looke Aright into yt within the vaile And yt sight will metamorphize us into the same Image of glory As by the Lord the Spirit.

Therefore my breathren Adde to yor reasons faith to faith power to power love of all men, to love Brotherly Kindenes to all saints, lett A man honor his brother & suspect himselfe weare yor harts together as the twisted threads of the ould tabernacle, say not I can doe nothing, but rather I can doe all through Christ, for ye precepts are twisted with promises, As silver & Gould together, observe all Christ Ordenences, Meet oft together, divide not about words, yett studdy to use wholesome Expressions. Honor one more yt sitts on the foote stoole of faith (in this point) then many yt naturally aspire to the high beloved seate on the throne of reason. Rather admire the Beame then stare on the being of god, watch least old lusts have new resurrections Amonge you. The Lord can make us waity peeres & wee are all in his ballance.

I send this paper in some hast not for disputac̄ons but for satisfaction. And I desire you to trye & hold fast the Good, it is not good to read many Bookes: yett I advise you to studdy Eagle Eyed [John!] Prestons Banke or bottome last teachings of the beings & attributes of God (which as Ellias mantle are left behind) I request but two things of you, one is yt you would nowe further the worke & Churches of god in Wales by yor Earnast prayers of faith for us all.

The other that you Considr what I write if any should wronge or wrest these lynes, I may learne howe to be silent here after.

The peace and grace & power & trueth of the Lord Jesus (who was & is to come) be with you All Amen.

(Addendum)
To his Honoured friend
Mr John Whittell
Chester.
to be comunicat.

I adde & beseech you (my deare friends) that though the poore scribe bee but a very small shell and as hee often iudgethe the chiefe of sinners & least of saincts, yet lett this increase deare & mutuall love, lett us hold fast our confidence, and keepe close in churchship, & go not off that charriot but walke wth our lord in white in that Garden (for we live in spring) Honour your officers as the angells of God, notwithstanding the infirmity of their flesh. Be not wise in yr owne eyes. We are all either too rash or too raw. let us beare burdens mutually, & conquer evill wth good. You are a heavenly lantherne to a populous citty Shine ye then more publiquly in knowl. honesty & . . . & Avoyd the traps of your owne table & particular callings. And while you waite, worke & watch. And when wee mention one another to the father mind wee that he that commaunds heaven & earth hath said even to us concerning my sons & daughters comand ye mee. Bee we comanded by him. Jehovah is King lawgiver guide & that ocean of Being without Banke or bottome.

His face shine upon you in Chester & upon us in Wrexham. Amen.

To His Honoured friend Mr. John Wittell to bee comunicated to them that are taught of God in Chester.

23
Llywodraeth Cromwell

(LLGC 11436D, ff. 1ᵛ—1—3ᵛ)

12m. 15d. 55

A third post from North Wales
The 1. was called A. W. F. G.
2. the humble repres.
This 3.

I am ashamed as a man to discover the nakedn of Wales (which is also too much the same) amongst the English, Irish Scotts French dutch & & but as a Xtian I am glad that the lords day dawns so fast. so as sent to discover the frailties of good p' ple to thems, & to the world. I may no longer forbeare to speake a litle to the mûch writing & printing of friends in Wales, for & against one another. I am glad of the light not of the fire that is mother of it. These demure contentions are not good but necessary to this time & absolutely accessory to the nature some friends live wth. I must open a litle of my heart in this to all. When I saw & read the first paper called Word for God. I said the enemy was in it. I & that I durst not subscribe it, because it would increase vaine ianglings & endlesse sinfull unprofittable replyes, wherein most people are apt vainly to lett their time run their hearts run their heads tongues hands pens all run out from God (in a sieve of vanity) in scribbling agst one another & when death takes hold of them they shall (& I wish I may not my selfe) sadly thinke how satan couzened us of our time, interest & opportunity to do reall good. **As for me**. I never durst iustify this man called prot. in all his wheelings and undertakings nor myselfe, nor some others that are against him in all things. In whom also with him & mee as it appears to mee much flesh is manifest. There is it seemes one of my name (but not I) that subscribed that called The Word for God. If wee had indeed The Word of God it would be a word for God too. But the trueth is we know litle of the living word of God, nor of the living God though we boast & talke much of him. But though the earth bee broken into pieces & factious fractions do abound, yet I hope the grace of God in many will keepe off malice. It shall not come to *emnity* nor the egge hatch, neither is it wisdome for the late wise Animadversions to talke so much of war as they do, lest thereby war be rekindled. Many by inveighing against divisions iealousyes quarells heartburnings &&. have increased them while they spake. Thus wee feed upon the forbidden tree of the knowledge of Good in time of ioy & Peace. As we did & on the other side of the knowl. of sorrow & evill in time of Warre. But the tree of life in the midst of paradise & also in the midst of us & of this creation. we scarce tast of that & if wee do gett tast Its gone presently: yet this tree is in the midst of Gods garden & eternall life in the middle of us for us.

reproove Southwals also.

I find the p ple in Wales quartered & lodged into many chambers as Ezekiel sth too, (**sufficiently divided already** into the outward chamber) many in the outward court. Indep. anab. cavall. prot. & some papists & others called quakers who seeme at least to be more pure than the rest. And now Churchbrethr. divided. Elders in envy.

They grope for the wall as blind, & grope as if they had no eyes, they mourne it like doves & roare like bears. But we waite for the Sun of R. by whom we shall see now lightly. (But And as for mee I am neither for nor agt this pres. Gov. I am for & against it, so I am for my selfe but this I am for the Gov. only as its prepar to a better, & herein all honest men I hope will ioyne without more words.

Word to protr 2
Councill 3.

My fears (as man) are many.

That satan would cozen us of our time talents & souls by talking writing printing so much of present Govern. wch as aforesaid I hope on us on all hands granted to be but a prep. for a better

That a strangenesse & distance on that account may grow betweene lovers of Xt & one another.

That the Protectours ears being filled with many noises on both sides may possibly become deafe to the true voice of God.

That all sorts abound most in their owne sense & cannot here trueth from one another as they would have him hearken to them.

That while we consider the Revelat. of Xt wee either presume we understand the Apocalypticall times & seasons of 666. 1260 or else we excom. that booke too much out of our thoughts as too mysterious notionall & impertinent for us of this age.

I feare, also that the litle love that once appeared from God among many will waxe cold wth many, for the many iniquityes.

Also that the glorious varietyes of Gods gifts & enlightennys upon us all that makes saincts as a pleasant garden wth many flowers, shall disturbe the spirituall unity for the sake of carnall uniformity, as it doth all over England. Moreover, that a party studdy too much to please the protector & others as much to wring & vexe foorth his corruptions & neither live nor act therein by the true eternall spiritt of serious love.

That wee sinke & soake our soules into bad thoughts of one another, & then make no consc. of sclandering every one his brother behind his back cum privilegio.

ô that I had a place in the wildernesse or a cave in the desert within or without that I might not heare or see what I heare & see among many called christian saincts.

I feare not war that awakens the drowsy but lest the fuell & burning of fire should not bring foorth the Son of God & of peace in their hearts who have expected much.

I feare while we pray for prisoners (as we should bee in bonds wth them that are bound) we are at that instant in worse bonds & prisons of selfe & passions & preiudices wch wee are not aware of.

I feare many by this present sunshine of prosp. & honour under this Gover. strive *too much to gett gold silver & lands for them & heirs* (as they say) for ever.

I feare Ordinances & institutions so called will through mistake make many destructions of peace & power of Godlinesse tho they be good men.

I feare that while men scruple to act under this Gov. the devill will so overact them & the countreys under it that debaistnesse shall still abound, & the mouth of wickednesse be still unstopt.

I feare that many Justices so called & other officers behave themselves like beasts & devills in the land of uprightnesse.

I feare we do disowne all good in them called cavalliers & countenance too much evill in them of our opinions.

I feare. The present churches & parishes too are so wedded to theire former iudgements & now so consolidated therein that the spirituall coming of Christ will fall on us as a thiefe in the night & strip many of all their religious cloathings.

I feare. That whilst some are seeking to heale the nation their owne churches & their familyes too, yea & their owne poore soules are sicke unto death.

I feare. That when they discourse of young Charls & the prot. competition, there will thousands of soules fall unprepared into the Jawes of the King of herrours.

I feare many have not rightly made their wills at home while they love so much to make out their owne wills (not Gods) abroad.

I feare. The presb. will be so blind now at sunrising as to thinke the Geneva dispensation must yoake all our necks.

I feare. That the cavall. will be so obstinatly blind that they will be separatist from the wellaffected of the nation & being fed wth poyson among themselves in their priv. conventicls will fall to a rupture to the destruction of that sect.

I feare that the blind confident papists will be so foolish as to follow their wise Jesuiticall warners so far as to plunge their owne soules & states to an irrecouerable drowning in all Britt as a millstone cast into the sea.

'A. W. F. G.' yw *A Word for God.*

'the humble repres' yw *The Humble Representation and Address to His Highness Of several Churches & Christians in SOUTH-WALES, and MONMOUTHSHIRE. Presented Thursday January 31. London . . . MDCLVI,* 14 td, (dim dyddiad cyhoeddi). Ymddangosodd *A Word for God* mewn print yn Rhagfyr 1655 ac roedd 322 wedi ei lofnodi. Er bod y copi printiedig, fel y gwelir, yn dweud bod yr *Humble Representation* wedi ei gyflwyno ar 31 Ionawr 1657 yn ôl ein cyfrif ni heddiw, y mae gennym dystiolaeth gadarn John Thurloe (*State Papers* IV, 505) iddo gael ei gyflwyno gan Walter Cradoc ar 4 Chwefror 1655/6, sef 1656 yn ôl ein cyfrif ni. Ac yn sicr byddai'r deisebwyr yn awyddus i'w gyflwyno mor gynnar ag oedd yn ymarferol bosibl ar ôl cyhoeddi'r *A Word for God.*

Mae'r llawysgrif hon yn neilltuol bwysig am mai ynddi hi y mae Morgan Llwyd yn dweud ar ei ben na lofnododd *A Word for God.*

'into many chambers as Ezeciel sth too', gw. Eseciel 8. 7–16.

'Sun of R.', hy Sun of Righteousness, Malachi 4.2

'666', gw. Datguddiad 13, 17, 18, 'nod, neu enw y bwystfil . . . a'i rifedi ef yw, Chwe chant a thri ugain a chwech'.

'1260', gw. Datguddiad 12.6, 'fel y porthent hi yno fil a deucant a thrigain o ddyddiau'. Cyfareddwyd llawer o Biwritaniaid (ac eraill) gan y rhifau hyn a'u tebyg. Tybient y gallent fod yn allwedd i ddatgloi dirgelion y dyfodol, ac ymhlith cyfeillion Llwyd a Vavasor Powell yr oedd y gred yn gryf y byddai datrys cyfrinach y rhifau hyn yn eu galluogi i ddweud yn union pa bryd y byddai ailddyfodiad Crist a'r milflwyddiant yn dechrau. Am y trafodaethau diweddaraf ar arwyddocâd rhifau yn y Beibl, gyda llyfryddiaeth lawn, gw. Colin Brown, (gol.), *The New International Dictionary of New Testament Theology* II, (1976), 683–70 4, erthygl 'Number'.

24

A Word for God

OR A

Testimony on Truths behalf; from several
Churches, and diverse hundreds of Christians in *Wales*
(and some few adjacent) against Wickednesse in
HIGHPLACES
With a Letter to the Lord Generall
CROMWELL.
Both, first presented to his own hands, and now published for
further Information.

Job 36. 1: *Suffer me a little, and I will shew thee that I have yet to speak on Gods behalf.*
Esa. 44. 8, 9. *Fear ye not neither be afraid: have not I told thee from that time, and have declared it? ye are then my witnesses. Is there a God besides me? Yea ther is no God, I know not any.*
They that make a graven image are all of them vanity, and their delectable things shall not profit, and they are their own witnesses, they see not, nor know, that they may be ashamed.

To Oliver Cromwell *Captain Generall*
of all the Forces in England, Scotland *and* Ireland

Sir,

Forasmuch as you have caused great searching of heart, and divisions among many of Gods People by a sudden, strange, and unexpected alteration of Government, and other actions to the great astonishment of those who knew your former publick Resolutions and Declarations; considering also, how (contrary to foregoing Acts and Engagements) you have taken upon you a Power by which your are utterly disinabled (if there were in you a heart) to prosecute the good things Covenanted and contended for, with so many great hazards, and the effusion of so much precious blood: and by reason whereof you are become justly suspected in your ends in time past, and actions for future to very many of those, of whole affections and faithfull services, you have enjoyed no small share, in all the difficult passages and enterprizes of the late War. These things considered by us, (as we know they are by many Churches & Saints) and there being a deep sence upon our Spirits of the *Odium*, under which the name of Christ, his Cause, People and wayes do lye (as it were) buried; and also of the exceeding contempt which the wonderfull and excellent operations of God are brought into; even those eminent wonders, which the Nations have been Spectators and witnesses of, and wherein your hands have been partly engaged; We cannot after much serious consideration and seeking of the Lord, many of us, both together and a part, but present to your hands the ensuing testimony, w^{ch} (however you may look theron) is no more then necessity exacts from us, for the clearing of our own Souls from guilt and discharging of our duty to God & men. Therefore we earnestly wish you to peruse and weigh it, as in the sight of God, with a calm and Christian like Spirit, and harden not your neck against the truth as you will answer it to the great judge, before whose impartial Tribunal you (as well as we shalbe very shortly cited to give an account of the things done in the body, whether good or evill. Where the true motives and ends of all your Actions will be evident, where no apologie will be accepted of, your flighting and blaspheming of the Spirit of God, nor for the hard measure you give his people, by reproaches, imprisonment and other oppressions; and where Pride, Luxury, Lasciviousnesse, changing of Principles and forsaking the good wayes, justice and holinesse will not have the smallest rag of pretence to hide them from the eyes of the Judge: Which things (whatsoever you say for your self) are (even at present) to be read in your Fore head, and have produced most sad effects every where. Especially, first, The filling of the Saints hearts and faces with inexpressable grief and shame: And secondly, The stopping (at least) of the strong current of their Prayers, which was once for you; if not the turning therof directly against you. To these we might adde (thirdly, The hardening of wicked men, yea the refreshing and justifying of them in their evill doings, and speaking against the Gospel, Name, and Spirit of our Lord Jesus Christ. And lastly, Gods signall withdrawing from you and your designs. Oh then! that you would ly down in the dust & acknowledge your iniquity, and return unto the Lord by unfeigned repentance, doing your first works, and that you would make hast to do so, leaft Gods fury break forth like fire upon you, and there be no quenching of it. This would rejoyce us much, as being reall welwishers to your souls everlasting happinesse, though we must declare with equall pity and detestation against your designes and way.

A Word for GOD

The wise God that teacheth the Fowls of Heaven, to know their appointed times, who directs his peoples work in truth, hath we hope directed us (after a long time of silence and earnest seeking the Lord) to expresse and declare what we find in our Consciences touching the transactions of this season; and though some may think (as we our selves have been tempted to think,) that this is a time, wherein the prudent should hold his peace, it being such an evill time, that men are made offenders, yea, Traytors for words: Yet considering how the Lords remembrancers should not keep silence, and fearing that if we should altogether hold our peace at such a time as this (as *Mordecay* said to *Hester*) deliverance would come another way, and we could expect no share in the enlargement of Gods people, or safety in the day of trouble: withall finding how self would prompt us (like *Issachar*) to see that rest is good, and outward prosperity pleasant, and show the same temptations (which we finde and fear many of our deare Brethren to be under) have set upon some of us, as to have mens persons in admiration because of advantage, and by good words, faire speeches and promises, to be deceived and drawn away in simplicity; especially, by the example of some eminent men (like *Peter*) in so much that many *Barnabasses* are carried away with their dissimulation, and as well Ministers as Military men willing to serve the King for his Work and Wages. However seeing every man must give an account unto God for himself; we have examined what particular duty was incumbent upon us, and how in faithfulnesse towards God and meeknesse towards men, we should perform the same: Moreover considering how the Saints did formerly bear their Testimony (not loving their lives unto the death) and by the blood of the Lamb, and their testimony did overcome; and how God did heretofore stir up some of his People (both in *England* and *Scotland*) to bear witnesse (to the truth and wayes of God) against the wayes and wickednesses of men) as a fore-lorn hope; though they were in comparison but a few; like *Joshuah* and *Caleb*, two of twelve; or like the two Witnesses, a small yet sufficient number. Observing also, that there are present Truths, and every work being beautifull in its season (as in the beginning of the late Wars) was the witnessing against the Book of *Common Prayer, Surplesse, Crosse* in Baptisme, and other Ceremonies (being superstitious things, imposed by the Bishops) and against Ship-money, Monopolyze, *&c.* (civill things) imposed formerly by the King. All which were afterwards Declared, Protested and Covenanted against; which Protestation and Covenant are fresh in the memories, and pressing upon the Consciences of some of us, even unto this day: Besides the Engagement, and the severall Acts of Parliament, made against Monarchy or Kingly government; all which now seem to be forgotten or neglected; and those that speak or write in defence of such things, as the Parliament, Army, and the Godly People in the Three Nations approved, asserted and purchased at a dear rate, are now accounted fanatick fools, disturbers of Civil States, and intermedlers in things that concern them not; under which notion many suffer imprisonment, and other tryals, as evill doers from those men, who now build what they did once destroy; and justifie what they did once condemn. Witnesse their own Writings, particularly the Declaration of the Officers and Souldiers of the English Army (whereof the Lord *Cromwell* was General) the words whereof are as followeth, *We are perswaded in our consciences that the late King and his Monarchy was one of the ten horns of the Beast spoken of,* Rev. 17. vers. 13, 14, 15. *And that we were called forth by the Lord to be instrumentall to bring about* *that which was our continuall Prayers unto God,* viz. *The destruction of Antichrift, and the deliverance of his Church and people; and upon this single account we engaged, not knowing the deep Pollicies of worldy States men, and have ever since hazarded our lives in the high places of the Field (where we have seen many wonders of the Lord) against all the opposers of the work of Jesus Christ, whom we have all along seen going with us, and making our way plain before us; and having these things singly in our eye, namely the destruction of Antichrist, the advancement of the Kingdome of Christ, the deliverance of his Church; and the establishment thereof, in the use of his Ordinances, in purity according to his word, and the just, civill, Liberties of Englishmen.*

These with many other expressions, both in the Declaration and severall other Papers of the Army, and Letters of the General, cited both in the Declaration of the Members of severall Churches, and Petitions of the Three Colonels; besides several other Papers which might be inftanced in; which we leave to all unbyassed men to consider; and compare with actions done by the same men since that time: but in pursuance of our duty to God, our fellow members and Countrymen, as we are Christians, having a right to the things of Christ; and as we are men, having a Right to our native Priviledges: We do Declare our reall Apprehensions and Consciences (which to the great grief of some of us) we have so long concealed, waiting if God might by his Providence alter our mindes.

First, That the sins and present condition of this Nation holds parallel in many things with the old Israelites after the mighty wonders of God, shewed unto them in their great deliverance out of Ægypt. For instance: They and we have soon forgotten God our Saviour, and the great works which he did; we have not set our hearts aright, and our Spirits have not been stedfast with God, but have gone back, and dealt treacherously, and turned aside like a deceiptfull bow; and not trusting to his salvation, have provoked the Lord to anger with our inventions; so that men have dominion over bodies, and over our Cattle at their pleasure. And we are in great distresse, for this is a day of trouble, and of Blasphemy, for the children are come to the Birth, and there is not strength to bring forth.

Secondly, That blessed Cause, and those noble Principles propounded, and prosecuted by the old Parliament, and the good People of this Nation (in the maintaining of which God did miraculously appear) are now altogether laid aside and lost; and another cause and interest (quite contrary as we conceive) espoused and maintained; For then the advancement of Christs Kingdome, the extirpation of Popetry, and popish Innovations, the Priviledges of Parliament, the Liberty of the Subjects, and an equall distribution of Justice were Declared and fought for; and Tyranny, Oppression, Injustice, Arbitrarynesse; Destroying the Priviledges of Parliaments we Declared and Engaged against: But how far some men have now receded from, and acted contrarily to the dishonour of God, scandall of Religion, great grief of many faithfull men, and the strengthening of the wicked in their principles, and justifying their practices, we leave to the consideration of all those that a sober and wise.

Thirdly, Moreover the unadvised and unwarrantable changing of the Government and swearing thereunto, doth (as we judge) put a necessity upon the chief undertaker thereof, to overthrow the very foundation of a Common-wealth: and to maintaine the things comprised in the said Instrument (whether right or wrong) and to turn the very edge and dint of his Sword against the faces and bowels of such as should or shall declare their consciences contrary thereunto.

Fourthly, As a consequence and fruit of this forbidden Tree, many of the choice servants of God and faithfull of the Nation (some Noblemen, Gentlemen, Ministers of the Gospel, Souldiers, *&c*) are imprisoned without knowing their accusers of having so much liberty as was granted by the Heathens to the Apostles, or the benefit of a fair and publique tryall, according to the fundamentall laws of this Nation.

Fiftly, Under pretence of necessity still to continue the heavy burdens of Taxes, Customs, Excise, *&c* upon the Nation; without (yea contrary to) the Consent of the People represented in Parliament, and contrary to thier own INSTRUMENT.

Sixtly, Notwithstanding all the fair pretences and promises of Reformation; yet what abhominable and horrible Impieties, Injustice and Oppression are there couched and covered under this new Form, from the Head to the Taile (as the Prophet saith) treading in the very foot-steps of their Predecessors; witnesse the receiving of the Honours, Profits, Customs, Benefits, Tenths, and First-fruits comming in formerly to the Crown; the exalting of Sons, Servants, Friends and Favourites (though some of them known to be wicked men) to the highest place and greatest preferment, which the good Rulers of old, as *Gideon, Nehemiah* and others did not do; because of the fear of the Lord, and the Bondage that was heavy upon the people: Witnesse also the unreasonablenesse of the Army to have so many Officers, which might easily be reduced to a lesser number, and both Officers and Souldiers for many years to receive their pay (even in a time of peace) when the poore Peasants or Tenants (who pay but ten shilling rent per *Annum*) doe pay out of their penury, to maintain them in their pompe and luxury,

Seventhly, We cannot without grief mention the sad effects of the secret designe of *Hispaniola*, to be the losse of so many mens lives, the expence of so much blood and treasure, and the endangering of this Common-wealth by Invasion; as also thereby rendring us a scorn and snuffe to the Nations round about.

Lastly, We do declare and publish to all from our very hearts and souls, that those of us that had any hand in joyning with the Parliament and Army heretofore, had no other designe against the late King and his Party, save as they were enemies to our Lord Christ, his Kingdome and people, hinderers of his work, and oppressors of the Nation, and that it never came into our hearts to think or intend the pulling down of one person to set up another; or, one unrighteous power to promote another: but we aymed as primarily at the glory of God; so likewise as the generall good of the Nation, and particular benefit and just liberty of every-man; and it greives us, that any just cause is given them to stumble at Professors, or complain that they are deprived of their Freedome, and severall wayes more oppressed, then in the dayes of the wickedest Kings; we do also believe in our heart, that (though the worst things are not without Gods permission and providence) yet that this Government is not of Gods approbation, or taken up by his Counsell, or according to his Word; And therefore We do utterly Disclaime having any hand or heart in it, and for the Contrivers and undertakers thereof, we suspect and judge them to be great transgressors therein; and so much the more, because they are Professors of Religion, and Declarers, Engagers, and fighters against the very things they now practice: And it is most evident to us, that they there by build again, what before they did destroy; and in so doing they render themselves and the Cause, Religion, Name and People of God abominable to Heathens, Papifts and prophane Enemies, which is a grief to our Souls to consider. We doe also detest the practices of these men in imprisoning the Saints of God, for their Consciences and Testimony, and just men; who stand for morall and just principles, and the freedome of the Nation and People; and their breaking off Parliaments to effect their own Designe. We do also from our Souls Witnesse against their new Modelling of Ministers (as Antichristian) and keeping up Parishes and Tythes (as Popish Innovations.) And we Disclaime all adherence to, owning of, or joyning with these men in their wayes. And do withdraw, and desire all the Lords people to withdraw from these men, as those that are guilty of the sins of the later dayes; and that have left following the Lord, and that Gods people should avoid their sin; least they partake with them in their plagues: Thus concluding our Testimony, We Subscribe our Names hereunto.

William Jones
John Morgan
John Thomas
Evan Jones
John Phillips
Thomas Jones
John Beevan
Thomas Lewis
Gabriel Lewis
Howell Thomas
Thomas Phillips

Lewis William
Lewis Reece
Reece Iohn
Howell Reece
Richard John
Richard Price
John David
David Morgan
Morgan William
Morgan Robert
John William

William Edward
Richard Roberts
Lewis David
Morgan John
Richard Thomas
Meredith William
Witkin Ricc
William Watkin
Reece David
Watkin David
David William

William Howels
William Waters
Howell John
John Price
Meredith Phillips
William Jenkins
Thomas Prosser
Jenkin Griffith
Howell Williams
Thomas Williams
Richard Howell
Watkin Price
William Powell
Thomas Powell

Lewis David
Thomas Edwards
Reece John
Jenkin Jones
William Iones
Jenkin Rosser
Rice Rosser
Nicholas Griffiths
Lewelin Beevan
James Powell
Mirick Morgan
Evan Meredith
William Jones
Meredith Rees

William Phillips
John Williams
Henry Thomas
John Jones
John Farmer
Henry Meredith
Trehern Morgan
Richard David
Evan John
Edward Evan
Thomas Evan
David Evan
Howell Waters
Jenkin Waters

John Howell
Phillip David
Rice Richard
Edward Matthews
Watkin Richard
Thomas Evan
Lewelin Jenkin
Jenkin William
Thomas William
Evan Lewelin
John Lewis
William Waters
Morgan David
John David
David Walter
Reece Jones
Phillip Jones
Jervice Jones
Edward Jenkins
Watkin Jenkins
David Thomas
Rice Jones
Evan John
David William
Henry Williams
John Bedward
Thomas Tunman
Robert Tunman
Roger Griffith
Thomas Morgan

Reece Jones
Richard James
William Hopkins
Lewis Jones
William Watkins
Richard Mils
John Thomas
John Smith
William Price
Vavosor Powell
John Williams
John Hammer
Moris Griffith
Edward Owens
Richard Griffith
Walter Davies
Thomas Gwin
Thomas Vaughan
John Powell
Rees Havard
Roger Thomas
Thomas Lewis
John Watkin
Walter Lewis
William Thomas
William Lewis
Richard Vaughan
David Jones
Rice Thomas
Henry Thomas

Thomas Price
Roger Williams
Iohn Baddam
Iohn Powell
David Roberts
Iohn Pugh
Thomas Parry
Howell Williams
Walter Price
William Bevan
Lewis Prytherch
David William
Lewelin ap Iohn
Ienkin Griffith
Peter Chidlowe
Arthur Chidlow
William Iones
Owen Humphrey
Evan Thomas
Samuel Brees
Iohn Lewis
William Beatsley
Thomas Morgans
Iohn Symonds
William Beddoes
Morris Williams
Iames Williams
William Matthews
Lewis Price
Evan Ellis

Samuell Williams
Richard Bromley
Richard Baxter
John Crowther
Francis Mason
Iohn Evans
David Phillips
William Evans
Thomas Ellis
Thomas Crowther
Thomas Fernell
Richard Irish
Henry Iones
William Phipps
William Becket
Daniel Brees
Francis Hanckock
Edward Irish
Oliver David
William Dabellis
Lewis Pugh
Richard Rogers
Owen Iones
Edmund Rosser
John Meredith
William Thomas
Llewelin Lewis
John Rowland
Lewis Williams
William Lewis

William Price
David Davies
David Price

Richard Morris
John Evans
David Powell
Walter Lewis
Richard Meredith
William Morris
James Haydock
William Bostosk
Phillip Russell
Edward Williams
James Morgan
David Rutherch
William Bayes

John Williams
Thomas Powell
John David

Iohn Rowbuck
Evan Watkin
Charls Lloyd
Hugh Thomas
Rosser Watkin
Thomas Griffith
Lewis Price
Morgan Lloyd
William Thomas
Lewis James
Iohn Thomas
Robert Thomas
Howell Watkin

Richard Tudge
William Fernell
Edward Gretholder
Iohn Tomkins
Thomas Tudge
Hugh Evans
Owen Lewis
Owen Iones
Edward Brees
Ralph Robothom
William Lewis
Iohn Powell
David Kadwalader
Rowland Tudge
David Evan
John Tibbots

Edward Williams
Howell Rees

Rowland Morgan
Phillip Gyles
Iames Watkins
Iohn Iames
Lewis Iones
Michael Watkins
Edmund Morgan
Rosser Thomas
Iohn Rosser
Thomas Iohn
Iames Iohn
Elias Thomas
Iohn Howell
William Iohn

Rosser Watkin
Daniel John
Thomas ap John
Gilbert Morris
Matthew Prichard
Edward Jones
Owen Edward
David Thomas
John Pugh
Howell Thomas
Reece ap David
John Bevan
Thomas Lloyd
Henryck Jones
James Quarrell
Edward Williams
Edward Moore
John Roberts
John Brown David
Alexander Powell
Hugh Powell

John Nicholas
Phillip Williams
Robert Sanctley
John James
Edward Roberts
Walter Thimbleton
John Fowler
Hugh Prichard
Henery Williams
William Win
Richard Saltonstall
Rice Jones
Richard Williams
Phillip Rogers
Richard Roberts
Thomas ap Thomas
Ellice ap Roger
David ap Edward
Lloyd Brian
Thomas Edwards
Francis Lith

James Park
John Meredith
John Owens
William Iennings
George Ienkins
William Heatley
John Lewis
Dauid Jones
Jeffery Parry
John Hughes
John Evans
Richard Jones
William Rider
John Ratlieffe
William Jones
Ralph Hopley
Hugh Price
Griffith Jones
Sixsmith
Mathaniel Edwards
John Meredith

A POSTSCRIPE

Reader

This paper had sooner come into thy hands, if the Subscribers hereof (who were willling to do nothing rashly) had not waited for further

Councell and direction from God herein then they had at their first intention of the publishing hereof and withall it was deferred for a time, hoping that God might some other way convince the Person chiefly concerned in it; and seeing God gave him time to repent, and yet he repented not, we have published this our Testimony. To which you might have had many more Subscribers (who were willing to own this Paper) if conveniency and Providence had made way for it to come into their view: There hath been great endeavours to stifle it in the Birth; to that end, some of the Subscribers were threatned with imprisonment, and Orders were issued out to imprison some (whereof one was secured) namely Mr. *Vavasor Powell,* who was taken by a company of Souldiers, from a day of Fasting and Prayer at *Aberbechan in Mountgomeryshire,* wherein many Saints were gathered together, which caused much sadnesse; yea and much heart breakings to them all; and he remained for some time a prisoner upon that account.

FINIS

25
Nodiadau ar y Word for God

(LLGC 11436D, ff. 2–3)

Marginall notes on the preface of the Word
for God so called to my deare
V. P.
11m. 11d. 55 or 56

lett love in mee prevaile with love in thee to answere candidly these querees which I now send to thee only & that only on the letter wth the style thereof to him called Protector.

Then next on the Word it selfe if the lord willeth it. Though I delight not in such things & such replyes.

Is this the Doore out of Babilon? or do yee not knocke at a wrong gate? Do yee bring honest saincts to subscribe their names who comprehend not the matter, (as they made the Jury sweare, then saith the Cryer, Jurat.) Do yee not falter in your wittnesse when you testifye against wickednesses in high places? When yee meane the very Monarchy it selfe & the high office of a Protectour which I Justifye not.

Whether Captaine Generall of all the forces in three nations as you stile him bee not in effect & indeed really equivalent with the Title of Lord Protectour.

Yee speake in Elihus words to Job. Suffer Mee a litle. Do yee not as oppressed rather speake to a seeming Prince. Though we shall certainly be better acquainted wth Jobs Case.

Do yee use wholesome and right words, when yee speake of unexpected alteration of the Gouernement. To whom was it unexpected? not to Cavalliers etc.

Yee subscribe to ends in times past & actions for future. But can yee not discerne two men in one man. Or can yee your selves tell what your ends were in times past or what your future actions will bee? Then are yee strong Christians.

Whether your many churches & christians (mentioned) bee infallible in their considerations (as yee say the saincts and churches have considered etc. yee say after much seeking & consideration. But can yee tell wn yee seeke God wth the whole heart.

Is the name of Christ. His cause, People & wayes confined to the Government of England? will yee shutt the sun in your chamber & say still againe & againe Lo here Only. when yee your selves iudge the poore quakers for seeming so to say?

Yee write & say. Many of us both together & apart etc. Are yee not all assured of one anothers seeking & consideration.

Yee say. Necessity exacts this from yee. Necessity is an exactor indeed now in the land. But is not your necessity mixed though your conscientious Honesty bee pure & right.

Whether divers of the subscribers & reproovers do not themselves live in reproachings, oppressions (by words) Pride, luxury lasciviousnesse, changing principles as the reprooved do. Or how do they demonstrate what the word Principles meaneth.

(Addendum)

And for Magistracy. Man cannot see the ground thereof unlesse he hath first exactly known who is Governr in his owne heart. For he that doth not know himselfe knoweth nothing as he ought to know.

Governrs vexe the governed. Also subiects grieve their rulers. So it hath beene a very long night But when shall both Governrs & Governed encourage one another lovingly & wisely in what is good in either. And deale friendly as well as faithfully while they reproove the will of one another also.

Hence it is wee in Wales & in the 3 nations ought to ioyne in all good things with the man called protector during his turne naturall life, & lovingly reproove him of his evill, for if hee sin being now a publique man It may bring mischiefe on us all & if wee owne it in him (as Dd's iniquity plagued the subiects) All say, wee ought not to flatter him nor yet to slap him without cause, & take heed we flatter not ourselves. For how can we well reproove another of wt we are ourselves in our places & proportions guilty.

Lett us then (having borne our testimony) say no more of others, but quietly wthout private mutterings tend oure owne worke & waite within ourselves on God who is wonderfull in counsell & marvailous in workings. And as we have turned the inside out to reproove others lett us turne our outthoughts in to rebuke ourselves & make sure worke there for God will turne all our insides out againe in such a manner before all men & all angells as will make us more ashamed of our owne selves, then we are now of our neighbors Governours or other relations.

Lett all flesh feare the Day of God now dawned for that will discover all as farre beyond our best consciences as the sun is brighter then a candlelight. Can wee not stand still a few months or years & behold the saluation of God. His righteousn. hasteneth & his promise tarrieth not, but his patience stayeth long wth every one of us for our repentance & hee waiteth that he may be gracious to England Wales & the whole earth and therein to us also he lifts up himselfe to show mercy.

Romes agents & all their Jesuits that are so much feared & talked of may now whirle for their game is over, & the all ruling providence will not lett mans witty blasts to turne the wheele. Howbeit the Pr. will suddenly depart out of this & after him though an enemy *shall fish in troubled waters*, yet the same spirit of glory & omnipotency shall carry on the begun designe (without in these nations but especially within in the spirituall who are among us of all kindreds & confused tongues & languages, & wn this come to passe.

And when this comes to passe (as the men & children of this age shall wonders now see) then remembred it will bee that a true spirit of prophecy (in the midst of false prophetts) hath a spring & a summer before this generation is ended in this life. The Jesuits shall smoother their plotts. Their wisdome shall hurle them downe to the pitt. The protestant fractions are running into one spirit of eternity, tho many be lost therein. Every man shall be so divided in himselfe that he shall find worke at home. The civill & ecclesiasticall (so called) shall keepe within their owne doors by warrs of [*neu*, because of] hailestones now powring foorth.

There will be no persecution for conscience but a punishment for abusing the light of him who is God by nature. One church shall now bee on earth & one shepheard shall fasten the nailes & use the goads & speake foorth the words of wisedome that shall bee masters of all hearts in all Christian assemblyes. And the time is coming & come to many when the mouth of iniquity & flesh in mens spirits shall be stopped. And opinionative churches in the outward court shall bee all broken downe that out of their rubbish the tabernacle of DD may be built. The building goes on in every one of the elect, where the sound of those hammers (outsmarting one another) *is not heard*, where the peace of God keepeth. The saincts walke not in the streets of Babilon where the devills coaches trundle in the spirit of this created world. Howbeit, the lame shal bee healed & those that wickedly or ingenuously halted shall be recovered or convinced. And so all shall see good cause to silence their lips & thoughts before the great pure and dreadfull lord of all heaven & earth. The witt & malignity of most countreys frustrated. The Protector strengthened to do his worke, with a measure of honesty towards God & good. The narrowspirited brethren tired wth tending for their ungrounded expectations. The false prophetts & prophecyes ashamed of themselves. The pure poore honest spirituall soules raised up on the throne to iudge all men & things. The temporall sunke into the spirituall. The outward thoughts turne inward.

26
The Humble Representation and Address

To His Highness Oliver *Lord Protector of the Commonwealth of* England, Scotland, *and* Ireland, *and the Dominions and Territories thereunto belonging.*

The humble Representation and Address of several Churches and Christians in Southwales *and* Monmouth-Shire.

May it please your Highness,

We should yet longer have contented our selves with praying and praising God for you in secret, and taken advantage from our distance, as to publique affairs, and from your Highness most Christian and favourable understanding of us, to have still forborn any address of this manner to you, but that a late printed Paper, entituled, *A word for God, or a Testimony, &c. from several Churches, and divers hundreds of Christians in* Wales, *&c* comming to our view (the largeness of which title, to those that did not compare it with the subscriptions, nor know that Country, might seem to involve under it the generality of the good people there) We therefore think our selves lowdly called upon to assure your Highness, that most of such as fear the Lord in that Country are not led aside with those temptations; but continue still, through grace, such as you judged them once to be, highly esteeming and honouring not only your person, as being before them in Christ; but also that Government and Magistracy, which God by most eminent and signal providences hath called you to the exercise of over these Nations, and cannot now but in the rear of some thousands of good people bear our testimony in this manner to it, as that wherein at present we believe the cause and interest of God so long contended for, the protection of the Saints, the liberty of the Gospel, the just rights of all the people, are, under God, imbarqued; And we cannot see if some, who are so earnestly set against this Government (and for no other visibly) had their wills, how these mercies can be preserved to us. And indeed (my Lord) it hath not a little affected us, that while you are sitting at the Stern, and wrestling with difficulties for us, any professing Christ (and especially from among us) should the while be doing the thing that tends evidently to sink the whole Vessel, Nor can you easily judge how much we are grieved, that your Highness should have any seeming occasion to think the generality of the poor Saints of *Wales,* who were once so much your joy, should now so sadly degenerate, as to have head, heart or hand in this unseemly Paper. And though we hope we should have hearts to bless God for you exceedingly, if we might but under you lead a quiet and peaceable life, in all Godliness and honesty (as who, having a heart to it, may not, and be also greatly encouraged from the authority) which is a mercy would have been valued at another rate by our Fore-fathers, and such as no Nation in the world besides, that we hear of, do enjoy; yet we cannot rest there, but must acknowledge that (which in private hath rejoiced our hearts) wee see other good things upon the wheel. Endeavours and waies taken to remove all oppression from the bodyes of men also. Godly Governours, appointed into all parts to protect the well- affected, and discountenance sin and wickedness, Taxes lessened as far (at least) as the safety and preservation of the whole could give way; Godly Protestants of Foreign parts owned and sympathized with in their Distress; Designs laid in the most probable way for the extirpation of Popery, and making further passage for the Gospel and Kingdome of our Lord in the world, which the hearts and spirits of the Saints, for these many hundred years have been engaged on; and yet we wonder Friends that seemed once to be of the same minde, should take the advantage that was too sadly given the Enemy, to pass so hard a sentence upon the Works of God, whose waies are in the deep, not weighing aright what experience might have taught us all ere this, that his usual course is to pull down where he intends to build, and to make instruments base and vile, that his own arm may be considered when he shall appear with them, and we humbly take notice, that not onely in this case, men run before God in prescribing wayes and times for the bringing forth the merciful dispensations he hath promised to these latter daies, seem to have a spirit to the work in their own time and way, but none in Gods.

And for what remains undone of all that was declared, prayed and fought for, we and the rest of our Brethren of this Commonwealth may, if we would deal faithfully with God and with our selves, justly acknowledge that our grievious Sins and our sad and unparrallel'd abuse of those manifold mercies already received, together with that monstrous pettishness, and too common an indisposition in divers good men to follow God, and to yield cheerfull obedience to him in your government (which doubtless is of his own workmanship) is the real proper cause why any good thing hoped for by any man is so sadly retarded and indangered. It is not our meaning to trace our Brethren in all the particulars mentioned in that Paper, as the imprisoning some Noblemen, *&c.* which we conceive to be the mildest course could be taken, and keep them from ruining themselves, and hazard the whole Nation with them; and we with; in naming such, with that respect they do, though Cavaliers and Enemies, our Brethren to magnify the opposition, do not forget the Spirit themselves were once of towards them, and all their Party; Not what they urge touching the continuing the Army, together with the Taxes, Customs, Excise, &c. even as they say in a time of Peace, without considering by what hands, under God, that peace and all the mercies with it, as it was obtained, is to this very hour (and as yet cannot, without a miracle be otherwise) conserved to us; Onely we are so far from undervaluing, that we must remember and own with them the noble principles that were in some of our Patriots in the old Parliament; and the frequent appearances of God for his cause and people during their fitting, and yet wonder our Brethren should so soon forget, their own sense of them in the latter end, how weary they were grown, of their Government, and how far they were then from judging it to be a dishonour to God, a scandal to Religion, or grief to good men, to have a period put to that Authority. But we greatly fear many of our dear Brethren take too much liberty to censure the manifest revolutions and actions, that the right hand of God hath brought forth amongst us, and to ravel into, and put contrary senses on those passages of providence, which themselves together with the generation of the Saints had once written *Ebenezer* upon; which God in his own time will (we hope) mercifully convince them of. In the mean space, as we have (through grace) some fellow-feeling with you in your burthens, so we rejoice in the goodness of God to you, that hath armed you with such a measure of strength, as in the middest of trouble enough from other hands to be able to bear with the numerous oppositions, contradictions and infirmities of the weak Saints, and while that Spirit that is in them (which perhaps they know not) carried them to be pulling down the Wall and hedge God hath set about them, that you should still continue a protection and defence to them and us, and not to be discouraged in the work of God under your hands, and we trust that the provocations, and evil of this late Paper (though it be very great) will not prevail over that glorious spirit in you, but that you will still in some likeness to your heavenly Father, be doing good for evil, and rendring love and compassion for perverseness, and so convince calumny it self. And God, even your God, will be with you in the rest of the works he hath given you to do; And (after we hope many years longer over us) reckon you amongst the Overcommers, and welcom you into his own eternal joy and glory, which is the prayers of

Your Highness most humble Servants and Subjects in the Lord.

Ralph Williams
Edward Harry
George Robinson
Hugh Rogers
John Nicholas
William Blethin
Edward Herbert
Thomas Martin
John Williams
William Arnold
John Watkins
Lewes Rogers
Robert Jones
James Kemeys
Alexander Jones
Francis Watkins
Walter William
Harry John
Lewis Richard
George Edwards
Morgan William
Hopkin Rogers
Morgan Rosser
John Bygan
Rosser Edward
Walter William
Rich. Howel

George Morgan
Richard Williams
Rice Jones
Richard Parker
Morgan Jones
John Gregory
Thomas Calles
Nicholas Peather
Robert Baker
William Richard
Lewis Evan
John Thomas
Knewill Thomas
Walter William
Charles Jones
Thomas William
Edward Hutton
John Baker
George Ambrose
William Packer
Edmund Jones
of Itton
Will. Richard jun.
Thomas George
Rice Williams
Thomas Jones
Walter Radock
Richard Charnock
Henry Walter
Walter Jenkins
John Taylor
John Perin
John Walter
John Jones
John Morgan
William Philips
Rosser Williams
William Rotheras
Richard Pen Mau:
Richard Namer
John Ace
Ienkin Tayler
Richard Bevan
Iohn Lucas
William John
Robert Curnock
Griffin Jenkin
William Pitcher
Francis John
Walter Howel
Andrew Lewes
Edward Lewis
David Jones
Francis Sincus
William Bide
Wroth Richard
Richard Buller
John Williams
Thomas White
James Morris
Roger Williams
Thomas Evans
Gresham Bray
Charles Jenkins
Philip Williams
John Davies
Iohn Morgan
David Morgan
Thomas Caple
Walter Richards
George White
Lawrence Nonney
William Iones
Iohn Iones
William Iones
Iohn Evans
Iohn Morris
Iohn Powell
R. Ouldaukine
Iohn Bowens
Iohn Daniel
Thomas Williams
Bedmill
Iames Iones
William Wrinch
John Morgan
Iohn Thomas
Ienkin Lloid
William Thomas
Giles Morgan
Rice Williams
Rosser Thomas
Harry Thomas
Edw. John
Thomas Williams
Thomas Arney
Iohn Roberts
Thomas Philips
Iohn Daniel juni
Rowland Thomas
Iohn Whithear
Thomas Daniel
Hopkin Thomas
John Morgan
William Price
Frankl. Matthews
Lancelot William
Evan ab Owen
Robert William
Walter Jones
Iohn Biyes
Daniel Higgs
William Richard
Iohn Thomas
Ienkin Byvan
Marma. Matthews
William Iones
Griffin Bowen
William Prichard
David Bayly
Iohn Retherought
Matthew Iones
E. Lewes
Iames Philips
Evan Griffiths
Moor Py
William Bayly
William Morris
Rees William
Morgan David
Richard Howel
William Howel

Iohn Knaeth
Iohn David
William Rogers
Iohn French
Iohn Powel
Edmund Ellis
Edward Gamage
Robert Puel
Henry Nicols
Iohn Gowler
Griffith Daryld
Robert Thomas
William watkins
Rice Davies
Morgan Thomas
Edward Bartet
Ienkin Edward
Evan Lewelin
Ienkin Elliot
Ienkin Thomas
John Nichol
Christopher Ienkin
George Matthew
Edward Thomas
Rice Samuel
Iames Walker
Edward Morfe
Edward Wrinch
John Day
William Morgan
Edw. Rowland
Edward Lloid
Henry Morgan
Mor. Tho. Gunter
Evan Jones
William Philip
Edward Gabriel
Miles Bruer
William Jenkins
Evan Rosser Tho.
Lewis Morgan
John Barckley
Tho. ap Thomas
Howel John

Matthew Cuffe
William Cuffe
Waking Nicholas
Waking Thomas
Leyson Thomas
Arnold Griffith
Charles Rebeot
Thomas William
Griffith Richards
Ienkin Evan
Thomas Davids
Anthony Lutton
Morgan Howel
David Lewis
William David
Griffith Howel
Rawleigh Fox
Thomas Grifith
Morgan Cook
Thomas Nichol
Richard Ienkin
Iohn Harry
Thomas Thomas
David Lewelin
Ienkin Griffith
Howell Prichard
Evan Howel
Thomas Iohn
Meredith Thom.
David Evan
Philip Thomas
John William
Morgan Williams
Patrick Walter
Gibbon William
John Howel
Nathaniel Ripid
John Evans
Samuel Lort
Robert White
Thomas Elliot
Henry Garlake
Edward Wills
Richard Lort

Morgan Griffith
Morgan Thomas
Edward Matthew
Edward Thomas
Morgan Lewis
Morgan Evan
William Thomas
Lewis Harry
Watkin Robert
Watkin Thomas
Rice Iohn
John Moses
Thomas Iohn
Harry Philip
Rice Iohn William
Edward Thomas
Lewelin John
Andrew Rosser
William Iohn
Lewis Iohn
Robert Phillips
Morgan William
Rosser Thomas
Iohn William
Morgan Bruir
Reinold Morgan
William Thomas
Watkin Jones
Edward Morris

From the Church of Christ at Langom in Pem broke-*shire, the* II. *Moneth,* 17. *day, 1655.*

Edward Carver
John Sayes
Christop. Jackson
Humph. Gunter
Erasmus Hicks
Anthony Stocks
John Lewis
Owen Young

Rosser Richard
William Richard
Water Howel
Knywilling John
Rob. Williams
Henry Williams
Will. Williams
Edmund Turban
Evan Rosser Tho.
Giles Lewis
Rosser Thomas
Lewelin David
Philip William
Edmund Harry
Philip Thomas
Rice John David
Philip Lewis
James Lewis
Morgan Rosser
Thomas Evans
Nicholas Watkin
Lewis Rice
William Evan
Rice John
James Rosser
Harry Llwelin
John Rees
Wil. John Rosser
Harry Lewis
Rof. Tho. Willia.
Tho. Edw. Tho.
Wil. John Morg.
Thomas Edwards
Thomas Jones
John David
John Thomas
Edward Morgan
David Morgan
John Davies Lew.
Rosser Watkin
John Lewis
Watkin Harry
Thomas Howell
Lewis Llevvelin

Giles Denham
Abel Bishop
Griffith Howel
Rice Price
Robert Tennant
Thomas Warren
Stephen Young
Joh. Elliot junior
Thomas Howel
William Hughs
William Steward
David Dyer Rof.
James Picton
Jenkin Jones
William Moyl
Thomas Wills
Thomas William
Elias Harry
Evan William
Thomas Morgan
Watk. Ioh.
Harry Morgan
William David
Lewis Levvis David
Thomas Evan
Thomas David
John Philip
Thom. Rovvland
Rovvland Robert
William Rishersh
Walter George
Henry Morgan
John Harbert
Joshua Miller
Thomas William
Watkin Benedict
David John
Lavvrence Reece
Hary Watki.
Edvvard Levvis
Harry Edmond
Harry John
Reynald Morgan
Rice John Levvis

Thomas Melet
John Luntley
Robert Peiest
Richard Brown
Stephen Love
Peregrine Philips
Thomas Smith
Richard Rayler
Edmond Thomas
Walter William
William Watkin
Tho. Griffith
Evan Lewes
Rice Harry
James Richard
Thomas William
Gregory David
Rice Philip
Levvis Rof. Wat.
Will. Benedick
Philip Thomas Reece
William Green
John Myles
David Davies
William Thomas
Morgan Iones
Wil. Iohn Price
Levvis Thomas
Iohn Thomas
Evan Bovven
Hovvel Griffith
Thomas Iones
Iohn Williams
Iohn Beaban
David Thomas
Thomas ab Evan
David Hopkin
Ovven Levvelin
David Hopkin
Evan Thomas
Edvvard Robert
Thomas Hopkin
William Nicolas
Iohn Morgan

Philip Rees
Edmund Evan
Iohn Jones Tho.
Edmund Morgan
Robert Matthews
Charles Morgan
Philip Ienkin
Willia.
William Morgan
Hugh Bayly
William Morgan
David Griffith
Owen Dowl
Thomas Hopkin
Richard Edward
Thomas Iohn
Ienkin Franklin
Iohn Knayth
Nicholas Tanner
William Rees
Moses Whityard
Reese Pue
George Williams
William Badcock
Evan Iohn
Edward William
Roger Thomas
Howel Iohn
Evan Lewelin
Iohn David
Leifon David
Iohn Davies
Morgan Jones
George Rood
Philip Ione
Lewelin Evan
William Philip
Richard Prees
Walter Griffiths
John Medith
Roger Morgan
Roger Prosser
Thomas Lloid
William Morgans

Wil. Wat. Rosser
Harry Evan
John Rosser
Evan Rosser
David Lawrence
Hugh Matthew
William Thomas
Mathew Evan Tory
Robert Edward
Iohn Givelin
Richard Else
George Harry
Hopkin David
Philip David
Griffith Bowen
Francis Williams
Howel Iones
Reynold Thomas
Robert Callow
William Philips
Iames Philips
Robert Morgan
David William
Morris Iohn
David Morgan
William Philip
David Ienkin
Daniel William
Ieavan William
Lewis Richard
Wil. Huddlifston
Abeding. Godfre
Morgan Awbre
Henry Griffith
Thomas Proud
Thomas David
Mirick David
Edward Lewis
Ric. John
Thomas Price
Watkin Ienkin
Tho. Williams
Rees David
Thomas Lewis

Sim. Butler
Harry Philip Iohn
William Thomss
David Thomas
Morgan Robert
Thomas Beevan
William Thomas
Griffith William
Vincent Powel
Will. Watkins
Thom. Watkins
Will. Watkins
Rice Powel
William Proserp
Owen Parry Iohn
Howel Iones
Lewis Thomas
Thomas Prosser
Watkin Thomas
Ienkin Morgan
Watkin Philips
Watkin Lewis
William Prichard
Thomas William
Thomas Ienkin
Wil. Watkin
David Rogers
Roer Iones
Watkin Thomas
Humph. George
William Price
Richard Powel
William Powel
Thomas Powel
William Parry

Rich. Io. Mredith
Iames Iames
Meredith Richard
Rice Griffith
Walter Thomas
William Philip
William David
William Iones

Thomas Pugh
David Pugh
Richard Williams
Edward Bruhord
Lewellin Williams
Thomas Fainton
James Philips
Anthony Rydley
Richard Coslat
Charles Rosser
Rog. Thom Badam
Phillip William
Morgan Rosser
Lewis Ienkin
William Morgan
Richard Gibbon
Wil. Joh.
William Badam
Thomas Edward
Lewis Foh.
Jo Howel
John Rosser
William Morgan
Andrew Morgan
William Hughs
Philip Lacok
Philip Pember
Richard Clark
Edward Morgan
Thomas Mason
Eustance Mason
Thomas Matthews
John Lurcot
Richard Heigh
James Lacock
James Crews
Walter Edwards
Roger Watkin
Thomas Prosser
Thomas Bevan
Thomas William
Thomas Watkin
Roger Prosser
Roger Philip
John Iones

Iohn Ienkin Ien:
Richard Creed
Io: Iones
Thomas Edmund
Watkin Ienkin
Ienkin Watkin
William Watkin
Rosser Morgan
Rees Iones
Edmoud David
Rosser William
Harry Lewis
Morgan Iohn
Thomas William
William Ienkin
Iohn Rosser
Morg. Renald William
Iames Watkin
Iohn Parry
Howel Watkin
Thomas Io.
Io. William
Renald Wil.
Andrew Ienkin
Iohn Lewis
Harry Rees
Watkin William
Oliver Gilbert
David Francis
Thomas William
Roger Jones
Christopher Price
Iohn Edward
Iohn Morgan
Iohn Richard
Thomas Lewes
Edw. Owsley
William Gunter
Rosser Ienkin
Iohn Parry
Thomas Rogers
Anthony Parry
Lewis Hughes
Morris Philip
Abergaveny

R. William
Robert Knaeth
Iohn David
Owen William
Thomas Lloid
Edward Frood
William Raterd
Rees Iohn
Evan Ienkin
Michael Howard
Robert Thomas
Thomas Rice
Daniel Howel
Ien. Griffith
Lewellin Morgan
William Iones
Humphrey Philips
Thomas Parry
Will. Watkin
Harry Owen Lewis
Rosser Evan Lewellen
Matthew Hodson
Preet Walter Prosser
Ed. William
Harry Thomas
Wil. Nicholas
Iohn David
Iohn Iones
Wil. Davis
Iohn Abbot
Wil. Prichard
Richard Rosser
Edw. Giles
Wal. Williams
Will. Morgan
Andrew Morgan
Samson Ienkin
Lewis Samson
Thomas William
Toshua Rosser
Richard Gibeon
Walter Will
Villiam Beran

Iohn Hugh Sen.

Thomas Prosser
Thomas Williams
Watkin Iohn
Rees Price
Richard Bevor
Howel Yohan
Thomas Lewis
Iames London
Thomas Landon
Iames Williams
Watkin Brown
Samuel Iones
Ien. Daukings
Iohn Rice
Thomas ap Owen
Iohn William
Ievan ap Owen
Dav. Wil.
Morgan Thomas
Rees Evan
David Evan
Iohn Ievan
David Richard
Wil. Rees
Evan Dan. griffith
Rees David
David Griffith
Iohn Evan

Walter Sampson
Richard Iohn
Peter Harry
Griffith Ienkin
William Thomas
Howel Lawrence
Thomas Richard
Reynold Tumlin
Walter William
Edward Water
Evan Griffith
William David
Thomas Iohn
Evan Thomas
Iohn Powel
Meredith Davis
Francis Davis
Philip Thomas
Rice Iohns
Drahern Evan
David Iohns
Dav. Matthew
Owen David
Rees Iohn
Morgan Iohn
Iohn Bowen
Griffith Humphry

Steven Hughs
Richard Ienkins
Evan Davies
David William
David Harry
David Morris
Wal. Richard
Harry William
Nich. Richard
Iohn Nicholas
Anthony Griffith
Thomas Morgan
Iohn Owen
Rees Thomas
Griffith Iohn
Dav Bowen
Owen David
David Morgan Thomas
Iohn Evan
Evan Morgan
Iohn Walter
Rich Hugh
Dav. Hary
Anthony Thomas
Ezekias Thomas
Iohn David
Griffith Hopkin

FINIS

27

Sylwadau ar The Humble Representation and Address gan Vavasor Powell a'i gyfeillion

(LLGC 11436D, f. 4)

(To Cradock)

Our ancient honourd & beloved friend. A late page called an addresse & subscribed among many others & as wee believe promoted at least, if not drawne by your selfe. The matter & style whereof doth very much affect our hearts & is the occasion of these plaine lines (in much love & faithfullnesse) hoping that former & friendly acquaintance wth the good old practice of thorough & home speaking will find acceptance with you. However we can really say that our respects to you together with the discharging our dutye as brethren has extracted wt follows from us.

That we wth many others cannot but greatly wonder how different you are in this paper from what you were use to bee. For heretofore you had favour & gift from God as not to respect mens persons or to flatter them which most pitifully & miserably & (indeed wee feare blasphemously) you & the rest do in that paper, giving oft to a mortall man such a Title as Highnesse which is due to none but God (which assumed title was accounted blasph. in the Hollandrs a few years since) using such glavering & hardening words that render you to those that have a mind to putt the most charitable & candid construction upon this Action, to flatter egregiously, & not wthout iust cause very offensive to us, & many more godly, whose paper you greatly mistake, construing the prisoners we meane to bee cavalliers (we no way intending such) & are magnifying the opposition (as you speake) of the spirit in the Protector & in your opposite subscribers by calling the one a glorious spirit & the other a spirit of perversnesse. And that so many lines & leaves should passe under yr hand without one word either of reprehension or councell is scarce credited by those that read it, & compare it with what they formerly knew in you. Withall we cannot but remember & remind you of what you have expressed to severall of us since the change of this Govnt. concerning your dislike thereof. Do you not rember how you showed halfe a sheet of paper written upon both sides to one of us, & said the one side contained arguments against the Govërnt. & the other side arguments for it. And need you (deare friend) bee minded how you spake to another of us that you saw evidently as the sun that the wayes of these men (meaning the Protr his councill & Army) tended to confound utterly all that interest of God & his pple among us. And another time in a publique sermon at

Jameses. That formerly if any officer wrote to his wife & etc. they mentioned the cause of God, but speake of Gods cause now to men they will aske wt you meane by the cause of God. And this now is the language over all Westminster & tell them I say so. And be not forgettfull (Good sr) how often you spake to many That Cradock was as much dissatisfyed as any man & that you were scarce looked upon (but loathed) by the courtiers for you had told ym to their faces more then was said at Allhallowes. How also did you preach & pray against parishwayes & tythes etc, and yet since you have had your hand in upholding them. Oh Sr How much do your deare friends (& some of your children) grieve to see such an eminent instrument so much decline & degenerate & be yea & nay? Oh that our hearts could feare & mourne in the thoughts of such a sad & strange change. For wch wee cannot but pray & grieve in secrecy. Especially if we can hear you are convinced & sensible as we hope you will bee. However Our lord is wittnesse that we desire not your shame but repentance, & shall remaine very desirous to heare as soone as may be from you, & shall be exceeding glad if by any means we may be instrumentall or serviceable to you or receave any knowl. or furtherance from you either for our soules or the worke of God.

Your very affectionate & reall frinds wellwishers & brethren.

John Browne. Hugh Pritch. Vav Powell
Rich Robts. Jn Meredith. John Robts.

'more then was said at Allhallowes'. Tebyg mai cyfeiriad sydd yma at waith Cornet Day a John Sympson yn darllen *A Word for God* i gynulleidfa o dros 500 yn Eglwys Allhallows the Great — yr eglwys lle bu Cradoc ei hun yn pregethu ynddi gynt. Carcharwyd Day ond llwyddodd Sympson i ddianc, gw. C. H. Firth (gol.), *The Clarke Papers* III, 62 — 22 Rhagfyr 1655.

28
Gwŷr y Bumed Frenhiniaeth

(LLGC 11437B, ff. 2–3)

17. 2m. 57

The Fifth Monarchy men (now so called) do aime aright at the true & last marke of all things even the exaltation of him who is all in all wth God & over man. They consider Daniels prophecyes compared wth the Revelations that testifye of things certainly to bee in the last dayes. They are beyond this pens expression saddened & aggrieved to see so barren a tranquility after so sharpe a war, & the parliamentary primitives & (as they iudge) prosperously & divinely caried on (as indeed it was) betweene Charls & Parliament now choaked up & suffocated by the interposition & apostacy (as they conceave) of the present Gov. They also long after & vehemently expect a death of this & a restoring of another. & to that end have made many prayers & encouraged one another to attend for better things now shortly to come. & though some of them be mild tame & precious hearts & others so furious & conceited that they canot owne each other in all things, yet they agree to have a change to the better as they hope. Now the fifth monarchy (whereof they speake) is certaine & the litle stone will beare all before it. & no nation shall be able to resist & controule it. But (marke) that this Fifth Governm on earth shall be the first Governm & the last dominion & not of a particular concernment or private interpretation. None must raigne but he who is first & last. Alpha & Omega. & whoever would rightly iudge of these things & bee assured of these matters must first of all know (& that first in himselfe) the first & last God monarch & potentate, & then he that would see these things & wt shall be hereafter must first come to, the end of nature & of all naturall things & nationall revolutions. (which few attaine to though many talke). Every one would have his owne sorted opinionists sett up but the most deep & most high God will not owne them because they are not come or will not (in their private & hearts concernments) come up to the life of God himselfe. And nothing besides his owne life in all will long stand in those last dayes: (This is written by a mind grieved wth all such partyes & factions as rove about lotts doore & yet canot gett in). Its well seene that the impartiall God who is infinitly acquainted wth nations revolutions is not such a sun as will shine onely & peculiarly at the doore or window of any mans or angells apprehension. But measureth all at once though many would measure him & comprehende his mind & will of these dayes. Once more its comanded Bee silent ô flesh before this lord for he is risen out of his holy habitation Dread him (thats his comand). Admire him (thats his worship) lye in the dust (o man) before him (thats best for thee).

Comend the good in all & live in peace within & without (thats best for others & thy selfe) This kings wheele will turne (& is turning still) & will shake off the thoughts of man & of thee ô Sts (so called) as it is thy vanity. For no vanity will he endure in thee, how gloriously soever thou professest feare him. Feare him, else thou shalt feare him. And if thou shalt say in thy heart. This is not to our purpose nor indeed to the purpose of God, thou shalt shortly know whether his word or thine will stand. He that writeth knoweth but in part that God spanneth the heavens, of highest apprehensions, & Hee standeth & measureth the earth of mens private opinions, & holdeth in the palme of his hand all the tempests of the seas of mens turbulent agitations. Hee is litle considered by profane & professors, That do not see who Hee is that triumpheth by life over death & by light over darknesse, & by crooked things brings to himselfe the straightest gloryes. He turns the shadow of death into a morning & awakeneth the halfe dead sleepy man to walke in the perfection of the day. Hee giveth mee life & being & so to another better then my selfe. Why should any then be discontented? Have wee not one father? Are wee not one bone & one flesh? Why should we not bee one spirit in every comon good? Why do wee back bite devoure or consume one another? And because all mankind are one flesh how is it that some hate their own flesh, theire owne friends, & their owne professions? Is not this from the devill the enemy of mankind & of Xtian kindred? Why should not this consideration allay & qualifye & bring to the Sabbaoth & to perfect peace both the oppressor & the oppressed? Are there not seven spirits before the Throne of God that worke before his face in the children of men? Do not those Worke towards only one sabboth in God? If one be come to the first second or third day of this great weeke should not hee that is but a beginer & furious & fiery be borne wth by him that is come to the fourth or seventh? & should not the beginer in these stop his mouth at the perfect. These things are so in thems. Why not in us?

Do wee know how things go wthin our owne hearts? or consider we the 7 spirits in ourselves? If we be not come to the sabbath & quiet rest in our selves, how shall we looke it out abroad? Why then do we fight wth one another that have a fight in our own breasts?

Where shall we be for ever if we dye before we subdue the enemy within our owne minds? If he be alive at our death whither will hee carry us when soule parteth wth body?

There is one alwayes neare if not deare unto us. Man understands him not because he stands not under him but above him by naturall corruption if rottenesse could effect it. Shall the spider measure the firmament? or the mole the heavens? Shall Adams rotten worme know God immortall or any family of the whole earth understand the omnipotent? No, not as much as the ebbing doth the tide? But there is a spirit in man which is God or of God in man & as that spirit knoweth all so he yt yeilds to him discerneth all. As its written yee are taught of God & yee know all things.

Wherefore, Heare ô yee people. Cease to build synagogues of private opinions (from which another as good as thy selfe differeth) Now gett up the great temple not a synagogue but that which hath roome for all the saincts of all times nations & opinions in it selfe. But whether this bee taken heed to yea or nay, lett it be remembred and upon record of conscience & memory against time to come.
17 2 Month. 1657.

(LLGC 11437B, f. 1)

Addendum

It is dangerous to act wthout the lords pure spirit, especially in things of eternall & also of present publique consequences, seene beforehand in this lords day.

Every spirit that hath energy in acting is not Gods. Some impressions are false, others limitting the holy one in one forme to appeare out of the grave are unsuitable to his acceptable will in these last consumating dayes. Division from the good (who is the only true God) in any is not the way to Canaan. & for brethren to dwell asunder in contrariety how ugly is it. Much more is it an abhomination to the father (the peace eternall) to see them spill the blood peace & safety of one another in their rashly apprehended dawning before his due time & spirituall attoning day hath prevailed wthin over their flesh in particular.

I do here not only advise but charge yee in the name of Jehovah who is to come; that yee do not forerun his steps, last yee loose not only your lives in the ruines of babells bloody contentions, but also yet more darkin & eclypse the glory that now is to rise. Rather attend as sufferers & bee not sons of Tumult. And though at first bloodshed is not intended, watch your steps lest ye come by degrees to what yee have not forseene. Deale plainly wth all men above board, & not couertly. & waite in peace upon the lord God. & so farewell in Jesus. But the funerall occasion I feare or know. will not bee a prosperous occasion. Do yee as the true spirit (not a false) shall direct. I know it shall offend none sober among yee that I send this as the present consideration, & day unto day shall shew knowl. Es. 30. 18.

Drafft anorffenedig yn llawysgrifen Morgan Llwyd.

Briwsion Cymraeg a Saesneg

29
Dirgelion y Galon

(LLGC 11438D, f. 2)

Fourth

In what spirit every thing is done is such a mystery as yee would do well to open if yee can. The deepe things of God are here concealed or sparingly touched in this Message. Because the Dogs would snarle at a *Pearle* as if it were a common stone throwen *at them* And the Turning of the Eye fixeth the spiritt of mankind. The true saincts in Humane words cannot comunicate the Thoughts but by Hints. And since now every sort of people are divided our next (yet present) worke will bee the plowing up & tearing of our owne whole hearts and to bewaile our condition in Egypt and Babilon and wildernesse, and not to professe more than is true and meet, nor bee such as swagger with scripture words in their mouth when they have hellishnesse in their hearts & beastly marks in their practice (for this is the very beast and Dragon mentioned in the Revealation) If these things were layd to & awakened within the Heart, then Many a poore soule would say after this manner. I have not words to expresse what I see. I do not carefully use the power of God alwayes with mee in all things to follow what I professe and say. I find many different thoughts and fires kindled in one heart, *in my owne heart.* I sinke under a Deluge of Apprehensions in mine owne thoughts. I Judge now of one thing after this manner & annon after another. I find two (if not three) Judges that would conclude in mee severally of one thing. I live in Doubts because I have not lived in Perfection. I feare to professe Perfection of Judgment before I have it. I find no easy lodging to my naturall mind in Babilon and yet there I am sollicited to bee because of the mixtures. I see all Divisions of Partyes factions and fractions without as so many Sieves of vanityes & vexations untill men come to the Eternall Distinction. Also I heare many talke idly of the Distinguishings in Eternity that have not seene what themselves are in the Judicious everlasting Eye. I am filled with noise without from all, as they are speaking of the great Day of the Judgment of God himselfe (by the lambe of God) and yet I heare them Judge before the time. I perceive how boldly they appeale and reserve all to the Day of God, but they care not (or they cannot) for present stand before their owne inward court,

Mar. 12. or 13. 56. A woman call our childr. by name begin at yongest. DDs feare of nose bleeding. Another at ludlow say Wm. Herb. should have 2 wives & named them.

Mae'n amhosibl penderfynu pwy oedd yr 'Wm. Herbert' yr adroddir sgandal amdano yn y nodyn atodol!

30
Sylwadau Beiblaidd

(LLGC 11433B, ff. 1–6)

10 Acts

9 : 3 thinges in those wordes hee made noe difference betweene us and them yt is ye godly.
1. There is a pure people and those bee the church indeede or that some in yor (?) world have a pure heart & these bee the church. There is none that have a pure heart but those that are of ye church and there is never a limb of the church or ye least in it but have a pure heart, & this is a pure heart that receaveth noe mixture within to poyson ye heart, and those that are pure they beleeve that they are one with god.
2. there is noe difference or strife betweene those that are of a pure heart.
3 thing in these wordes are there is noe way to have a pure heart but these that make X there head 23 Job: 27: those that say I have sinned, the lord will forgive them & though some doe not say I have sinned, yet when they come before the lord there conscience will say I have sinned though they say not soe here. I have sinned aghainst the light which is in mee, and that hee hath got noe profit of his sins, after wee have our pleasures and fulfilled them what profit have they done us. God begat us out of his owne will . . . wee goe to pray or to doe our worke or calling or when wee doe go to reade or speake looke whether you doe these in your owne will and ye will of the lord 1 James 1. Why is it hard to know the difference betweene the 2 wils in man Ans ye will of man is bottome but ye will of god in man is bottomlesse but not when wee rise in the morneing . . . the minde and will doth run out and doth not keepe in as a truant doth from schoole, there is soe much purity & in one and soe much purity in another yet they all made but one kingdome & one church and it is ye kingdome and Church of God Saith the Apostle some are of one opinion another of another opinion, but you that have a pure heart is with x

yn digio yn dragwyddol pan ddaw didd farn i fidd 2 dan yr i, digter duw yn erbyn pechod ag digter dyne yn erbin duw pa fodd y mae dine yn digio wrth duw pan foe ganddo ef ddim i ddiwedid wrth y ef. duw gwirionedd ag heb anwiredd ynddo hynny iw heb anwiredd i rhyny ag gimer aful ar i air ef, yn i fers nesau Q, pa faeth ddynion iw rhyny ag sith yn galw i hynnen yn blant iddo ef? Att, Mae nhwy yn anghofion ag yn gimion yn i ffirdd mae duw yn wastad yn gweithio ag yn gwneuthur daionni yr da ag yr drwg ond mae rhynny ag y sith yn galw i hynaen yn blant uddo ef nae wnane nhwy dda am dda pryn ag yndi idi nhwy ddim tebyg iw ef ag etto i fynnan i galw yn blant i dduw. ag yn oes neb yn blodonni yn arglwydd yni idiw ef yn debig iw arglwydd ag cymend y sith yn dy galon di yn debig i dduw cymaid y sith yn blodonni duw, ag cymaid nid sith mae honny yn i ddigio ef i rhaid iti feddwl ath fyddi di debig i dduw nes y bidd ef debig i ti, ag nid iw bossibl i une enaid y sith nid yn debig i ddiw fod gydy duw i ddou ar i didd farn arglwydd agor imi nid wit ti ddim yn debig imi ag i oddu ti yn tobed y fiddwn i yn debig i ti certh oddi wrth y fi: Psal 50 gollyngaist dy safn i ddrigioni, ag ath dafloedd i plethu ddifaith ag i ti fethaist i lawr gydy rhyny oedd fel dy hynnan ag i ddiwedest yn erbyn dy frawd, ag er hynny ni ddiwedis i ddim, ond oedd angel yn scryfenni pob peth i lawr. ag pathu ni yn i cymerid pen ag ingc ag yn gosod y pechodu i gid mewn nie diwrnod ni fedru di ddim mae ef yn ynbosibl etto mae duw yn rhoi ag yn i scryfennu nhwy i gid ag yr arhos iw amy dafru i ti dybied i foddwn i fel ath ti.

Q.3. Pa beth y mae duw yn gwneuthur am i bobl. Att. 1 mae ef yn i cadw fel canwyll i lygad. Att 2 mae ef yn codi nhwy i fynny fel y mae Eryr yn codi i nerth meth yr arglwydd i ddafru ini ath godi i fynni etto i ddafru i ti wingo ath sodlu Att 3. y fi y llenwes ef a phethu da, ag bob pechod yr ydin ni yn i gwneuthur mae nhwy o flan yr angl . . . sanctaidd i gid ac o flan cythreliaid, ag mae ef yn ddiwedid Iago ine yn troi oddi wrth y i ohono pa beth iw Jesusun. mae ef yn arwithocai beth inion 4 pa beth iw ni yn gwneuthur dros. duw considrwch hyn y mae

Job 23. 27.

Where there is one that seeth his sin hee doth 3 things
1. hee acknowledgeth It
2. hee acknowlidgeth it in his heart 3 hee acknowledgeth that hee hath got noe profit by it, and there are 2 roots 1 the root of sin 2 the true vine and the one acknowledgeth his sinne and the other doth not. hee seeth that there is not profit in it and if wee doe not see ye first roote wee shall have noe benefit in ye second & hee yt seeth his sin & confesseth it the lord is readye to forgive It and hee shall see that hee hath got noe profit by it. I hope if it were asked what are you better of all ye thinges yt you have heard & spoken & if you are not ye better you deceeue your selves. 3 thinges would come with this free will is ye cause of the new birth of his owne free will begot hee us mans will is mans bottome but the will of god is underneath, it is bondage for Ever but ye will of god is at libty and wee ought to consider 1. What is our end that wee come to here is it because wee have time spare now more than another time then saith god thanke mee that thou hast time too spare if it is soe onely saith god I will spare my light, thou hast bin indifferent for mee & I will withdraw from thee 2 What in thee doth here there are 2 natures in thee ye inward nature 2 thy one wil and ye reason why wee doe not understand some scriptures because wee doe put our owne wil to here wee ought to watch least the

old nature may not get agst . . . that ye new man may rule in thee and governe thee.

wrth Mr Lloyd Text 1 Cor 2 Cha mae ef immossible i dyne wrth i swnwir i hynnan i ddiall pethu ysprydol. ag mae rhai yn darllen ysgrwythyr y mae ag y mae ef yn egglur iddo ef ag tippin bach ar ol yn dowill dymae yr achos am fod yr meddwl naturiol yn gryfach nag yspryd yr arglwydd ag ar amser hwnnw mae ef yn dwyll: ond pan fidd yspryd duw yn feistr imewn dyna'r amser mae ef yn eglur ag dewch i ni edrych pa bethy sith orhau yn da feddwl: mae 2 feddwl 1 feddwl aniannol hwnnw iw nos yr enaid 2 feddwl ysprydol iw yr didd ag cofiau pa beth y sith yn feistr i mewn ag nid oes un dine da na drwg y all wrth i feddwl naturiol ddiallt pethu ysprydol ynghylch pethu ysprydol ag diall pethu ysprydol. mae 3 maeth o bobl yn yr ysgrythur y mae 1 rhai yn diall ddim 2 eraill yn diall ychidig 3 eraill yn diallt llawer Q pa beth iw dirgelwch y doethineb A peth iw 1 mae ef yn i galw nhwy doethineb, ag peth bynnag ag yr ydych chwi yn discwil yn benna hwnnw y rhoiff yr arglwydd i chwi 2 Meth paul doethineb iw y nerth oblegid ymple bynnag y mae y doethineb y mae mawrnerth 3 doethineb iw y dirgelwch dy di fab duw nid cig a gwaed a gonosoedd hyn i ti moth X 3 ni welodd lygad ni glywodd glist y 3 fforth mae dirgelwch yn ymddangos 1 ni welodd y llygad 2 ni gliwodd y glist 3 ni ddiallt mor galon.

Paul's, 3 way of inteligens man hath (1) seeing 2 heareing 3 understanding & wee are alwaies to see what thing is upermost for this is ye Reas. why ye minde doth not understand ye scripture bec ye naturall minde is upermost and many wonder when they reade a scripture that they doe not understand, & some doe understand it and presently after they doe not ye same what is ye Rea: ye scripture is ye same and ye man is the same but ye minde and heart ar not ye same ye naturall mind is in within & that time wee cannot understand ye scripture for there is noe man good nor bad with his owne naturall minde can understand spirituall thinges neither I hath seene noe eare heard nor entered Into the head of man yt is not mans natur all wil nor understanding can understand spirituall if it were asked have you any faith you would say yes a little is it such as a Idle husesye sweepeing the house but this is ye misery and woe that ye devil doth keepe the heart under his master over it all ye weeke faith the devil do not say we sinned for that is a shame to thee take heede of saying soe saith the devil but a beleeveing heart saith I will to beleeve that X died for mee & wt then that I must bee sanctified & the devil saith god never intended thee, & wee must kill this man in us. Rom 1d 14 there are some dainty thinges men doe have and hee names them by 3 things, 1 fruits 2 goodly 3 lovely I here & reade & speake, I hope and trust in them wel saith ye lord I will take that from thee they are cald goodly because the minde thinkes there is something in them dainty because they are some choice thinges but this cuts the heart they shall never come to thee againe

& (can never) snatch at things & the fruits of this world as a greedy doge & it saith if I cannot have it to day I will have it to morrow (no saith the lord) I will take it away and cut it off from thy mouth & wee thinke they are goodly and dainty & wel saith the lord I will famish thee and then thou shalt say I have sinned & now wee feede the corruption & then it overcomes us but the lord saith I will starve babilon, there are goodly religious fruits in this world but the lord will take them away if you were upon your death bed and remember all yr sins and seeke to make a supper and content your selves for one quarter of an hour ye conscience would say noe, 1 James: 1d of his one will begat hee us, wee are (not borne of flesh nor bloud but of god his one will was free.

Mae'n amlwg mai nodiadau ar bregethau yw'r rhain a dywedir bod un ohonynt gan 'Mr Lloyd' — ai Morgan Llwyd yw hwn?

31

Ysbrydion yn Abertawe

(LLGC 11438D, f. 2.v)

Rein Bowen, Swansey.

Febr. 28. 55. A woman neere Sus Brough told mee she was troubled with a sprite in the house. Shee heard it usually before midnight but not her husband. Her husbands cozen Germ. was an old angry scolding woman dyed about 4 years agoe. Shee lives about a stones cast off her. The husb. dreamt that the daughter sought to wrong him. And the daughter replyed. It was to helpe her mother. The sprite whizing breaketh wind over her head, & once came in crying Hurt, & crept from off her heart to her neck & there broke forth where a notable scarre is. A papist (tenant to Andr. Ellice) would have her to their way & shee should bee free. Shee used their blessed water on some side of her bed & the sprite came to her another way not over the water. The old dead woman had hid some moneyes from cavall. in time of warre.

This woman was advised to sett Criâfol over her head but it profitted not.

Hi ddaeth atti (ai llygaid yn gâead) ni ddywad hi ddim. Fe gelodd hon y naw ceiniog am dorth nis yr ail nos fe ddaeth (dybyge hi) y marw a thoes yn ei arffedog, ag yno hi ai talodd iw merch. Ei merch ai gwelodd yn cuddio box ar rhaw yn yr ardd gan glywed hi yn dywedyd ni wŷr neb faint o arian etc. Mae un pen ir tŷ yn uwch nar llall (llei roedd yr hen wraig) ebr y naill un wrth y llaill. Mae gwaeth na hyny ebr y llall, ysgwyd tidau heyrn bob nos.

March 14. Both came to me, Susan denyed (her eye not good) angry stout. She had sd after the 9d was paid, pray more for she will come againe to tho. yr husband. So it came. And the man saw her wth a great knife seeke to kill him. Upon enquir of that Susan replyed wt if it be to take my mothers part. Shee denyes also that shee ever saw the pot where the money was hid by her mother. Her looks are grim. No smiles nor name but most high. Her husb. threatned to strike in the head if he had beene here. He on a lords day reading by the fire putt book under elbow & told Janet shee was not of his faith yett sd hee offeiriad or hen ffydd, for fe ai rhwymwyd dros hyn a hyn o amser.

Mark ap Edw. & Janet Vch Jn Hugh his wife
levi Hughs & Susan his wife wt wrong
did this family.

32
Esgyrn Pregeth

(LLGC 11433B, f. 10)

1. Sons of God. 2. manifestation of them.
3. its waited for. 4. not by creatures but by the expectat.
the quintessense of all the third first vice versa.
obser. 1. creatures have an earnest peny. 2. creature ioyne with sts in three things. 3. creature or breath of creat. long for the prime creat. man in restauration, as hee was first in the fall. 4. Share his sons eminently Creat. longs not so much as for sts freedome.
begin in the end of these 4
1. This creation is Xt first fruits that we know of, except election.
2. Sts. the first fruits of Christ Jam. 1. 18
3. Some sts the first fruits of others as Jer. Rom 11, 16 Rom. 16. 5. I. Cor. 16, 15.
4. The spirit.

The first fruit of sts. soules.

5. Creatures have now an earnest peny of great freedome.
ergo wth us. they subsist 2 praise 3 beleeve live by faith 4. grone or pray.
20. Who shall have the book of my verses

Ens. Roberts
Howell Thom.
Ben. Rich.
Walt. Thimbl
Hugh Prich.

Rom. 8. 19, 20.
1. the creatures not creator is subiect.
2. subiect to vanity.
3. in the bondage of corruption, putrifye,
4. not willingly.
5. yet submissively to God.
lives in a Kind of hope ernestly expecting.
groaning, travelling, prayers future
1 delivered sym had yet not deliverance
from bondage to slaves of satan
Rom. 11 ult
2 into sts liberty wch is glorious
3 upon sts deliverance turne backe

Yr oedd Howell Thomas yn un o'r pregethwyr teithiol a benodwyd o dan Ddeddf y Taenu i weithio yn ardal Edeyrnion, T. Richards, *History of the Puritan Movement,* 150.

Sefydlwyd Benjamin Richards (neu Prichard) gan y Profwyr yn Llandegla, T. Richards, *Religious Developments in Wales,* 22; cyflwynwyd ei olynydd, Samuel Jones, gan y Brenin, 30 Gorffennaf 1660. Ceir cofnod ym mhapurau'r Sesiwn Fawr (Wales 4, 25/1) fod 'Benjamin Prichard of Seaswick clerk other Benjamin Prichard of Seaswick co. Denbigh, blacksmith' wedi ei gyflwyno 21 Medi 1661 am fod yn absennol dri mis o'r Eglwys.

Yr oedd y Capten Hugh Prichard yn un o gomisiynwyr Deddf y Taenu a llofnododd y *Gair Dros Dduw.* Er hynny, rhoddodd Cyngor y Wladwriaeth 100c iddo yn 1659 ar gyfer talu ei filwyr, T. Richards, *Religious Developments in Wales,* 234.

33

Cyfarwyddiadau i Argraffydd

(LLGC 11430B, f. 1)

To the Printer of this Welsh paper

1. Let it be in octavo in good large paper.
2. Let the character be the same wth the inclosed.
3. Let no alteration be made in words or sense.
4. Let the capitall letters be observed.
5. Let the sentences be kept distinckt.
6. Let the proofes be rightly ffixed in the margin.
7. Let not sentences usually begin in the end of a line.
8. Let 1650 of them be printed.
9. name not Duflyn and let there be no letters after it but Terfyn instead of Duflyn.

34

Trefn Llywodraeth

(LLGC 11438D, f. 6)

1656 The heads of the bill for Gouernment

1. A King
2. house of Lords.
3. A freedome of parliaments.
4. The number of the house of lords 70, not under 40.
5. Regulating of elections.
6. lawes for parliament to observe.
7. A certaine Revenue.
8. A privy councell of honest men.
9. To punish disturbers of ministers.
10. Protestant Religion to be setled at home & abroad.
11. Confirmation of sales.
12. to preclude the late Kings party from trust, And all of you to take the abiuration or to be banished.
13. That he shall choose his successor.

heads of next proposed

Gouernment.

35
Rhai cyfeiriadau

(LLGC 11433B, f. 8^{v})

27 Vat 14

200 140
340
8691
8691

291 proponindae
Joh. Kinge Baker,
of Bussleton

Marg: Herbert,
2 Butchers row.
Ann Powill. be
Name. Mayde,
by ye Castle-gate
livinge wth Cox.
Juan Water—man
of Sherbourne nr.
Rimton.
Geo: Brookman's
wiefe of
Bussleton
George Brookman.
Sargeant Barnes.

Llythyrau

36

Ri(chard Baxter) at Morgan Llwyd, 10 Gorffennaf 1656

(Llyfrgell Dr Williams, Llythyrau Baxter, Cyfrol 1, ff. 53–4)

S^r

It is so naturall to man to desire to know, y^t I take it for no boast to tell you, y^t I earnestly long to be acquainted with so lovely a thinge as Truth. And if I know my heart, I know not ye worldly thinge, y^t I should account too deare in order to ye obtainment: And expience tellinge me y^t dearest truths do oft afford ye sweetest Comforts, hath pmoted my hearty willingnes to entertaine it at any rates, so it be in order to my ultimate end. But here's my unhappines! I can easyer wish for it y^n reach it. I doubt not but many love it as well as I, y^t yet differ from me in many pticulers. And I dare not say y^t I have never so neglected ye Light as to forfeit it: for though I knew nothinge by myselfe yet I am not therby Iustifyed. The impfection of my knowledge I am deeply sensible of: but O y^t I could reach higher! wch I wish not meerly for ye Love of Light; but alsoe as it is ye necessary inlett of Love: for I find if I could but know God more, I should Love, desire & Labor more. And Concerninge ye state of my soule wch you enquire after, I shall as truly acquaint you with it as I can. In ye great Essentialls of my Religion, I consider two things: 1^0 whether they be true? And in this I am no Seeker: for I am satisfyed: e.g. y^t there is a God, a Life after this, y^t X^t is ye way &c: 2^0 By what evidences I may see more of ye Truth of these things, & be confirmed more in y^m? And in this I am still a seeker: As alsoe I am, for further Grace to impve those truths. And y^n for ye more subservient truths many of y^m I know past doubt, & there am no Seeker: in regard of very many I am at a loss, & am still to seeke: as alsoe I am, for ye clearer methodizinge & disposinge of some well knowne truths. And as for meeknes & sobriety, I have not so much as to boast of; but truly I can say y^t I am conscious of abundance of darknes in my soule, & y^t I would thankfully (even with a thousand thankes) entertaine y^t advice y^t would helpe me to a Cure. But y^n this is my Case! I have not a Commandable Intellect: I cannot believe things, because men would have me beleive y^m; & y^n they are offended: I have not ye Command of my owne app^{r}hensions: Its only evidence of verity y^t can Command it; for wch I waite on God in ye constant & laborious use of those wch I have taken to be his meanes; & all y^t I have attained to is this: 1° to be more stablished y^n ever in ye essentialls; 2^0 to see many subservient truths; 3^0 to have y^t Light for ye methodizinge y^m wch sometime I had not; 4^0 to longe after ye knowledge of ye rest wherin I am at a loss, 5^0 And to love those y^t unite in ye essentialls & greatest Common truths. So far am I from beinge pufft up with these attainments (though I am much troubled with pride) y^{t} my strongest temptations have beene to be yet more scepticall, & to Doubt of allmost all, through ye Consciousnes of my Ignorance in all. You would aske me why I Condemne ye generations of ye Quakers? 1^{0} Because they seeme to me to deny much y^{t} God hath delivered us in ye sacred Scriptures, & to deliver much contrary: 2^{0} Because they shew a designe to bringe ye most humble painfull Ministers into hatred & Contempt with their hearers, wch I litle regard for ye Ministers sakes; but w^{t} a people should we have, if they were cast aside? [ms. were cast aside?] & how faithfull do I know many of y^{m} to be to ye interest of their peoples Soules as far as they can discerne it? If they be in any Error, ye way of Charity is to reduce y^{m} in meeknes, & not to seeke their extirpation, to ye apparent hazard of ye flocks; 3^{0} Because they come in a Spiritt of malice & revilinge, as far as I am able to discerne; wch is not ye Spiritt ye truth ꝑceedeth from. These are some of my Reasons: if any of y^{m} be bad, I am willinge to know it. Ffor ye hints you give of y^{e} (Revealed immanent Essence & ye two wills of God &c) I must confess to you I cannot understand yor meaninge without more words or light. S^{r} I'le deale plainly with you! I have met with one learned man y^{t} said somewhat towards a change upon my mind, & I have lately read Sr Hen: Vanes booke, & look't into some of Behmens [y llsgr. yn aneglur] but they all deny satisfaction to my Vnderstandinge, by two miscarriages wch they are Commonly guilty of: The first is y^{t} they purposely & wilfully hide their minds, deliveringe most things in Allegoryes (even when they speake in Scripture phrase) & avoydinge plaine & ꝑꝑ termes. No man is so great an enemy to Truth as he y^{t} obscureth it. My Vnderstandinge is darke enough after all helpes: I have no need of Riddles to hinder my discerninge. I am resolved by ye strength of Grace, could I find truth more fully, to owne it bare face'd in ye open world without feare or shame w^{t}ever it cost me. God is not God if he be not sufficient to secure those y^{t} he engageth for him, & to see y^{t} they be no loosers by him. He y^{t} serveth a God y^{t} he hath Cause to be ashamed of, or to be afraid to owne, doth not worship ye God y^{t} I doe. They are envious to men y^{t} would hide ꝑ^{e}tious truth, & y^{t} under ꝑ^{e}tence of revealinge it. The 2^{d} Error is y^{t} they will not open to me ye whole fabricke & systeme or body of truths wch they ꝑfess to have attained: but will only drop here one & there one, y^{t} I may receive y^{m} by degrees. This way I find unlikely to take with me: ffor till I see ye Concatenation of truths & tendencye of y^{m}, & whither they lead & where they will end, I find much unsatisfyednes in my mind. If therefore you have attained further y^{n} I, & are willinge to do me ye office of a true freind, deale plainly & fully with me, & I will do so by you. I do here vehemently ꝑfess to you y^{t} let ye name of it be never so odious in ye world, I will thankfully entertain & openly ꝑfess any truth of God, whose evidence I can discerne. But y^{n} I must intreate of you these two things: 1^{0} y^{t} you will give me in some smal Connexed [?] Systeme of y^{t} Body of truths which you would have me to receive, beginninge at ye Principles & putt me not off with incoherent scraps: for it is ye nature of Truths so to befreinde one another, y^{t} ye hidinge of one may be a meanes to hinder ye reception of many: 2^{0} y^{t} you will studiously avoid Allegoryes, metaphors & uncouth phrases except where necessity compelleth you to use y^{m}. If you shall yeild to this I shall take you as a plaine & faithfull freind, & nothinge shall be more wellcome to me y^{n} any evidence of Divine truth from what hand so ever: But if you shall shun this course, I feare my dull understandinge will remaine in its former darknes. But still I shall wait on God for his discoveryes.

Yo^{r} Brother
Ri: Baxter.

July 10th
1656

'Sir Hen: Vane' oedd Syr Henry Vane yr ieuaf (1613–62), gwleidydd Piwritanaidd amlwg, gw. *DNB*. Ei lyfr, yn ôl pob tebyg, oedd *The Retired Mans Meditations, or the Mysterie and Power of Godliness* (1655).

'Behmen', wrth gwrs, oedd Jakob Böhme (1575–1624) y cyfrinydd Lutheraidd a fu'n gymaint dylanwad ar Forgan Llwyd. Gw. E. Lewis Evans, op. cit., 1931 pennod VI. Cyfeirir ato fel 'Beaumont' yn llythyrau Peter Sterry at Llwyd, rhifau 68–9 isod.

Cefnysgrifiwyd (54^{v}.) 'An Answer to a Letter from Mr Morgan Lloyd Pastor of the Church at Wrexham in Denbighshire'.

37
Ri(chard) Baxter at Morgan Llwyd, 31 Mawrth 1657

(Llyfrgell Dr Willliams, Llythyrau Baxter, Cyfrol 1, ff. 57–8)

Kederminster March 31. 1657.

Deare S[r]

I received not yo[r]s till this day March.31. 1657. Yo[r] loueinge & free communication must needs be acceptable, & obligeth me to gratitude, as every truth doth to a ready Entertainment. That you judge me a louer of truth & willinge to arrive at higher knowledge, I take for no great Commendation: for Truth is naturally y[e] object of o[r] understandings, as Goodnes of o[r] Wills, & y[e] Understandinge naturally is inclined towards it, however y[e] p[r]dominancy of carnall inclinations, haue made us averse to sanctifyinge truths: but yt is not as they are truths, but as they are Cross to fleshly interest, & are aboue & against y[e] naturall & carnall mind. I confess I haue so stronge a desire after knowledge, y[t] I thinke I could easily compass sea & Land, I meane, lay out y[t] litle strength I haue, in any certaine meanes for y[e] attainment; & yet so much of this desire as terminateth in y[e] meere delight of knowinge, & is not sanctifyinge, & leadeth not y[e] mind to God for God, I take to be but naturall. But alas, I find desireinge will not doe! I Study & Pray, & Pray & Study, & reach upward, but I cannot reach y[e] thinge yt I desire. My eager inquiryes into inferior truths, haue long beene moderated; but w[n] I am on my knees, & speake to y[t] God of w[m] I haue so low app[r]hensions, & w[n] I would feine haue more liuely & cleare conceptions of his blessed Nature, & y[e] invisible things, but cannot attaine y[m], this is my burden, & oft times a great temptation to despondency. I know y[t] as y[e] matters of y[e] world are trifles in comparison of y[e] least spirituall verityes & employments, so the lower sort of spiritualls are smal things in compison of y[e] pure knowledge & loue of God. An as y[e] highest complacency in y[e] Divine pfections wth the fullest sense of Gods complacency in me, (as a stone in y[e] buildinge of y[e] new Jerusalem, & a member of y[e] Glorifyed body of his Son) with y[e] exercise of these in everlastinge Praises, is y[e] Heaven y[t] I expect; & Intuition mut be y[e] Inlett or first stop of y[t] Complacentiall fruition: so I know, y[t] it is my Ignorance of God & distance from him, y[t] here keeps under my affections, & depriveth me of y[e] foretasts of heaven on earth: And could I but see more of God, & liue more in his Loue, I could spare abundance of inferior notions & speculations w[ch] I find but like all Creatures, empty & insipid, further y[n] God appeareth in y[m], or they lead to him. I know in p[t] (alas I am taught by long & sad expience) how litle I can doe myselfe to reach to this Divine knowledge, & I thinke I lye empty at ye feet of God, desireinge ye free Communications of his light: but yet I am amazed wth darkness & distance. A thousand times my heart groanes forth these wishes [0 for a clearer sight of God! how can I Loue him more till I know him more! O y^{t} I knew more of ye fountaine of Life, & ye everlastinge state of soules with God, though I were a foole to all ye matters of ye world!] And yet I am where I was. I daily look upwards & gaze towards ye altitude, but my sight falls short: I am studyinge ye height & bredth & length & depth & faine would know ye Love of Christ; but I find it passeth my knowledge. Yet (y^{t} you mistake me not) I speake not all this of ye matter to be knowne, but of ye manner or degree of knowinge. I must needs say y^{t} I take ye holy Scriptures conjunct wth ye booke of nature, for a sufficient objectiue Revealation [*sic*], & I dare not so much as aske of God to shew me more y^{n} Scripture & ye creatures doe Reveale, lest I accuse his doctrine & standinge lawes, & established way of teachinge ye world, & lest I be guilty of pryinge into forbidden mysteryes, & goinge beyonde my sphere, & falling with Adam by a desire to know: for things secret are with God, but things revealed are for us & o^{r} Children: It is not therefore for not knowinge more y^{n} God hath written in Nature & Scripture, y^{t} I am thus distrest; but it is because I know not ye most necessary p^{t} of y^{t}, with y^{t} cleere heart warminge, quickeninge knowledge wch ye nature of ye thinge requires: I am most wantinge in the knowledge of y^{t} wch I doe know. I can recite many truths about ye divine nature of ye mystery of Redemption, & ye everlastinge state of ye saints, but my knowledge of ye subject is darke & smal, while I ptly know ye sence & truth of ye Propositions. In this darkness I am apt to hearken / to any y^{t} pfess to attaine higher discoveryes, y^{n} ye rest of ye world: but when I haue oft drawne neere y^{m} as a learner in hope & great expectations, I haue found y^{t} many would thrust upon me their owne conceits without any evidence for proofe, & expect y^{t} we beleive y^{m} & take their doctrines on ye creditt of their wordes, layinge us downe some new contrived frame, and sayinge it is ye truth of God, & angrily rejectinge us as sons of darkness, and strivers against ye light if we doe not receive it. When I must confess myselfe exceedingly undisposed to receive any doctrines on ye creditt of any man, without Scripture or Reason to prove it to be of God: especially when I see so many undoubtingly confident y^{t} they are ye children of light & truth & have ye illuminations of God who contradict both Scripture & one another. And thus beinge discouraged in my expectations from men, I am faine to waite on God alone, in ye use of those ordinary helpes y^{t} he hath vouchsafed. I confess ye importance of yor first letters put me in some expectations of receivinge some extraordinary helpe by yor Communications: for I plainly pceived you had much to Communicate: but I now pceive you are pleased to withhold it, & silently deny ye great matters y[t] I so earnestly requested of you. Yo[r] pious spirituall lines are very gratefull to me; but had you granted my request, it would haue beene a much greater kindness; though it had beene but in one sheet or halfe sheet of methodicall Propositions, summarily containinge y[e] truths w[ch] you would communicate, or at least haue directed me to some booke where it is done. But I plainly pceive y[t] yo[r] disposition & mine in y[t] are contrary: you are reserved, & thinke meet to conceale yo[r] mind, & while you magnifye y[e] truth, you tell me not w[t] these truths are, w[ch] you desire I should receive; & how y[n] am I ever y[e] neerer receivinge y[m]. But If I know any thinge w[ch] I judge necessary for my Brethren to know I am most carefull to make it as Publique as I can, by a speedy & plaine & free disclosure; & I cannot endure to hide it, but must cast it into y[e] world, whether they will heare it or refuse it. And I know so well y[t] truth loues y[e] light, y[t] (to deale freely with you) I cannot but entertaine those teachers with some suspition yt refuse y[e] open light, & carry on their worke in darkness, & thinke men must be cheated into a beleife of y[e] truth under some other p[r]tense, as a foolish patient must haue physicke secretly put into his meat, yt he may take it, & not know what he takes. This is not y[e] way of y[e] Gospell. Truth feareth nothinge so much as to be hid. And he y[t] is loth to reveale it, least it lose his creditt, or prove his trouble, hath so low thoughts of his owne opinions (supposinge y[t] they will not beare his charges, or y[t] their creditt is to be buryed rather y[n] his owne, or y[t] they haue no such evidence as may breake through y[e] darkness of opposition) y[t] he may well excuse others yt are not forward to receive y[m]. Now breifly of w[t] you haue here communicated. 1[0] I resolvedly close wth y[e] Catholike Church in Catholike verityes, & am no more for or ag[t] any sect or pty, y[n] I am confident they are for or ag[t] y[e] truth. And there is no pty y[t] ever I opposed but I would quickly joyne with, if I could find y[m] in y[e] right. 2[0] The neernes & yet inconsistant distance of Truth & error, is past doubt. 3[0] The infinite essence of God, over through & in all (as well as y[e] Saints), & y[t] of him & through him & for him are all things (w[ch] as you call a fitt text, so you may see how I favo[r] it, on my seale) is a truth yt all Christians are agreed in. And y[t] ever sober man should call it [Scepticisme to see him who is invisible, or Atheisme to know him who is God by nature] is incredible, or y[t] w[ch] I never heard; for Scepticisme & Atheisme are y[e] cleane contraryes to these. But 4[0] I yet conceive y[t] man may know a thousand fold more of Gods will, y[n] of his Essence: for alas, its litle yt we know of his Essence: but to know his will, is but to know what he willeth, y[t] is, y[e] object & pduct of it, w[ch] is abundantly revealed in his word & works & events. 5[0] That some things of God are impossible to be uttered I grant: but of those, I am content to be Ignorant; for it is not y[e] will of God y[t] I should know y[m]: & y[t] w[ch] is aboue us thus, is nothing to us. That some things are hard to be uttered I grant: but these call for y[e] greater diligence in teachers & learners, & y[e] more condemne those yt wilfully / obscure y[t] w[ch] is so obscure in itselfe, w[ch] they should doe their best to illustrate.

That some are unlawfull or inconvenient to be told all, I am not satisfyed: If you meane it of any thinge contained in Scripture or ye visible works of God: for these are Revealed allready by God to all: & if all understand ym not, it is not bec[ause] God hath not told ym, but because they are dull of hearinge, & receive not wt is revealed to ym. To say therefore yt these should not be told all, is to accuse God yt hath told ym all in his words & workes, & commanded his ministers to Preach yt word to every creature. Yet I easily grant, both yt higher truths are not to be inculcated on men yt be not prped by lower; (but yt is not a concealinge ym, but a prudent orderinge or worke yt we loose not or labor); & yt such a one as Paul may haue a pticular supnaturall Revealation, intended only for himselfe, wch it is not possible or lawfull for him to utter to others. But yts nothinge to or matter. The truths wch you adde, about ye Trinityes beinge within & without all, & ye necessity of knowledge, admiration & stability, are great & prtious; & if I could advance to a liuelyear knowledge of ym I were happy; but there is so litle roome for an intimation, yt materially these are unknowne, yt all Christians are agreed in ym beyonde all dispute. These Pearles, & prtious Stones of ye Citty of God, we magnifye all with one mouth; though all haue not ye same intense apprhensions or inward workinge sight & tast of yt wch they confess. The same I say of Gods being wholly & every where at once: Its confest by all. And though ye error of ye wicked Atheists be ye denyall of it, yet ye error of ye wicked Hypocrites & heart Atheists in ye Church is but ye secrett denyall, or not beleivinge it with a workinge effectuall faith. Our Babylonish contentions (as you speake) I doubt not are fed by Ignorance of God in Xt, & by every sin, but materially they consist not in any of these matters, wch all are agreed in. I verily beleive yt ye mystery of ye holy Trinity runs through all ye veins of true Theology, & yt ye right Methodizinge of it, must be from ye workes of ye three in one: yea & yt some Image of ye Trinity is on ye face of Nature itselfe, & in ye nobler pts of it, somewt Conspicuous (as ye movinge-power, ye light & heat of the Sun; ye Vegetative, Sensitive & Rationall facultyes in man: ye Posse, Scire, Velle in ye Rationall, with abundance more doe intimate.) Or at least we may here see somewhat to quiett Reason itselfe, as concerninge a consistency of Trinity in Vnity. The necessity of *Mortifyinge ye fleshly mind*, is another truth wch all Christians are agreed in; & therefore I hope you would not make it any pticular hoñor[?], of ye Quaquers to hold yt wch we all hold wth out Controversye. If all practise not wt they hold, yts nothinge agt ye Doctrine, but ye pson. Sure you had more yn this wch you appved in ye Quaquers as their peculiar, when you would aske me, why I was agt ym? But doth not their unsound Doctrine about ye Trinity & Xt in speciall, & ye Scriptures, shew yt their mortificn hath had no such success for advancinge their knowledes [?] as you intimate. In ye last point I much differ from you. I am prswaded yt ye foundations of all true Churches prsent or past, were laid in an eternall interest (as you speake); & yt therefore, though hostile ptyes may trouble ym with some velitations [*sic*] about some pinacles of ye temple, yet it shall stand as built upon ye Rock. Christ only is ye foundation of all these Churches in ye primary sence, & secundarily ye Prophetts & Apostles, & we have his pmise yt his Church shall be so built on this Rocke (even Christ) yt ye gates of Hell shall not prvaile against it. We all agree in ye antient Creed, ye old test of Xtianity & in much more: we all beleive ye same Scripture to be Gods word. All Xtians in ye world, united in Xt ye head are, wth me, ye Catholike Church: And if there were no Church there were no Xt. No body, no Head: No Kingdome, no King: No Schollars, no Master: No Spouse, no Husband. Indeed ye prsent Churches know but in pt, & differ in pt & will doe: but note their Agreements, before you note their differences. I haue heard many blame ym, but wn I haue drawne neere I could not learne ye way to better ym, nor find ye reprovers more pfect yn others. If we blame men for beinge men, or ye Churches for not beinge pfect in knowledge & love, yt is because they are not yet in Heaven, & Glorifyed, we doe but tell ym of yt burden wch they groane under / & must doe till ye day of unburdeninge & deliverance, & wch orselues must beare as well as others. They yt see not ye Reconcilinge Truth wch ye shattered Churches must unite in, are fitter to Lament yn to Reproue or Divisions & Ignorance. And they yt doe see this Reconcilinge = Truth, & will not openly, speedily & plainly declare it, are most reproveable ymselues, as denyinge ye Communication of yt greatest mercye to ye Churches in their distress; & passinge by us in or wounds, & seeinge us in or needs, & shuttinge up ye bowells of Compassion from us. Deare Sir pdon ye plixity & beare wth ye freedome, of

Yor Brother
Ri: Baxter.

---

cefnysgrifiwyd (58v)
'To Mr Morgan Lloyd Pastor of the Church at Wrexham'.

38
Hugh Courtney at Morgan Llwyd, 3 Ebrill 1649

(LLGC 11439D, f. 22)

Dear Sir

I recd yrs this post, Indeed hurking much to the noyses without, I have formerly found by sad experiences hath deafned the eare to whispering within. Wee have since or being in towne walked with Mr Cradockes Congregation who freely & joyfully embrace us, much benifitt wee might enjoy by them had wee harts suitable to receeve & mercyes, how great an advantage it is to have fellowship wth sts. They that fully enjoyh it know how too prize it, the want of it by reason of a sinfull bashfulnesse in mee, renders mee as uselesse to others soe also uncomfortable to myselfe. You have inclosed besides the Moderate a petition wch much satisfies me for I was a little troubled at the pre --- of or present Parliamt agt Lilburne & the rest not having seen his booke I am persuaded it is expected by all upright men waken for certayne from Ireland that Inchequin for or after joyning wth Ormond have refused to engage agst Jones. Wee are here well blessed . . . god but desirouse to bee with you wayting to have a way opened for us.

With kindest salutes to you & yrs not a little censible of yr prsent tryalls, I take leave.

Yrs
Hugh Courtney

3[d] Apr. 1649.

The act for a fast the 29th instant were sent by Coll Twistleton

For Mr Morgan Lloyd.

Hugh Courtney. Gŵr o Gernyw (T. Richards, *History of the Puritan Movement*, 92). Fe'i penodwyd yn bennaeth milisia gogledd Cymru, 22 Mawrth 1651. Yr oedd cyn hynny'n ddirprwy lywodraethwr Biwmares ac wedyn yn llywodraethwr Ynys Môn. Yr oedd yn un o gomisiynwyr Deddf y Taenu ac yn aelod o Senedd y Saint, 1653. Er ei fod yn un o edmygwyr Vavasor Powell, ni allai lofnodi'r *Gair Dros Dduw* oherwydd ei fod wedi'i garcharu yng Nghastell Carisbrooke o Chwefror 1654 hyd Ragfyr 1656. Bu yng ngharchar wedyn o 13 Ebrill 1660 hyd 19 Mehefin ond cafodd ei ryddhau ar yr amod ei fod yn gadael y wlad (W. R. Williams, *Parliamentary History*, 3, a T. Richards, *Religious Developments*, 177–8, 205, 218).

'Coll Twistleton'. George Twistleton, mab John, Aula Barrow, Swydd Efrog. Fe'i ganed yn 1618. Priododd â Mary, merch William Glyn, Lleuar, Sir Gaernarfon. Bu'n AS Môn, 1654–5, 1656–8, Ionawr hyd Ebrill 1659. Bu farw 12 Mai 1667 yn 48 oed a chladdwyd ef yng Nghlynnog. Yr oedd yn llywodraethwr Dinbych 1646–1660 (W. R. Williams, op. cit., 4).

'Mr Cradocke' oedd Walter Cradoc (1610?–59).

'Lilburne' oedd John Lilburne (1614?–57), arweinydd y Lefelwyr. Yr oedd y Senedd wedi dyfarnu'r ail ran o'i lyfryn *England's New Chains* yn fradwrus ac yntau wedi'i garcharu yn Nhŵr Llundain ar 28 Mawrth, gw. *DNB*.

'Inchequin' oedd Murrough o'Brien (1614–74), Iarll cyntaf Inchiquin a chweched Barwn Inchiquin.

'Ormond' oedd James Butler (1610–88), deuddegfed Iarll a Dug cyntaf Ormonde.

'Jones' oedd y Cyrnol John Jones, Maesygarnedd.

39
William Erbery at Morgan Llwyd, heb ddyddiad

(*The Testimony of William Erbery* (London, 1658), 235–39)

For Mr Morgan Lloyd.

Sir,

Yours of the twenty ninth of the fourth month, I received at Roth near Cardiff this 12 of August; and I return an Answer in silence, seeing we are both in the Eternal Spirit, with the spirits of just men made perfect, where there is no need of speech to communicate our thoughts or attainments each to other; being taken up into him who is our All, and all in All.

There the Mystery of the Resurrection begins, and the Apostle goes on in that height from, I Cor. 14. 28. to the end; that this is the Resurrection, not that last and general of the world, but the first Resurrection; the rising of the Saints, or of the dead in Christ, who shall rise first: I say, That this is the Resurrection only of the just, and not of the unjust, nor of All, any man (even without the Spirit of Revelation) may judge by reason, and reading of that Chapter; where the rising of the spiritual body to incorruption, immortality, power and glory, is the glorious appearing of the second Man, the quicking Spirit, the Lord from Heaven (in us) to the heavenly Image; which is the third estate of the Saints now approaching, and the latter part of your Letter points at.

This I call the third dispensation, or last discovery of God unto and in men, differing from Law and Gospel—order; yet comprehending both, and above both, yea above all: for here all men and things are nothing, but God is all and alone, yea God is All in all.

This third dispensation, as all the Prophets and Apostles did write and wait for; so in this I wait in silence, with God (though I speak sometimes to men) for a full discovery of him in me, and to all the Saints with me; for when the Lord my God shall come or appear, all the Saints shall come with thee, Zach 14.5.

The Earth-quake there spoken of is at hand, 'tis the same mentioned in Babylons final fall, Rev. 16. 18. 19. for a threefold fall of Babylon is written, Rev. 14. 8. Rev. 18. 2 and vers 21. And that the third or last fall of Babylon, will be in the fall of this form of Church-fellowship (so called) you may see in your spirit, and in some printed scriblings of mine: therefore for Order, Ordinances, Officers, Churches, Societies of men, all are in Babylon, in confusion of Tongues; that's out of order, etc. though many of the Saints conceive they are come to Sion already.

Babylon is a Mystery (as you shall see with God very shortly) Babylon or the Beast is the mystery of man, that's the woman also, or the Whole, the man of sin: and Christ is the mystery of God, God manifest in the flesh, in his flesh & in ours; (for we and He are perfect in one with the Father) and as the Beast is the Wisdom of man, and the Power of man in the Church, that's the seven Heads and ten Hornes, etc. so Christ is the Wisdome of God, and Power of God, which was in the Church, and is, (though not known) and is to come; for that's his name, God with us, Christ in us the hope of glory which is to come; when the mystery of God shall be finished or fully known to men at the sounding of the seventh Trump, which is the last Trump, the Trump of God, when the great Trump shall be blown, etc. which is the last discovery of God.

When this great Trump is blown, those who were ready to perish in the land of Assyria, and the out-cast in the Land of Aegypt, shall come and worship the Lord in the holy Mount at Jerusalem, Isa. 27. 13. That's the new Jerusalem which shall come down from God out of Heaven after Babylons fall, and freedome of all the Saints from that double boundage now upon their Spirits. Not only of gathered Churches, but of scattered Saints 'tis spoken; of the one as ready to perish, and the other as out-casts, in Assyria and Egypt too (as I said) that's the twofold captivity we are all carryed away in, till the great Trumpet be blown.

Then the dead bones shall rise out of Babylon; and God will open the graves of his people, who shall all come forth out of their forms and flesh, when the glory of the Lord shall cover them, and they live in the Eternal Spirit together: then the sticks also, the divided societies of Saints shall become one, etc. for that's the third dispensation, called the dispensation of the fulnesse of time, when all things both in heaven and earth shall be gathered up into one, all the Saints of highest appearances, and of lowest performances, both those of Legal tempers and Gospel attainments shall be gathered up into one, into that glory, into God himself.

This Resurrection of the dead, the Apostle had not attained to, though pressing toward it: and Peter was waiting for it in the new Heaven and new Earth; for the old Heaven and old earth, (both Legal and Gospel-dispensation) vanish away in God; yea, there's no more Sea, (saith John) no more of that dividing and destroying Principle in man; for that's the Sea, which has made the Saints not onely to clash one against another, but every one to be as an Isle to himself, and so indeed it must be in Babylons fall, not a man to be found, Isai. 13. 12 but every man flyes to his own Land, vers. 14 (to live solitary and alone in his own light, that light which shines in every man, and every man in his God) but every one that is found shall be thrust through, and every one that is joyned with them; (that's not in the Hebrew) but every one that is joyned (in Babylon) shall fall by the sword, vers. 15.

There's no building of Temples in Babylon, nor joyning there in

Church-fellowship; for that will fall, and we with it, till we retire alone into our selves, or the Spirit rather in us; and this we must be, every man apart by himself; every Family apart, and their wives apart; man and his wife, though nearest and dearest flesh, must be separated, when the Spirit of Grace and Supplication (or favours) begins to appear to take us up into glory.

Then the multitude of the Isles shall rejoyce, when the Lord comes to Raign, Psal. 97.1. the Raign of God and of Christ, or the Saints with him, being the same with their Resurrection, the first Resurrection, Isai. 60. 1. Ezek. 37. 25. 26. Zach. 14. 5. 9. For as by the great Trumpet they are gathered one by one, Isai. 27. 12. so this shewes that all the Saints shall be found as so many Isles, every one alone by himself, made so by the Sea; but the Sea shall be no more when the new Heaven & the new Earth comes: then all the people of God shall become one Land, one Continent, wherein the Lord alone shall live; this is the Land so much spoken of by the Prophets, the Land of the living, the land of Israel, who are promised to be brought to their own Land, (being now in a strange Land, in Babylon) but he that scattered Israel, will gather him; and the Saints who are now scattered in and by their gathered Churches, yes all the scattered Saints with them shall be gathered up into God, who indeed is he who scatters as well as gathers; we do nothing, we can do nothing, but in him who is All in all.

In this Mystery of the Resurrection, all your Questions in the Letter will be answered, your doubts satisfied, your darkness cleared, your Captivity ended; for it is the glorious liberty of the children of God, the manifestation of the sons of God, the appearing of the great God in us, when we shall be like him, see him as he is, know him as we are known, see him eye to eye; as he sees us, we shall see him, see his Face, and his Name on our foreheads; that is, we shall not only see God, but men shall see God in us; for all that see us shall acknowledge that we are the seed which the Lord hath blessed: the blessed seed is Christ the Son of God, so all the Saints shall be in the glory of the Father, when the Son shall be subject, and God All in all.

This is the Adoption and Redemption of the body, the Resurrection of the body when the body, now natural or soule—ly (as the Greek reads it) shall be raised spiritual, the Eternal Spirit appearing to be all in all.

This will be in every one of us in particular (for we must be gathered one by one) and this will be in all the Saints in general, who are the body, the dead in Babylon, the dead body of Christ there; But thy dead men shall live together, with my body they shall arise, etc. Isa. 26. 19. together with is not the Hebrew; which reads, Thy dead men shall live, my dead body they shall arise, etc. that is, when the Lord God, in us all, shall stay us all, & all flesh to himself, our gifts our graces, and all shall be slain to God, and by him. His sword, his spirit, the fire shall do it, we must all dye, come down to the dust, lye there, as the dry bones (not so much as flesh or skin upon us, much lesse strength, spirit and life) yet we shall live, though now dead, yea the dead shall live: that is, as none see God but the blind, none hear him but the deaf (deaf to man and to self) so the dead alone can live, and they live in death, who find themselves the dead body of the Lord: my dead body they shall arise; Awake and sing ye that dwell in the dust, etc. in the lowest estate of flesh, when the first man Adam is turned to dust; when we are nothing, we are all in God, and God is all in all, and in this we may sing together: For the second man bears the Image of the heavenly, which is the third dispensation typified in the third daies Resurrection of Christ, as I shall tell you another time, with God.

I'le say no more, 'tis love, 'tis the Lord that makes the dumb to sing, and the tongue of the Stammerer to speak plainly. or elegantly, as the margine reads it, Isa. 32. 4.

Your lives were so to me full of divine elegance, of love and delight: truly 'tis my love to you likewise, and the Lord in me, has made me in much haste to stammer this much unto you; I am now silent, yea dumb; the Lord God, who rejoyceth over you with singing, will sing and speak himself with delight in you: There I leave you and all the Saints with you and your beloved wife; whose I am as I am,

Yours,
WILLIAM ERBERY

40

William Erbery at Eglwys Gynnull Wrecsam, heb ddyddiad

(*The Testimony of William Erbery,* 103–4)

To the gathered Church at Wrexham.
Beloved brethren,

The following Letters I call Night-light, for nothing else has shined forth to the world, or to Saints, since the Apostacie. (a) Watchman what of the night? watchman what of the night? the morning cometh & also the night, etc. Morns of light and love, have oft arised to the Saints even in Babylon, but a night of darkness has immediately followed or a mixture of both, light and darkness, day and night has continually succeeded in this confusion wherein we have been, and are as yet; yea, more of the mystery of Babylon appears this day within us, which makes me believe, we are in the day of God already though we know it not, for 'tis known to the Lord alone, whose day has not a certain constant shine, but is neither light nor darkness, 'tis neither Day nor Night, but in the evening (when the Sun sets, when mans day ends and our light goes away) there shall be light, or God appears to all: this is a secret; our sweetest retirements, and rest at present is in the night, then we have most of our loves or delights in the Lord; for all the night long we lie in his bosome, (and he lies between our breasts) there he leaves you, who is in Truth

Yours in the bowels
of Christ Jesus
WILL. ERBERY.

(a) Isa. 21. 11, 12. This was spoken about Babylons fall, verse 9 for the Apostasie was a night to the people of God, who were as the watchman waiting for deliverance from their spiritual bondage, typified by Dumah ver. 11. Edom or Esau, was of kin to the true Church or Jacob, but yet a false brother; therefore a burden or destruction is prophecied against him, and in him against the false Church-state.

(Daw'r llythyr uchod o'r gyfrol *The North Star: Or, Some Night-Light Shining from North-Wales.* With some dark Discoveries of the Day of God approaching, that is, the second coming or appearing of Christ in us the hope of Glory).

41

William Erbery at Morgan Llwyd, heb ddyddiad

(*The Testimony of William Erbery*, 105–10)

1. For Mr Morgan Lloyd

SIR,

Your second Letter is exceeding welcome to a friend of yours, who is now the Lord's prisoner, and has been so indeed, these many daies, and years also, in the Spirit.

Truly, he would not know any thing of man any more, and all that he knows of God at present, is, that he is known of God, or God become his knowledge; this also, but in much confusion: therefore (Dear Sir) expect not clearness from a man that dwells in Babylon.

All my life at present, and liberty also, is, to serve the King of Babylon, and to be quietly subject to God in this captive state, wherein himself hath brought me, who is my life and glorious liberty.

This glory (even God himself in the midst of my flesh) makes my flesh to suffer, and to dye daily; till he be so manifest in flesh, and revealed in me to be All in All, and in all the Saints the same.

Till this be, he who is first must be last, and he who has the first dominion or power, shall be the weakest, the least, and in the lowest dungeon (with Joseph and Jeremiah in the pit without water) and their feet not only stick in the mire, but they shall cry out aloud, as men in prison out of their grates, (of flesh) or as a woman in travel ready to be delivered (of spirit).

The Lord God calls to the man, Is there no King in thee? is thy Counsellors perished, Is all thy knowledg humane and divine dead, thy wisdom and power departed, thy rest and peace fled? for pangs have taken hold upon thee as a woman in travel; this the flesh would fain put off, and be as wise as it was, and as easie: but, be in pain, O daughter of Sion, etc. that is, the man in whom God begins to discover himself in glory, with love and delight, must be content to be as a woman in travel. 'Twas so with Saints in the Gospel dispensation, when the man child, the mighty power of God, was brought forth in them: 'twas so also in the suffering-Saints since the Apostasie, when after many pangs and pains of a woman in travel, the man-child was brought forth, Rev. 12. 2, 3. 'twill be so much more in the third dispensation, after our deliverance from Babylons captivity, a man shall travel with child again, as a woman in travel, till the man child, David the King be brought forth, Jer. 30. 3, 6, 7, 9. that is, God will so be brought forth in our flesh, that we shall go out of the City into the field, not only out of all Churches and common societies; but we shall go even to Babylon, and there shall we be delivered; delivered of God, or God brought forth in our flesh, that is All of flesh without or within, God will confound, and so redeem us to himself into the glorious liberty of the sons of God, Rom. 8. 21, 22, 23.

But the Son of God is he you enquire after, the hypostasis of the Lord Jesus, etc. I see by this, you are with me in Babylon; for who knows the Son but the Father? the Father in you may shew you the Son, and the Son revealed in you will shew you the Father. This knowledge of God and of Christ comes not by reading, nor yet by Scripture, but by the Spirit of Revelation, though the Scripture also speaks the same.

And yet what the Apostle writes of himself in his highest knowledge of the Mystery of Christ, was but in part; what he knew, as what he prophesied (that is, preached or writ of Christ) was but in part, therefore his Epistles to us will give out but a partial discovery of God and of Christ; yea, all that Christ spake of himself in the Evangelists was but in parables: therefore no plain discovery or manifestation of the Mystery of Christ can be had from the Epistles or Gospels: Hitherto, saith he, I have spoken to you in parables, or proverbs, but I will shew you plainly of the Father, that is, when he should depart or disappear in flesh, then they should know him in the Father. And the promise of the Father or power from on high, even the power of the Godhead that was in his flesh, should appear in theirs, that's he in them, and they in him, John. 14. 20 Luke 24.49. Eph. 3. 19. compared.

To know then the hypostasis or substance of the Son, is to know the Son in your self, that is, God even the Father, in our flesh as in his, as you may see in my little Book, Neither Truth nor Error, nor light nor darkness, but in the evening there shall be light.

The light of the last times will clear up the mystery of God even the Father, and of Christ, which has been clouded all along the Apostasie; for in the sounding of the seventh trumpet, the mystery of God shall be finished or fully known. Again, in the new Jerusalem, the Lord God Almighty, and the Lamb is the light thereof; that's God and Christ. Besides, the walls of the City had twelve gates, and in them the names of the twelve Apostles of the Lamb, Rev. 21. 14. 22, 23.

These twelve Apostles of the Lamb, may be the Ministery of the Spirit in the last times in some suffering men, who shall rejoyce in Babylons fall; for the Heavens with the holy Apostles and Prophets are called to reioyce over her judgments Rev. 18. But as the testimony of Jesus is the Spirit of prophesie, so the heavens are the Saints of the most high, who live not below in forms or flesh, but in the Spirit from on high waited for, Rev. 22. 17. Yet the testimony of the twelve first Apostles, and of the Lamb also, is at hand to serve you, that the hypostasis of the Son, is the glory of the Father, or God even the Father (dwelling in the flesh) is the substance or

Godhead of the Lord Jesus. For, as no man can say (or confess) that Jesus is the Lord, but by the Spirit: so that Name above all Names, even Jesus, to be God over all, is given him of God, to the glory of the Father, Phil. 2, 9. 11.

The hypostatical union of the Son then is this, that the Father is one and all with the man, the man Christ Jesus is one with the Father; for the Father in him was all in all, and he nothing, or could do nothing, but as he was in the Father, and the Father in him, doing all his works, and words.

And because God even the Father cannot be known in his own naked Being and Godhead, but as cloathed with flesh, therefore the Son that was born, and the child given to men, was none else but the mighty God, the everlasting Father manifest in flesh.

For no man hath seen God at any time, but the only begotten Son, who is in the bosome of the Father, he hath declared him, not in word only, but in works which the Father did in him and by him; for the Son could do nothing of himself, etc. And because the Father spake all in the Son, God in the Man, therefore the Man Christ Jesus is called the Word of God (for God was that Word, as the Greek there reads, Joh 1.1) that is, God even the Father, being manifest in wisdom and power in the Man, the Man Christ Jesus is called the Wisdom of God, and Power of God.

Thus Christ also was that Wisdom of God, Prov. 8. 22, 23. God coming forth with wisdom and power, in the Creation of all things, and of man; and as power is the glory of man, so (the glory of God appearing with power in Christ) John saw his glory the glory of the only begotten of the Father full of grace and truth.

And as Christ the Divine wisdom and power was set up from everlasting, Prov. 8. 21. that is, from the beginning ver. 22. So Christ is called he that was from the beginning, Joh 1. 1. I Joh. 1. 1. I Joh. 2. 13. not begotten from eternity (as men say); but because the eternal God even the Father brought forth himself, with wisdom and power in the beginning, wisdom was said to be in the beginning brought forth, Prov. 8. 24. or begotten, as the Geneva Translation hath it, or born, as another translation reads. And thus Christ is called the heir of all things, by whom all things were made, or made forth; that is, all things manifested from the beginning, were in that wisdom and power that was in Christ, called therefore the beginning of the Creation of God: For all things were of the Father, so by Christ are all things manifest, and made forth in the Creation, and in man, I Cor. 8. 6.

But as wisdom was said to be set up by God, and God appointed Christ to be heir of all things: so it pleased the Father, that in him should all fulness dwell, Heb. 1. 2. Col. 1. 19. Prov. 8. 23. therefore the fulness of the Godhead in Christ, that wisdom and power in him, was by the Father's pleasure and appointment, not natural to the Son (as Schollars speak without Book, for no Scripture saysit) nor yet was it proper and peculiar to him only, but for us also, he being set up for this very purpose with all fulness of glory, that out of his fulness we might receive grace for grace, and to be filled with all the fulness of God: yea, as we receive grace for grace, so glory for glory; that glory or grace of union which the Son had with the Father, that have we perfect in one with the Son, Gods love to us being as to his beloved, and our life with Christ in God, Joh 7. 22, 23.

That which has brought confusion upon all Christendom in the knowledge of Christ, is not only the ignorance of man's union with Christ in God; but that personality of Christ in the Godhead, according to the traditions of man, and metaphysicall speculations of God or vain Philosophy (as the Apostle calls it) by which the Mystery of God even the Father, and of Christ, is exceedingly clouded.

But if we knew the Mystery of God even the Father, and of Christ in the Spirit, it would shew Christ in us, that's God in our flesh as in his, Christ as God being one with the Father, and Christ as man being one with his brethren, who are not only one flesh with him, but of his bone and of his flesh; though he be the elder brother, and above his fellows.

Thus the Scripture (speaking of God, and Christ, and the Spirit) must be spiritually understood; not in a carnal sense, as three distinct persons, but as a threefold discovery, or making forth of that one God to Man. God in himself, of whom are all things, is the Father: the same God and Father manifest in flesh, is the Son; that mighty God powefully acting and exerting himself in flesh, is the Spirit. Thus the Word being said to be God, and God sending his Son, and the Son sending forth the Spirit, are spiritually to be understood, Again, the Son giving himself, sending the Comforter from the Father, etc. all this (as Christ said before) is parabolically spoken, or in a figure: the Word was not with God, as one person with another, for God is the Divine Nature, and God sent not his Son, as a man sends his servant, a distinct person from himself, and from a distinct place, as men imagine: but as the glory of God is that which appears in all things; so God even the Father coming forth with glory in the Man Christ Jesus, is God giving or sending his Son, called also his servant.

Again, saith Christ, the glory which thou hast given me, I have given them: Observe first, The glory was given him, and he giving that glory to us, is nothing else, but as God is pleased to reveal his Son in us; then the glory of God that was in Christ is revealed in us by the Spirit; and by the Spirit to the world. The Spirit (as I said) being called the power of God, or God powerfully exerting himself not only in the Creation (for so 'tis the Spirit simply) but this spirit or power appearing in us also (even in the Saints) as in Christ, in our flesh, as in his, is called the holy Spirit.

This also is the sense of that which Jesus saith of the Spirit, I will send you another Comforter: for as the Father sent the Son, so the Son sends the Spirit, that's himself in Power, for I will not leave you comfortless, I will come unto you: 'tis called another comforter, because 'tis in another appearance, for he that is with you, shall be in you, that is, when the power of God in my flesh, now with you, shall appear in you, then the Comforter is come, and the Spirit sent, John 14, 20.

By all this it appears to me, that what you ask concerning the hypostasis of Christ, must be only answered by the Spirit, which will speak the Father in you to be the hypostasis of the Son.

The Letter of Scripture shews this abundantly, but I must be brief.

1) The hypostatical union is this, *viz.* the man Christ Jesus one with the Father, that's the Son: for the Son the second person, is not said to be one with the man, (as men do say) but the man one with God even the Father is the Son.

2) The Spirit is given to the Son, and the Son is said to receive it from the Father, therefore called the promise of the Father.

3) The Son is said to send the Spirit from the Father.

4) The Spirit proceeds from the Father, not from the Son, though sent by him, Joh. 15. 26.

My dear friend, ask no more of man the things of God, but seek him and all in your self; where you may find him and all. There wait to see the morning Star, The sons of oyl, or two witnesses, with the seals opened, the Trumpets sounding and the Vialls full of wrath poured forth on all that is flesh within you, that nothing but pure spirit may appear, nothing of man, but God may be All in All.

Only this I observe, that as in the seventh Trumpet the Mystery of God is finished: so the seventh Vial poured out, one says, 'tis done; thus Christ when his sufferings were ended, or done, crys 'tis finished, Joh. 19. 30. when our inward flesh is more crucified to God (as Christ was) when we are come up to full fellowship with his sufferings, and conformity to his death, we shall arise and live in the life of Jesus, then all the seals are opened, we hear no more of the Trumpets, nor the sound of war, nor sense of wrath.

Your last question is, what manner of persons ought we to be in this age? Your own retired spirit will tell you, and the eternal spirit taking you up, first to the mount, to see Christ transfigured in glory, then into the Garden, to be not only an eye-witness, but a companion of his sufferings in you, will shew you.

Those three Apostles who were witnesses of both, even Peter, James, and John call upon you, First, To be pure in heart. Secondly, Holy in conversation, Thirdly, to be patient, or (as the margin reads) long-patient, or suffering with long patience) to the coming of the Lord, Jam. 5. 7. Farwel

Your loving Friend,
WILLIAM ERBERY.

42

William Erbery at Morgan Llwyd, Mai 1653

(*The Testimony of William Erbery*, 113–15)

2. For Mr Mor. Lloyd.

Sir,

Tis your love, and the Lord in you that gives you that liberty to write so oft to an abhorred man and in bondage, every way unworthy of this favour, especially from those who (with the Church of the Jews) think themselves free, and so far from Babylon: but though the sons of Sion lye in the dust, yet the time is come, that he will have mercy on her, and raise her sons to wait for that glory to be revealed in them, Christ in us is the hope of glory, God being in our flesh as in his: though our flesh as yet be the grave wherein the Lord is laid, and our life is also hid with him in God; yet God in us will rise, and his glory so be revealed on us, that we shall rise, and shine as surely, as the Son was raised to glory; the glory being the same, though not now manifest in us, as 'twas in him when risen. None but the Women, the weakest Saints, see the resurrection at hand, which the present Apostles and Ministers of the Gospel laugh at, and look upon as idle tales. Luke 24. 11. Truth is yet dawning, and the day of God is yet darknesse, and not light to those who live in man's day, whose Sun sets at noon, that they cannot see Ezekiel's inward gates, nor yet the outward porch of God's house, being not ashamed of their whoredoms, Ezek. 43. 11.

This is man fallen into flesh and blood (as you say) for the Whore loves the flesh of man, and of many; so good men do this day, having lost their sight and spiritual hearing in the noise of the multitudes of this world, in the wordly sanctuary and earthly thing.

'Tis well your soul is escaped, and can fly among the fowls of Heaven who are called to the Lord's feast, to feed on the flesh of Kings and Captains, &c. Rev. 18. 18. However I would not, you should be a Swallow or Dove, mourning; for that's Babylon's plague; nor yet on Hezekiah's sick-bed, as one dying, when life (as you write) even the Tree of life, &c is appearing in the Paradise of God.

'Tis not notionally or after the flesh; I hope your expectance is of those living waters, and flouds of the Spirit coming forth, or the flowers in your own garden. Christ spake once as Joseph, by an Interpreter, when the Spirit of Interpretation was in the Church: but now that gift being gone, he speaks himself in us, unless he be indeed silent, and we deaf to his voice.

Blessed be God that some men can say, and see the Father, now revealing himself as the natural Father, nourisher and enjoyer of this world; for as all things are of him, so all men are in him, &c. the everlasting Gospel will more manifest this mystery.

Therefore you add, 'Tis joyous (or Gospel) that the Eternal — will works with delight in the everlasting power, which cannot be resisted, as you say. True; but God in weakness, and God in strength, is a distinction our Divines never taught you: For God the eternal power gave his life for us, and he who was the wisdom and power of God, became so weak, a worm, and no man.

That was the will of the Son, to be crucified through weaknesse, and that he had a body prepared for suffering was the will of God, and the delight of Christ. In the light of this Sun (as you say well) we shall be as nothing, for God will be al [sic] in all to us, as to him who could do nothing of himself.

Vanity and levity, &c. may then appear on our spirits, when our pure flesh is so crucified, though curiosity, obscenity, and base lusts will be more crucified in such, then in some who are alive before men, and seem to be Angels.

I'le say nothing now of the holy City, nor the stout-hearted in it; who are so, beacuse not come to the brink of eternity, nor have ever heard the Angel swear, that time shall be no more.

The deep things of God, and heavenly Mysteries lighting into a foul heart, heighten and harden it more, because notional or not understood; but falling in truth, into a broken and contrite spirit, tears it in pieces; 'tis well, and the way of God to make it whole, this way.

Purity of spirit I minded you of as my self, not without me, but as you are in me with all the Saints; you shall hear more of this, when the Father alone speaks to you, and man no more.

Your Letter I printed for publick use, because I count you as one of the Angels of God, who are (as you said once) to millions every day, so is not that what we speak to a particular Congregation or company.

Again, I would not be a Hermite cloystered in a Church, but fly through the world that's more than publick preaching; though this I do also; if we lose by either, 'tis our gain, and we find our selves again in God, when we are at a lost condition, and have not the wit to save our selves.

'Tis by the Lamb slain in us, we have the Seals opened to us, and by the blood of the Lamb in us, we also overcome the world, with spiritual wickednesses in high-places; and though the eys [sic] of the Lamb are fixed and inward, as the four Beasts were full of eys within, yet the eys also run to and fro the whole earth, Rev. 4. 8. Rev. 5. 6. Zach. 3. 9. Zach. 4. 10. compared. Your waiting in silence contradicts your preaching, as well as your coming forth in print by me; but in both, you may be in your own earth, under your own Vine, and under your own Fig-tree sit in silence.

That the Scriptures are not afraid to say, the Trinity is in all the Saints, I have not yet heard nor read in the Letter, but wait to be revealed in us by the Spirit, not as a noble company (as you say); for that has offended and confounded most Christians these many ages and generations in their forms of Divinity; therefore I forbear to speak any more of this, till the time come that there shall be but one King in all the earth, and one Lord, and his Name one.

Then no Rogues, nor worldly, fleshly, selfish lusts of men shall appear in his presence; yea, the beasts of the field, even Dragons and Owls shall honour him, when Jacob shall be given to the curse, and Israel to reproaches.

This is all of the Spirit that hath moved on my waters: if you see an Angel to come down and stir in other mens Pools, pray put in; for henceforth I sit still, and am silent to you in God.

The last part of the Letter I understand not, onely the last line, wherein I am learning to rest with you, and to remain yours in love,

WILL. ERBERY.

London, May 1653.

Gw. Medwin Hughes, 'Llythyrau William Erbery', *Cylchgrawn Llyfrgell Genedlaethol Cymru* XXVI (1989–90), 17–26.

43

Philip Eyton at Morgan Llwyd, 22 Hydref 1656

(LLGC 11439D, f. 33)

ffor his Esteemed
ffrind Mr Morgan
Lloyd at his House
at Brin a
fonon in
Wrexham
post payd

Deare Sr.

Yours I received last weeke and for your care and respects had theirin to my bussines I thanke you for I hard from Collonell Puckenfield sence your last to me, he seemes desirous to Lengthen ye time as to arbitrators but he would have me pick upon another in youre Rome What ye reason their of might be I know not unlesse it be to free you from your troubel or otherwise to keepe from vew some papers yt passed from him to me. I call to mind yt word wch sayes yt hee that Hastneth to be rich falls in to divers snares now a word of passege ye time yt ye Parliament spends is wholy taken up about ye manageing of ye warr with ye spaniards, and contriving of wayes to rayse moneyes to yt end with as littell Burthen to ye Nation as possible may be some part of our fleet is Come into ye Downes as they came they discovered a fleet of Dunkerkers but our shipes being foule and theirs newly maned out, ours could not over tacke them it is reported yt ye sylver prizes is come to Plymouth but noe certenty of that, ye lawers yt are in ye House are much troubled yt ye Act for Registers in ye several Counties should passe theire in shortly a Tract of one Mr. Stellam Minister in Essix to come forth in Answer to ye severall Bookes set forth by ye peeple that is called Quackers it will be large I shall send you one when it is come to vew I desire not to forget your labor of love for me but shall alwayes be ready to owne it when opportunitie offers it selfe my deare Respects to Mrs. Lloyd and ye Rest of my deare frinds

With you remaine

Yr very Affectioneat
ffrind to love and
Serve you
Phil. Eyton.

London 8^0
22th 1656

'Brin a fonon' yw Brynffynnon, y darn o ganol tref Wrecsam lle'r oedd Llwyd yn byw. Yr oedd y cyfenw 'Eyton' yn gyffredin yn yr ardal, yn wir yr oedd y twrnai Kenrick Eyton o Eyton Isaf yn byw ym Mrynffynnon at ddiwedd y ganrif (A. N. Palmer, *History of the Town of Wrexham* (1893), 53–4). Ond nid yw'n eglur prun ohonynt yw awdur y llythyr hwn.

'Mr Stellam Minister in Essix' oedd John Stalham, ficer Terling, Essex, o Fai 1632 nes iddo gael ei ddiswyddo yn 1662, ac Annibynnwr. Bu farw cyn Awst 1677. Y llyfr y cyfeirir ato oedd *Marginall antedotes to be affixed over against the lines of R. H. and E. B. their pamphlet, intituled The rebukes of a reviler* (1657). Y ddau y mae'r teitl yn cyfeirio atynt oedd y Crynwyr Richard Hubberthorne ac Edward Burrough. Gw. *DNB*.

44
Robert Hughes, o Westminster, at dderbynnydd dienw, 15 Mawrth 1659

(LLGC 11439D, f. 30)

Sr

After I waited for severall weekes past I missed the opportunitie to send to you by Mr Robert Evans who hath sett forth here hence betimes this morning, I suppose my Mr . . . (in his lr̄e wch he writt unto you upon Thirsday last) hath given you a full acct. of things, & how ye squares goes here. I have not much att this tyme as to ye publick to acquainte you wth save wt I mentōned in my last lr̄e, the Parliamt. doe goe on wth their busines and transac̄c̄ons but very slowly, Chute (their Speaker) fell ill last wee soe yt they were faine to appoint another to supply his place for the present untill he recovers some strengeth. This man's name is Longe who likewise fell sick yesterday, whereupon ye House did adjourne untill to morrowe. I am informed that there be greate many yt doe sitt in this present Parliamt, who would faine make England yet a Commonwealth once more, ag y mae ei llaferydd nhwy hyd yn hyn yn i Cyhuddo . . . That yt is ye only thing they aime att, I was tould yt ye Commonwealth . . . have sent to ye Courtiers att Whitehall to Certifie unto ym yt they are . . . dissatisfied wth a single p-son to Govern as some doe make yem yet som. . . . there be wch they could not well beare wth. Wherefore they d. . . . yt the Courtiers should appointe 6 sober men to come & meet . . . of them to treate abt it & to heare their objections, but it ser. . . . Courtiers are pretty high in yt. they did not onely dissappr. . . . frowne & slight their offering. Magor Genll. Overton was sent . . . Parliamt to ye Isle of Jersey who upon Wednesday last com. . . . some say in an unhandsome posture wth 5 or 600 people . . . but they had noe Armes & abt 40 or 50 Coaches others . . . many wch is more like to behave however he would . . . higher power carried into prison & wth in a little . . . & this week he is to have his tryall before ye Par. . . . This is all att present save to tell you that Mr his lady & his son are in perfect health, from yor friende.

Robert Hughes

Westminster 15 dy I^s moneth 1658.

'Chute' oedd Chaloner Chute (bu farw 17 Ebrill 1659). Fe'i penodwyd yn Llefarydd y Tŷ Cyffredin, 27 Ionawr 1659. 'Longe' oedd Syr Lislebone Long (1613–59), recordydd Llundain a benodwyd yn Llefarydd, 9 Mawrth 1659. Am y ddau, gw. *DNB*.

'Magor Genll Overton' oedd Robert Overton (bu farw 1668). Yr oedd yn cydymdeimlo â syniadau Gwŷr y Bumed Frenhiniaeth a chafodd ei garcharu ar Ynys Jersey, heb brawf, am fod Cromwell yn amau ei deyrngarwch. Gw. *DNB*.

45

Samuel Hughes, Abertawe, at dderbynnydd dienw, 3 Hydref 1656

(LLGC 11439D, f. 34)

Most loveing friend,

Grace, mercy, and peace bee maintained by you, multiplyed in you, and manifested more and more unto you from God who is ye giver of all good both internall, externall, and eternall, unto all men allmost externall, but unto none but his choice vessells, & beloved Saints internall, and eternall, and may hee bee pleased to say, soe bee it. After My deare mother received your kind letter, in which your good and Godly counsells were not a few, for which wee are all greatly bound to blesse the Lord, and prayse his most holy name, for such a rare blessing, as you are unto us, not onely in giveing us such good counsells, but perswading of us to accept of them without which, wee can hardly atteine unto everlasting Salvacōn I have here according to my bound duty and your chiefest desire wrot a few lines unto you, partly for the respect I beare unto you, and for your entire love of my deceased father, whose memory with mee cannot bee extinguished; and partly to congratulate you for all your kyndnesses unto us, and especially for this great and matchlesse love, in shewing us the true and onely meanes whereby our hearts may bee brought into that everlasting way, and then In what posture wee ought to behave ourselves; oh that God the giver of every good, and perfect gift to such of his children that unfeignedly serve him, would give us hearts soe to doe, for which as well as for your health, and prosperity, and your good wife's, I (as well as my mother, and sister) am bound, and many wayes engaged to pray earnestly for, whilest wee have a day to live.

Soe not willing to bee overtedious unto you, I commit you unto the protection of ye almighty, whose I am, and whom I from my heart desire to serve, & remaine your friend to love you for ever.

Samuel Hughes

Let not your prayers be few for mee, but let them bee multiplied, praying to God, as I myselfe oftentimes doe, yt hee would make mee such a one as desire to walke in my fathers stepps, & to follow him as neere as I can, yt I might enjoy life everlasting, & yt by remembring my creatour in ye dayes of my youth, I might goe to the happinesse that my father enjoyed, & by liveing in a state of grace here I might enjoy a state of glory hereafter, & may the lord bee pleased to say soe bee it.

Let us desire you to remember or love to Mr. Ambrosse Mosten, and to John Robert & his wife, & Edward Cynricke & his wife, & to my aunt

Alse, and her daughter my cousen Sara, & thanke her kindly for her love unto us in sending us tokens, if wee could find any convenient way we would send some small tokens to her againe, Remember or love to my uncle Thomas & his wife, & all my cousens, to my uncle John & his wife, & to all our Christian friends,

I wrot unto John Robert once before, and therein mentioned you, but as I suppose neither hee, nor you yet received ye letter, but I pray excuse my barrennesse in writeing unto you, being yet but a young beginner, and let us heare how you & all or friends are (thankes bee to God) wee are all well at this present writeing, and if you can possibly remember or love to Phillippe William, & his wife, & you may tell them from us that his brother is in good health, and wee heard noe lesse but his mother is well.

Swansea this 3d of this 10th month 1656.

'Edward Cynricke', hy, Edward John Kenrick (John oedd enw ei dad). Trwyddedwyd ei dŷ fel man addoli i'r Annibynwyr o dan y Declarasiwn, 1672. Yr oedd ganddo dŷ yng Ngwersyllt a dau yn Wrecsam, yn Hope Street. Un ohonynt oedd y 'Talbot' ac mewn ysgubor yn perthyn i'r tŷ hwn y bu'r Annibynwyr yn addoli tan 1762. Bu Kenrick farw yn 1693. Bu ei weddw farw ym Mehefin 1693 ac fe'i claddwyd yn Rhos-ddu (A. N. Palmer, *Older Nonconformity of Wrexham*, 47–8). Ŵyr i Edward Kenrick oedd yr Edward Kenrick a briododd â Susannah, merch Hugh Owen, Bronclydwr, ac a fu farw yn 1741. Gw. *Bywg.* o dan 'Kenrick (Teulu), Wynn Hall, Sir Ddinbych, a Bron Clydwr, Sir Feirionnydd'.

Ambrose Mostyn (1610–1663?). Un o Biwritaniaid amlycaf y gogledd. Mab Henry Mostyn o Galcot, plwyf Brynffordd, Sir Fflint. Graddiodd BA, 28 Ionawr 1630, o Goleg y Trwyn Pres, Rhydychen. Bu'n ddarlithydd ym mhlwyf Pennard, Morgannwg, o 19 Ebrill 1642 ymlaen, ond ar 20 Gorffennaf 1644 gorchmynnwyd ef i bregethu yng ngogledd Cymru a neilltuodd Pwyllgor y Gweinidogion Llwm 100c iddo am bregethu yn sgil ymgyrch fuddugoliaethus Syr Thomas Myddleton (T. Richards, *History of the Puritan Movement*, 65, 67). Ac eto ar 27 Gorffennaf 1646, rhoddodd yr un pwyllgor 50c iddo am bregethu yn Abertawe a'r cylch (ibid., 65). Yn ôl y *Broadmead Records*, 514, ef oedd sefydlydd Eglwys Gynnull Abertawe. Yr oedd yn un o gymeradwywyr Deddf y Taenu ac yn y blynyddoedd nesaf bu'n cydweinidogaethu gyda Vavasor Powell ym Mhowys. Ar 16 Hydref 1656 gosododd y Profwyr ef ym mywoliaeth Holt, Sir Ddinbych, ac yn Rhagfyr 1659 daeth yn olynydd Morgan Llwyd yn Wrecsam. Gweithredodd fel ysgutor ewyllysiau Walter Cradoc a Llwyd. Cafodd ei ddiswyddo o Wrecsam yn 1660. Bu farw yn Llundain ond y mae ei gyfoedion yn anghytuno ynglŷn â'r dyddiad. (Am wybodaeth lawnach, gw. *Cofiadur* (1962), 62–5, ac E. Calamy, *Account* II, 714–15.)

'Phillippe William'. Yr oedd 'Phillip Williams' ymhlith llofnodwyr y *Gair Dros Dduw* ac fe'i cyflwynwyd i'r Sesiwn Fawr yn 1660 fel anghydffurfiwr, *Gweithiau Morgan Llwyd II*, 323.

46

Eglwys Henry Jessey yn Llundain at Morgan Llwyd, 10 Awst 1656

(LLGC 11439D, ff. 28–9)

ffor Mr Morgan Lloyd
Minister of the Gospell
at Wrexham
in North Wales
post paid H. Jesse

The Church in London with H. J. called of God our Father into Communion wth his dear son Jesus Christ to ye dearly beloved Brother M. Lloyd, wisheth Grace & peace in beleeving. Beloved Brother, yor lines of love, inviting us to further fellowship with ye Father & his Dear Son Jesus Christ, & to al his; & not resting in outwards, but pressing much more after inwards & spiritualls, are very lovingly accepted, having been read amongst us.

Through ye Exceeding Riches of his Grace, this hath been & this is, ye bent of or souls, & oh that it were more so continually!) That from the warmth of the Love of our God & Father in the son of his Love, we may abound in all love more and more! in Love to ye Father yt begot us again to a lively hope of far greater things than in this life we enjoy, in Love to JESUS yt loved us, & washed us from or sins in his blood. In Love to his Good Spirit, yt reveals to us this Love, and fulnes of ye Mystery of the Father, & of the son; of wch we long to know more, knowing nothing as we ought to know. (In Love to all his Ordinances & appointments, ye meanest & most despised of which have somewhat of his Image upon them); because they are his Commaunds Jo. 14. 15, & 15. 14, & because he delights therein to communicate more of himselfe to his; yt therein humbly wait on him, & have an especially eye to himself. Though we would not idolize any of them, as too many doe; so we would be far from sleighting or vilifying or neglecting any such meanes, as he vouchsafes us, for help to such poor weak ones, as we are sensible yt we are: least we should seem to be like Ahaz who accepted not such favor as ye Lord offered to him Isa. 7—13—Thus to avoid one Extream we would not fall into another, as ye Ranters & people called Quakers do; & so do some precious souls, whom we owne & love; but love not ye Course therein. We know this, yt we know but in part; & are learning to love all yt are Christs, though differing in things of Lesse moment; according to Christ's Love to us, when we in knowledge & practise, differed from what we now know & do.

Touching ye Vials yt you mention, some of us have judged, & do still, yt none of them in yt Prophetical Order, are powred out, nor shalbe til ye Witnesses shal have fulfild their Witnesse, & be slaine, & rise againe. That Prophecy seems sealed, til neer ye time of the end. Then many shal run too & from, & knowledge shal be encreased. Blessed ar such as read & hear such things alright, & make a right spiritual use of all, eying most their death & burial & rising with Christ, & conversing wth him in al his ways & Ordinances; & walking humbly & joyfully wth Our God & father through him. For this, as we would remember you al, so we desire al yo rembr. us frequently to or father in Christ, who hath loved us, & wil love us to ye end. In whom we desire to remaine.

Yor very dear Brethren & fellow servts
H. JESSEY
Will. Crees
Tho. Theobald

Colmā Street Lō. 10th
of VI Mōn 1656
Signed in the Name & by
the Congrt. of ye Church.

If further light be given to any of you abt. ye Trumpets. Vials etc. yt you would communicate to us is desired.

We herewith send you this lr from a Church in Kent, not as approving or justifying every clause in it, yet because of many passages yt are precious.

(Addendum)

Bro. Loyd
I had pd 6[d] for yor Lr to us. But after ye Porter allowd 3[d] back, taking yt outside (yt being but one seale) to show ye Postmr. Or Church writ to you both. We hear not yor Ry

Mr. John Goodwin Rembd. not yt he had any lr from you.
H.J.

My very dear bro; I salute in or L.J. you yr wife, Sr Ric. Saltonstal & my Lady (wth thanks for or Kind entertainment) & or Chrian friends wth you.

I spake to Mr. Jo. Goodwin for Ansg you: he said he remb not yt even he had a Lr or a word from you, or yt ever he saw you, so he Knows not what it is you expect his Ans. about.

This L. brought us to Lon

H.J.
25th of VMo. 56.

For Mr Morgan Lloyd,
at Wrexham
in
North Wales.

Henry Jessey. Ganed 3 Medi 1601 yn West Rounton, Swydd Efrog. Cafodd ei addysg yng Ngholeg Sant Ieuan, Caergrawnt (BA yn 1623, MA yn 1626). Ordeiniwyd yn 1627 a bu'n ficer Aughton, Swydd Efrog, 1633–4 nes ei ddiswyddo. Daeth yn weinidog Eglwys Gynulleidfaol Southwark yn 1637 a derbyniodd fedydd credinwyr ym Mehefin 1645. Daeth yn 'athro' yn Eglwys Fedyddiedig Swan Alley, Colman Street (lle'r ysgrifennwyd y llythyrau uchod) yn 1654. Yr oedd yn un o'r Profwyr yn 1654. Cafodd ei garcharu yn Nhachwedd 1661 ond ei ryddhau'n fuan a chael ei gymryd eilwaith i'r ddalfa yn Awst 1662. Cafodd ei ryddhau yn Chwefror 1663. Yr oedd yn ddarlithydd yn Eglwys St. George, Southwark, pan gafodd ei ddiswyddo yn 1660. Bu farw 4 Medi 1663. Yr oedd yn bresennol pan gorffolwyd Eglwys Annibynnol Llanfaches yn 1639. (A. G. Matthews, *Calamy Revised* (1934), 298–9.)

John Goodwin (1594?–1666). Yr amlycaf o'r dadleuwyr tros y safbwynt Arminaidd ymhlith y Piwritaniaid. Cafodd ei ddiswyddo o Eglwys St. Stephen, Coleman Street, Llundain, 1660. Yr oedd yno er 18 Rhagfyr 1633 ond cafodd ei atal ym Mai 1645 a'i adfer yn 1649. Cafodd ei addysg yng Ngholeg y Frenhines, Caergrawnt (BA, 1616, MA, 1619) a bu'n gymrawd yno o 1617 hyd 1627. Cafodd ei eithrio o'r *Act of General Pardon*, heb fygwth ei ddienyddio, 18 Mehefin 1660. (A. G. Matthews, op. cit., 227.)

'Sr Ric. Saltonstal & my Lady'. Yr oedd cysylltiadau agos rhwng Richard Saltonstall (1586–1658) a Sir Ddinbych. Yr oedd ei gyfnither, Hester Saltonstall (merch Syr Richard Saltonstal (1521?–1601), Arglwydd Faer Llundain, 1597) yn briod â Syr Thomas Myddelton (1550–1631), Castell y Waun, un o noddwyr ariannol 'Beibl Bach' 1630. Llofnododd Richard Saltonstall y *Gair Dros Dduw*.

47
Henry Jones, Dulyn, at Morgan Llwyd, 23 Mai 1655

(LLGC 11438D, f. 7)

Dublin ye 23rd May 1655

Presious ffreind,

I have had ye hapines somtimes to Inioy some lines from you. Although I cannot say of what benefit letters have bine to me thorow the unfrutfull-ness of my hearte I would I could write somthinge, or Receive somthing that would convince me of some Evill & shortnes in my walkinge to ye holy & pure ways of the lord It may be sd of most of or letters & writeings as Job said to his ffreinds *how Axeptable are Right* words but what doth yor Arguinge Reproove I have Cause to be ashamed of my fformer Course in writinge wch was more to sett *ffoorth parts & words to be Admired by ye* Ignorant then Aney holsom Reproof or Advise to muche wise the simple and for somtims *Darken Counsell by words* without knowledge, or as ye Apostle calls you swellinge words of vainitie, or Knowledge that puffes up. but I Ernestly bege of god that we may all learne to seeke yt Knowledge that is I pure & then peasable for without puritie we most Expecte noe peace.

Deare ffreind ye bearer my Couzin is sent for by his ffather. I Know not wher he doth Intend to dispose of him if with you in Wrexham I shalbe glad thereof hopinge the lord may Renew his former love to ye lord & his truths, wch thorow or two *little wachfullnes over him* I find now much beclouded I desire you would wach over Robin & call him to give an Accounte of what he hears he hath had a large memory to Remembr sermons. I hope ye lord may Implant somthinge of them in his poore hearte & alsoe macke him worthy to stand in the Evill day: my Deare Due Respects to Deare Daniell Lloyd, Capt prichard Sontlej Kathrin & Lowrey Williams and all that doe exell in vertue Among You Ye blessinge of ye lord Remaine upon yor heads is ye prayers of yor unworthy ffreind.

Hen: Jones

Eliz: powell desirs her deare sone to be Remembrd with thanks for An Answer to this in another.

Brawd John Jones, Maesygarnedd, oedd Henry Jones a Dirprwy-lywiawdwr Dulyn yn 1653. Bu farw cyn 1664.

Llofnododd Daniel Lloyd y llythyr 'from the Church of Christ at Wrexham' yn llongyfarch Oliver Cromwell ar ôl buddugoliaeth Caerwrangon (3 Medi 1651), gw. *Gweithiau Morgan Llwyd II*, 266. Yr oedd yn un o gomisiynwyr Deddf y Taenu ac yn aelod o Bwyllgor Atafaelu gogledd Cymru. Fe'i claddwyd mewn cae gyferbyn â fferm Pen-y-bryn yn Abenbury ac ar garreg ei fedd ceid y geiriau, 'Here is asleep Daniel Lloyd, Servant of Jesus Christ, interred November 19th, 1655'. (A. N. Palmer, *Older Nonconformity of Wrexham*, 30–1.)

'Capt prichard' oedd Hugh Prichard.

Nid hawdd penderfynu pwy oedd 'Sontlej'. Yr oedd Roger Sontley a Robert Sontley i'w cael (*Gweithiau Morgan Llwyd II*, 266). Bedyddiwyd Roger, mab Edward Sonlley (*sic*), 26 Mawrth 1622 a dau Roger arall, meibion John Sonlley (*sic*), y naill ar 7 Rhagfyr 1626 a'r llall ar 15 Ionawr 1627. Yn wir, ceir tri Roger a tri Robert 'Sonlley' ymhlith bedyddiadau Wrecsam rhwng 1623 a 1643, gw., A. N. Palmer, *A History of the Town of Wrexham*, 257.

48
Cyrnol John Jones, Dulyn, at Morgan Llwyd, 9 Hydref 1651

(LLGC 11440D: The Letter Book of Col. John Jones, 12–14)

Dearely beloved in the Lord Jesus,

It pleaseth the Lord to excercize his poore Creatures under various dispensacõns, and all to bring his owne glorious purposes to passe, for good to them that are called according to his purpose, Rom. 8. 28. Att this time, when the Mouthes and hearts of all the S'ts are filled wth songs of deliverance, The Lord hath bene pleased to visit my poore family with sad afflicc̃ons, my deare wife being brought by sicknes to soe low a Condicõn, as made those aboute her to iudge that her course was finished, but the Angell of his presence was with her, bearing up her spirit in the full assurance of his eternall Love, and the spiritts of the S'ts very active in their Addresses at the Throne of grace for her. In the middest of her weaknes yor l'res of the 17th of the last moneth came to our hand, wherein shee did very much rejoyce, causing them to be read over and over in the presence of such as came to visit her, and reioycing in yor sweet Reproofes, and wishing that her heart, and theirs who, informed were layd open before you, to remove such hard thoughts as you might have of her. And if it became me to plead in her Justificacon comparatively (for what flesh can be iustifyed from any one sin) I might instance many Arguments to evince her indisposition to height and priority, even almost to ridiculousnes in respect of or conversac̃on in the world, and deportments proper to particular stations, consistent wth religious observances, and if such deportment had bene observed by such as bore that testimony to you of her, if I guesse the party aright they might have testifyed her tendernes of them, using them more like Children, then Servants, endeavoring to cover infirmities, and not denude them. Passion is an unbridled Monster, wch many a gracious Soule cannot Governe.

Although it hath pleased the Lord to exalt himself above the Nations in England and Scotland by casting downe the powers of the Earth, and giving his Sts honor to bind Kings in Chaines, and Nobles in Fetters of Iron, yet here wee labour under more darke Appearances, our God in his Wisdome permitting the Enemy to grow numerous, insolent, and bould about 10 dayes since, they tooke the towne of Rosse, (except ye Church, and a house, which was fortifyed) plundered it, and made the Inhabitants pay 700 l. to save it from burning, and they quitted it upon approach of some of our forces that way. They have forced severall other small Guarrisons, they dayly waste and burne our Quarters, and take the opportunity to committ all the wickednes Sathan can invent, while the maine of our forces are ingaged in the seige of Limerick and Galloway. And all this to teach us that he is the Author of those great workes he hath done of late, whereof wee are witnesses. 2ndly to humble or selves under the mighty hand of God, who cann in a moment dash in peices all the Nations of the Earth. 3dly that wee are in his hand as the Clay in the Potter's hand, it is he that gives courage, and casts downe the spirits of men. 4thly That if wee goe not out in the strength of our God, the Ashes off or enemies ruine is sufficient to destroy us. Wee have here some few S'ts who thirst after the water of Life, and long for more discoveries of or everlasting bridgroomes love, & for more enjoymts of his blessed presence, and if the Lord, would open a way would much reioyce in yor Company and helpe, although yor Stay should not be long. Heere is worke for you and deare Mr. Powell, and some more of our Brittish Nuntioes to divulge the bridgroome's message, and make knowne ye Mistery of that union that is betweene ye bride and her head Xt Jesus, and what is ye brightnes of the father's glory.

Wee are here much under the letter of Gospell dispencacōns mingled with Clay — humane prudence, weakesighted, not able to behold the native brightnes of the son of Righteousnes. The inclosed paper may informe you how seasonable yor presence had beene wth us at this time, or may be yet.

What becomes of poore Merionythshire, is that Countrey denied the tender of gospell Mercies? Is there noe prophet, noe Messenger of Xt yt will make Duffryn Ardidwey in his way? Where is Mr Powell, Mr Lloyd, etc., that once thought it a mercy and a high priviledge, to bee accompted worthy of being driven to the Mountaynes, & desolate places, that they might have liberty to preach the Gospell there. Yor office and duty is to encounter wth sinn and the power of the prince of the Ayre, and where is there more sinē to encounter wth where more ignorance, where more hatred to the people of god? where the word Saint more scorned? than in Merionythshire. The more the difficulty and opposition, the more is the power of the spirit of the Lord Jesus in Gospell Administrac̄ons manifested and the Instruments honoed I dare not goe no further then Queres in this matter, not knowing where the weight of ye worke lies. I am now called away, my deare Love to yor Wife, & ye rest of or Xtian friends where you are.

Yor unworthy brother
in the Lord Jesus,
Jo. Jones.

Dublin, 9^{d} 8^{m} 1651

I desire to be remembred to Mr. Baker, & his wife, with thanks for their kind enterteynmts.

Am John Jones (1597?–1660), Maesygarnedd, Dyffryn Ardudwy, gw. *Bywg.*, *DNB* a John Lloyd, 'Colonel John Jones, Maesygarnedd', *Cylchgrawn Cymdeithas Hanes a Chofnodion Sir Feirionnydd* II (1953–6), 95–104.

'Mr Powell, Mr Lloyd' oedd Vavasor Powell a Morgan Llwyd.

'Mr Baker & his wife' oedd Thomas Baker o Sweeney, Croesoswallt a'i briod Elizabeth, merch y Cyrnol Fenwicke. Yn 1649 yr oedd Baker yn siryf Swydd Amwythig ac yn 1653 yn aelod o Senedd y Saint. Bu farw yn 1675 ac fe'i claddwyd yn yr ardd yn Sweeney. Yr oedd Richard Gough (1634–1723) yn *The History of Myddle* (gol., David Hey, 1981), 158–61, yn canmol Elizabeth fel 'a lovely gentlewoman of a masculine spirit, and noe meane beauty' ond braidd yn sarhaus o'i gŵr—'noe comely person of body, nor of great parts, and litle education, butt hee was very rich in lands, woods, money and goods'. Nid clod iddo oedd bod 'yn great patron and benefactor to all independent preachers, such as Vavasor Powell, who comonly preached every day in the weeke'. (Ceir nodyn arnynt yn *Montgomeryshire Collections* 8 (1875), 304–5, ar ôl llythyr oddi wrth Baker at y Cadfridog Mytton, 25 Mai 1653.) Yr oedd chwaer Elizabeth yn briod â Humphrey Mackworth (1603–1654), llywodraethwr Amwythig, 1654. Yr oedd yn byw yn Betton Strange, gerllaw Amwythig. Fe'i claddwyd ef yn Abaty Westminster (*Montgomery Collections* 7 (1874), 364–5).

49

Cyrnol John Jones, Dulyn, at Morgan Llwyd, 20 Mawrth 1652

(LLGC 11440D: The Letter Book of Co. John Jones, 43–5)

Deare Beloved

To Mr Morgan Lloyd,

Yors of the 25th of ye last Moneth, and the paper their inclosed, and the other of the third of this Moneth, I received, and have thereby received much refreshing consolacons. I purpose (if god sees it good) to follow yr Advise concerning my Sonne, as being indeed the most suiteable to my desire, and reason, considering the advantage he will have thereby in Conversation, and his aptnes to sadd and solitary disposition, wch probably would encrease amongst strangers. The Lord I hope hath fully possest his heart, with a desire to know his will, & to become conformable thereunto.

Wee are here under weake, and darke dispensacons, litle appearance of growth in any, the ground wee stand upon slippery, the stac̄on wee have attained unto is but on the floare of the house you menc̄on, and or spirituall strength not competent to keepe us from gooing backe from that measure of inward Revelacōns, spirituall quicknes, fervency of Seale to the glory of or maker, & love to or Bretheren, wch formerly did appeare in some of us, Wee are striving about Huskes (even to bitternes) and thincke wee doe well, & neglect the whollsome food, Wee may say with that Eunuch, how can wee understand thy great Mistery within us, and the Pathes of the eternall god in the deepe Waters, without a Prophett to Reveale the same unto us. This comfort Remaines firme, that although wee are weake, darke, deformed and peevish, Wee stedfastly beleeve, that wee are compleatly strong, wise beatifull, and meeke in the Lord Jesus, who is our sunne or Sheild & or Life, our light, or strength, and Rocke, from whoom wee were hewen, Consider those that have a hundred Milstones, day, and night about their neckes (The Affaires of the world being such) lett yor Charity be ample towards them, lett yor love pitty them, and yor prayers helpe to buy them, when they find their owne spirits in a dead sincking Condic̄on. They may find the spirits of the Sts. supplying their Wants, & putting up Requests for them at the throne of grace, this is my Condic̄on, & I beleeve many more, there are two tempers, I observe to reigne at this time, the one in the saints, their narrowheartednesse towards such as are without, leaving so litle Roome for that vertue Charity to spread her Wings, and restrayning Christian love from its full influence. The other is the people of ye world by their ready Conformity, and forward seeming Seale to ordinances, and duties striving for the forme of Words, that thereby they might be made acceptable to the people of God, and be accounted of them, because the way to worldly prefermt. while their hearts are full of the world, minding nothing but worldly things. If the Lord Jesus would Administer light, life and strength to discover, and avoyde these evills, It would be a great Mercy, I have but litle time for, and lesse knowledge to enlarge in this Matter, The Lord Jesus sanctify unto us the measure he gives, and it will suffice, I would heartily mourne with you for the absence of your pretty Babe, but he that gave, and tooke away, hath mercies enough in store.

Yors in all faithfullnes & Love

Dublin 20th March 1651/2 J. Jones

I long to heare what Mr Powell found in Merion: I have had sad Complaints from thence. I am afraid there wants Discretion and Christian Love, and Moderation in Cousin Robert Owen, but I hope he is free from having the Countreyes Monies sticking in his fingers, some of the greatest gentlemen in the Countrey informed me soe much, and desired of mee leave that they might compell him to come to an Accompt wch I hope he will doe voluntary & give satisfaccon to all Rationall & honest men.

50

Cyrnol John Jones, Dulyn, at Morgan Llwyd, 1 Mawrth 1652/3

(LLGC 11440D: The Letter Book of Col. John Jones, 103–6)

To Mr Morgan Lloyd,

Most Deare Ffrind,

Devine Providence hath soe ordered that of late we have not had opertunity of Mutuall Correspondence by Lr̃ẽs soe that wee in Ireland are in some high expectacõn of some glorious manifestacõn of our father's outgoeings with his sts. in England in owneing theire honest sincere, & Pious Endeavours to Establish Truth, Peace, and Righteousnes in the land, upon that lasting foundation of Justice: wch will make all the Nations Round about them, who are guided and governed by Corrupt, Carnall selfeish interests, to stand in feare of them as being a greate nation, and a wise, & understanding people. Deu. : 4. The spiritts of the saints in Ireland, have beene lately in the persuite of one of the wild boares of the fforest whose sent hath beene lost for many ages past, although he lodged nigh us even in our hearts, it is a fforgetting of what the lord hath done for us, & of what our Eyes have seene, A sinne that brought grevious plauges upon gods people of old A sinne that turnes our Counsells into ffolly. Psal: 106; 12: 13: a sinne of ingratitude agt god, wch seemes to be reckoned more haynous than Murther: 2 Chron: 24: 22. It is note-worthy serious Consideracõn in the psl. above v, 13. They soone forgott his workes, & wayted not for his Counsell; This not wayteing for the Counsell of god in our undertakings is heere mentioned as a Concomitant sinne to that of fforgettfulnes, or rather as a Punishment for the same. It is a fearefull thing to undertake any designe without wayteing for gods Councell in it. It is a sinne of Impatience in not being willing to attend and wayte for his Counsell, our desiere to be disolved with Paule and to be with Christ to behould his glory, argues a heavenly frame of spiritt and yett wee have noe warrant to putt those desieres in execution by shortning our dayes. If wee can Constantly remember what the lord hath done for us, and with what a high hand he went in and out before his people in our dayes, wee shall have faith enough to beleeve that he will guide us by his Counsell, and lead us by his power through all difficultyes. The lord is still pleased to owne his Cause and Instrumts in Ireland Inis Buffin, and all the Rest of the westerne Islands are delivered into our hands, upon Condicõn of haveing leave to goe into spaine. Thus theire land spues them out, the high Courts of Justice are terrible in inquisicon after Blood, in soe much that the murtherers hearts fainte, and theire Joints tremble even to admiration, such is the Maiesty of god in that great ordinance, This hath caused some hundreds, and thousands to runne out lately, and begin to appeere in Considerable numbers and have beene made instruments to reproove sharpely the Carelesness and security of some of our fforces, But I am Confident their Distruction is not farr off. I desire you to remember mee to Deare Mrs. Lloyd, and our Christian ffrinds with you, and lett my boy and Eliz: know that god Contineus health unto us.

Shall poore Ireland have noe assistance from the neighbouring Churches in walls, must Christ fetch instrumts further off; what doe wee knowe butt that the saints in walles may yett fall into, & under psecutions and that they may Come wherein they shall wish that they had layd a foundac̃on for a hideing place in poore bleeding Ireland, wee have the findest weather that ever was knowne, and in the begining of aprill wee shall begin our progress through the land, at which tyme our frinds if any of them come over will have an excelent opertunity to vew the land, I had noe answere from my Deare frind Mar Powell in this matter, The lord direct your hearts aright. St Fhelin O Neale Created Earle of Tyreone by the Uttaghs, according to theire solemnityes, Prince of Ulster by ye Popes Comission. Genll of all the fforces of Ulster & Leinster by comission from ye Lords of the Pale: and the Prime, and Chiefe Actor, in ye horrid Massacres, and Rebellion by Comission from the late Charles Stuart was Iesterday triyed & Condemned, and all the saide tytles made good by Evidence at his tryall. Soe lett all thyne Enemyes pish O Lord.

Dublin ye 1st of
March 1652.

Jo. Jones

'St Fhelin O Neale' oedd Syr Phelim O'Neill (1604?–1653), Iarll Tyrone, gw. *DNB*.

Mae llythyr John Jones wedi'i ddyddio 1 Mawrth. Tybed a yw'r dyddio'n gywir? Ar 6 Mawrth 1652/3 y dechreuodd prawf O'Neill a chafodd ei ddienyddio ar 10 Mawrth.

51
Cyrnol John Jones, Dulyn, at Morgan Llwyd, 30 Awst 1653

(LLGC 11440D: The Letter Book of Col. John Jones, 137–9)

To Mar Morgan Lloyd.

Deare & beloved

your little booke is in the Presse, butt haveing butt one Presse, and many Publique Declarations in Printeing, there was a necessity of Post-poining that impression for some tyme, I have some thoughts of Printeing your letter in the Close of the other, but Truly Dearest frind, I find some Expressions in it, Espetially in the Paragraph at the topp of the first Page, and in the Parenthisis of that Paragraph, That I Cannot possibly under-stand as yett, in any sound or safe sense, and that hath made mee to Pause upon those intentions of myne, untill I Receave a little more light from you therein,

Pretious ffrind I have had many trembling and aking thoughts con-cerneing you, least the Lord should Deprive the poore, Rich, sweete Cluster of saincts in Wales, of those Edifying and strenghtning Refreshmts which formerly the enioyed by yor Ministry, (and I hope doe still enioy) by Reason of those seraphick and High Expressions you have of the thinges of god, wch (allthough to you apprhended as a greater Measure of light, then is attayneable by ordinary Gospell administracōns yett) To others (who cannot wach those high Misteryes) they are butt Darkness & Confusion; I doe acknowledg that if wee have not an inter-nall speritt to carry us out above the letter of the word, and outward administracōns wee have noe acquaintance with the Mistery of Godlynes, butt I humbly Conceave that it is our Duty to hold forth what the lord Discovers unto us of that Mistery by the plaine, sober, sound Expressions of the Holy Ghost in the word; And to studdy how to make knowne unto others what the lord Discovers unto us, by the plainest & most intelligible Expressions that wee cann, I have beene an Eye, and an Eare wittness of the snare wherein the tempter hath Caught many, by theire being Carryed into these speculations, as houlding the Scripture to be an useless thing prayers, and other Gospell administracōns to be low & Carnall, and to be excersised by those only that are in the state of Bondage, That the speritt within the saincts wch is mortall is the lord Jesus Dwelling in them, That Christ is noe other way to bee apprehended by faith, then as a speritt Dwelling in the saincts, That all the rest of man that is his Body and Soule is mortall, That nothing that the saincts doe is sinnefull, That they are most spirituall who cann comitt uncleaness, and other vile sinnes without

Cheque of Concience and thereby putt theire saide tenents into practice, And truly had I not had the examinacon of them myselfe, with others both in England & Ireland, I thinke I should never have beleeved that such Notionists had beene given over to such vile assertions; The Lord give us a speritt of wisdome & sobriety to Discerne the wyles of sathan, who on the one hand indeavors to Delude us with insignificant Ayry noions, makeing us beleeve (like a man in a dreame) that wee fly above the Clouds when in truth wee are butt filled wth empty vapours, and are indeed in the Lowest and Darkest posture of men, and on the other hand, to pswayd us that Christ is heere, and Christ is there, that the substance of our Religion, is in this forme or in that forme, and that he that is out of such a forme, is out of ye Church of Christ, and thereby Acting his proper Diabolicall office of Babe and Contention amongst proffessors. The Lord Deliver us from his snares, and keepe and preserve in us a speritt of faith, prayer, and the feare of the lord.

One word is my owne particular.
Dublin August ye 30th 1653.

'your little booke is in the Presse'. At ba un o lyfrau Llwyd y mae'r geiriau hyn yn cyfeirio? Y pwynt cyntaf amlwg yw fod gan Morgan Llwyd *ddau* lyfr yn y wasg yn Nulyn erbyn diwedd Awst 1653. Mae hynny'n glir oddi wrth eiriau John Jones, 'I have some thoughts of Printeing your letter in the Close of the other'. Dywed John Jones ymhellach ei fod yn petruso gweithredu oherwydd 'I find some Expressions in it, Espetially in the Paragraph at the topp of the first Page, and in the Parenthisis of that Paragraph, That I Cannot possibly understand as yett . . . '. At prun o'r ddau y mae'n cyfeirio wrth sôn am 'Expressions in it'. Ar yr olwg gyntaf y mae'n cyfeirio at yr un y mae'n ei alw'n 'your little booke'. Y ddau bosibilrwydd yw *Llythur ir Cymru Cariadus* a *Gwaedd Ynghymru yn Wyneb pob Cydwybod*. Pan ddywed ei fod yn ystyried 'Printeing your letter', y mae'n naturiol cymryd mai *Llythur ir Cymru* . . . sydd ganddo o dan sylw. A 'little booke' oedd hwn—rhyw wyth tudalen a hanner. Y mae *Gwaedd Ynghymru* yn ymestyn tros ryw dri thudalen ar hugain. A ydym i gymryd felly mai *Gwaedd yng Nghymru* a gyfansoddwyd gyntaf? Ni wna hynny'r tro oherwydd yn y *Llythyr* (*Gweithiau Morgan Llwyd I*, 123), dywed, 'Dyma'r llythyr cyntaf a ddanfonais i erioed attat ti mewn print . . . ' Felly, teg tybio fod hwn eisoes ym meddiant John Jones pan gyrhaeddodd *Gwaedd Ynghymru.*

A beth am betruster John Jones ynglŷn â'r cynnwys? Mae'n haws credu fod y tri pharagraff cyntaf yn *Gwaedd Ynghymru*, gyda'r ychydig eiriau sydd mewn cromfachau ynddynt, yn peri trafferth i John Jones na'r darnau cyfatebol yn *Llythyr ir Cymru.* Ac y mae'r geiriau sy'n dilyn yn y llythyr uchod yn tueddu i gadarnhau'r dybiaeth hon. Yr oedd J. H. Davies (yn *Gweithiau Morgan Llwyd II*, 316–17) yn barod i osod *Llythur ir Cymru* yn 1653 ond i osod *Gwaedd Ynghymru* yn 1655 neu 1656. Awgrymai Saunders Lewis (*Meistri'r Canrifoedd*, 157) mai ym Medi neu Hydref 1653 yr ysgrifennwyd *Gwaedd Ynghymru.* Dichon y gellir mentro ei ddyddio rai wythnosau ynghynt na hyn, ond ar ôl *Llythur ir Cymru.*

52

Esther Jones at Morgan Llwyd, 19 Hydref 1655

(LLGC 11439D, f. 3)

These
For Mr Morgan
Lloyd att hi house
at Wrexham
present.

Hon[d]. Fr. Dol: 19; 8 m 1655

I shall disire you to thanke Coll. Jones for his kind & sympatheticall lre. to Mr Ellis Hughes for truely it was above my meritts & thoughts to have recd. such kindnesse from him or any else, for yt which I should feare is least I should let them slip unnoted, or not recd. on ye same acct. as they are given (viz) on Xts. acct. (for my proud heart is unthankefull) wt Mr Ellis Hughes will doe I doe not know for he was from home then, Wt ye effect will be I shall be like to give either of you notice. Since my seeing of you I find much struggling & striveing wthin which is judged to be between Consc. & an unbridled will, my spt. is still in close prison, as one yt were in a wide house full of rooms, not knowing how to get out but slips & runs form one darke wll. to ye others, & yet cannot find ye doore, yet. can he not rest, soe its with me Ye mind would now persist into one truth hopeing to find ye light of liberty there, anon to another soe tossed from one thing to ye other, but cannot rest, nor wait till Xt opens ye doore. I find my selfe to be among those (yt have not ye heart i ofyn nag i ofni) but yt I would be a naked shrubbe. In speakeing to my family I have much stirrings for I find its my duty then when I am abt it, there be such reasonings, thou doest not belleve thy selfe wt you wouldest presse on others, ye motives move thee not, ye promises nor threatneings affect thee not, thou walkest not in & according to the counsells thou sayest to others, thou hast not yt feare & awe in speakeing as you shouldest etc. soe yt there is no peace or joy in doeing it (nor omitting it) & ye doing is as ye omitting. I hope now I shall heare from you in writing (something to my condition which is ye earnest desire of yr friend.

Esthr Jones

I pray let me heare from you If you have any thoughts abt. my condition to be impted for it may be yt is ye way God would use to humble & affect my heart.

E.J.

53
[Esther Jones] at Morgan Llwyd, yn Nyffryn Ardudwy, 25 Medi 1655

(LLGC 11439D, f. 39v–39)

Answerd in part

These
For Mr Morgan
Lloyd at Duffryn — ardydwy or else where
— in his owne hands present - with trust.

25th. 7ber. 1655.

Dearely Respected,

You moved me to write to you severall tymes wch I really intended, & soe promised but in very deed I know not what to write, for I am put to stand where to begin wth my selfe, or how to expresse my condition for I know not wt to thinke or say of my selfe (or soule) Though I had not a heart to speake (for some kind of shame, or I know not wt) yet I am not loath to lay my state something open at present in writing. I was one yt came to make a profession lightly (upon wt grounds I cannot well tell), in yt profession I grew flourishing in all manner of outwards & commons, being most apt to catch knowledge & soe exceeding most therein (never reflecting in) & came to a kind of eminency & to be noted for severall things, which did soe fill me wth thoughts of my selfe, & blew me to much high concetednis (my mind & heart still fishing for creditts & applause among men) whereby I did deceive my selfe & many others though I doe not remember yt I did purposely & knowingly appeare to men wt I did not (through deceit) suppose my selfe to be. This knowledge began to wither & those flourishings became all dry, & my heart began to appeare most heard. Then I was even a dead barren tree haveing nothing to say to others, that I had really & experimentally tasted, wth this I began to apprehend yt I never knew what it was to act truly for God's glory, to hate sin & have ye heart humbled & made thankefull for wt it had, but wt kind of an apprehension it was I know not, for it made not yt impression it should on me, for still my heart went harder & harder, darker & darker, whereabout's (finding yt ye heart could not move for promises or threatnings) I began to question & suspect whether ye Scripture was truth, or whether there was such a one as God, or heaven or hell, still I found something wthin not yeelding to it, & yt yet not able to resolve & overcome ye contrary, thus I laid long in sore pressures & some pangs, not knowing well of my selfe, Sometymes I seemed to overcome such thoughts quite, but when I came to apply any truth yt might be convince-ing for me this bubled up & made it weake to ye worke. And ever since yt tyme (which is a while agone) I knew not wt to thinke or say but I found my heart rageing mad, full of blasphemy, lust, & all the iniquity of ye streetes. I find my selfe full of distractions & thoughts contradicting one another & yet still carried outrageously out of all order jumpping from this to ye thother thing, settling on nothing, nor searching any thing to ye bottom. I find such slothfull carelessnes crept (since & after) to my heart yt my heart doth not regard any thing, cares not wt become of soule or body, feares not any thing really, nor wthall of late (which I something admire) I doe not find much stirreing in me for sin, (but as it were sleeping in a kind of slothfull full distraction of mind) only I perceived very late my heart eagerly lusting to creditt or pride (wch I judged not to be my master lust) I find a light (though cold & heard) discovering ye smallest sin, but not bringing wth it such a hatred as causeth an earnest striveing agt it or a loathing of selfe for it. I suppose now yt the notion & forme of knowledge I had heretofore is a strong barre to keep off ye power of ye word now for when any thing is spoken, it will hardly be a new unknowen thing but wt was had & for through custome, & formality ye heart is as knowing all things. & soe when I read ye Scripture I find yt a kind of yt overly understanding I have thereof makes ye heart to disregard & disaffect it. Indeed I cannot judge how much hurt that knowledge of ye lre of ye word doth me, but ye evill is in me, because my heart is frothy & full, & most proud, for truly I doe not find yt I can say yt I have a true sense of any need I have of Xt, mercy, or grace, whereby it is evident, yt my heart was never opened, or touched to ye bottom, but only it sworn in a common sense & common enjoyments & yt which is ye worst an indifferency for anything that is above them. I thought I loved ye professours of ye gospell, but I doe find now they (especially such as are most strict & searching) are ye people yt my heart riseth agt & will have me be offended wth, for sincerity & holy strictnes are burdensome to such a heart, I cannot find any joy or comfort in any thing when I refect on my selfe, & consider ye grounds thereof. There is such staggerings & tossings in my mind that almost no evill is too heynous to be admytted as some-tymes off late, when I had been tossing up & downe in ye waves of horrible darkeness & blasphemy, about ye scripture, yn came severall thoughts, yt I should make my selfe away, severall wayes, & otherwhile yt I should flye ye Country & the like, whereby I find yt I am as blind as a stone in all thinges, especially I am altogether ignorant of Xt & his workeings; That which I want is certeynty of understanding, for I see not a reallity in ye scriptures, I meane, yt God, & heaven, hell, sin, death &c. are not made reall to me. There is not yt cleere reall convinceing sight of God & ye thinges mencioned in ye word. I heare not God promising & threatneing (as ye word of God) I see noe sin bringing hell & eternall woe, but ye mind sometime supposeing such thinges to be, sometime not, ye heart hovering in ye secret Atheisme, & quarelling agt. ye word because such a power hath not been manifested as did make it yeeld & silence all ye objections thereof; I want also a brocken, humbled heart, for if ye heart were broken & humbled it would not be as it is, still rebelling & quarelling, & waning weary off, & unconstant in all good dutyes, haveing such an indisposednes in it to every thing yt is good & as it were crying who is ye Almighty yt I should obey him & wt profit is to pray to him? If it hates sin it would not be loath to have it discovered & searched out, but in all thinges I groop for something as it were by hearesay & not enjoying yt which in a way is apprehended (which is a death) But wt will be ye end I know not (& my heart cares not), this I write & it should be my sorrow yt I have such a slight ungrieved *spt* in writeing such sadnes wthout a deep affectation thereof in my soule). I say this & write I suppose (& desire it to be) upon this end viz To see wt God may doe throw you towardes ye settleing of my heart in ye truth & bringing of me out of this prison of hankering in Atheisme & heart blasphemy yt I may praise God, & be truely affected wth my sins & misery, to see wt may be sd by you towardes ye gaineing of a right & sure apprehensione. I told you I knew not how to expresse my selfe rightly for its impossible for me, but I thinke somwt. of wt sad experiences I find in my heart, yea I have not had a heart dareing (for feare or shame) to unbosome my selfe thus to any one beside (though it may be I thinke somewt thereof to 2 or 3 more, who not knowing all said little or much to it) If you would know any particular further in explanac̄on I will send it you, for I doubt I write much confusion If you have anything to write by ye bearer yt yu shall be moved to send doe it, or as soone as you can, otherwise pray for him yt hath not a heart to pray for himselfe who would desire a heart to love you in truth.

I am writeing ye coppy about ye word now, & when I finish it I shall send ye originall towardes Wrexham I meane to if . . . will grant it for he claimes some interest in it as he tells me, soe yt you must send something to him abt it by . . . Another thing I perceive to be very often in my thoughts yt I am given up to hardenesse & blindnesse of heart & yt a secret sentence is passed, for I find most of ye signes of such in me, yet I doe not find an awe thereof, nor such a striveinge agt it as should be, nor yet a true or solid relyance on God for ye contrary I find yt my heart will give up a way to performe any duty in family or calling, nor is there liberty in conscience to omitt but an uproar.

This ltr I writt thinkeing to send it to Dyffryn, but heareing yo intended to call att my house I left it wth me, but finding it otherwise I send it desireing to heare from you in hast haveing not tyme to adde.

I am (E.J.?)

54

Holiadau i Gredinwyr Wrecsam, gan James Parke

(LLGC 11439D, f. 24)

To all the professors in Wrexham that deny the light of Christ to bee in everyman, these quearyes are propounded in love to be answered by them or any one of them: and sent to any of the people called quakers in wrexham to be conveyed to mee.

1. What that true light every man is inlightened withall, if it be not Christ?

2. What ground hath any to presse people to followe and obey a light that is not Christ?

3. What is the Candle of the wicked that by much sinning and disobedience comes to be put out?

4. What is the candle of the Lord?

5. How come people to be darke or darkenesse, but by shutting out and resisting the moovings thereof?

6. Whether christ now bee in the world yea or nay, if in the world is not hee the light thereof?

7. Whether Christ bee the head of every man or not, if hee bee what such a head is hee a darke one?

8. Is that light of the world which is the life of men, naturall, which excerciseth the conscience thereby, making manifest to man the evill deeds of darknesse?

9. Is the conscience god or was it created by god, then why do you put it in the seat of god, making it equall with god who exerciseth it and is lord over it, and light in it?

10. Is not this sufficient to lead to salvation all that followe and obey the moovings and leadings thereof?

11. Whats the seed of god the sower went forth to sowe?

12. Whats the manifestation of the spirit given to every man to proffitt withall?

13. Was not the seed the same that was sowne on all the grounds though it did not effect the same thing in all?

14. What is that which shines in mans hart, to give him the knowledge of god that may bee rebelled against and not comprehended?

15. What is the tallent of gods grace given by him to people to Improove for his use, which many do not improove, so it comes to be taken from them?

16. What is that that god gives much of to some, where and of whom he requires much, and to others litle, and so litle required of them?

17. What is that was a light to Davids feet, and a lantherne unto his paths?

18. Who are ignorant of the way and pathes of the light but they that love their evill deeds, who hate and rebell against the light?

Written by all your soules friend, formerly owned as a brother, and knowne amongst you by the name of

James Parke.

James Parke (1636–96), aelod o Eglwys Gynnull Wrecsam a droes yn Grynwr (gw. *Bywg.*, *DNB* a Richard Davies, *An Account of the Convincement. . .* (1710)). Eraill o'r gynulleidfa a gerddodd yr un llwybr oedd John ap John, Roger ap John, Bryan Sixsmith, John Meredith a Catherine ferch Edward, Rhuddallt Isaf, un y bu ei chartref yn fan cyfarfod i'r Crynwyr, gw. G. F. Nuttall, *The Welsh Saints 1640–1660* (1957), 65–6.

55

Vavasor Powell at Morgan Llwyd, 23 Ebrill 1657

(LLGC 11439D, f. 31)

23d of ye 2d Mon 57.

Though you have as good as interdicted me to write to you, yet I hope never to entertaine such thoughts of you (whatever you doe of me) as to iudge you unworthy to be owned, remembred & desireably embraced: & your company & counsell to be highly esteemed, & al-beit I feare I may use the words of ye Apostle 2 Cor. 12. 15g. yet I shall not forget Solomons Exhor: Pro. 27. 10. I confes I did much wonder at severall expressions in your last letter, as that you accounted those reall acknowledgemts of mine; but complements especially when you yourself had but a little before used ye same in effect to another brother in a letter: Oh brother! you should have beene willing to have measured my corne by your owne bushell, & you may yet possibly be convinced that you correspond by letters & otherwise with some (tho greater yet) that have not loved you more, nor padventure experienced soe much as poore V.P. But why should I be troubled seing its ye fathers' will to imbitter those creatures that I feare I have overmuch esteemed, (yea adored) & since its not my lot alone in theese days to be thus accounted; yet I shall greatly rejoyce to heare of your welfare, & to be & doe ye same to you (& more) then ever I have done & it wilbe small ioy to me & other saints to heare that beloved & blessed M.LL. dos degenerate soe much in his Doctrine, as to hold many of the old Arminian & popish principles, as freewill perfection &c. or ye Socinian D. as to enervate ye power of Christs death or intercession. I doe not say you doe, but looke you to it, or to comply & correspond with good men for advantage sake, & for outward gifts, or to refuse wt ye Saints could, & would give, to accept of a Salary from those that wrest it out of ye bowells of ye poore. I trust when you, & us (as you oft speake) come out of Babilon, we shall yet review old things, & when we compare them with ye old we shall say ye old is better. I hope this plaines will not be construed censures, or ly's, but that god will account them expressions of faithfullnes to your soule, & that they wilbe a testimony carying trust in them to your conscience, if flesh be silent, & evill surmising, & priudice set apart; however it satisfies me, why I write them & I hope at our next & best meeting, they will at ye worst be accounted but ye wounds of a friend:

Yors as before.
V.P.

Whoever your informer was concer. Capt Wms & myself was much mistaken, for we had neither head hand nor heart in yt simple enterprise. I recd ye Welsh paper, if there be more as I thinke there is, I will send them to you.

'yt simple enterprise'. Diau mai cyfeiriad yw hwn at gais Gwŷr y Bumed Frenhiniaeth i godi gwrthryfel yn erbyn Cromwell yn ystod gwanwyn 1657. Llwyddodd ysbïwyr y llywodraeth i ddilyn y paratoadau ac arestiwyd y cynllwynwyr pan oeddynt yn barod i daro, 9 Ebrill 1657. Eu harweinydd oedd Thomas Venner a gododd wrthryfel eto yn 1660 a dioddefodd ei grogi a'i chwarteru yn Coleman Street, 19 Ionawr 1661. Am hanes manwl y cynyrfiadau hyn, gw. P. G. Rogers, *The Fifth Monarchy Men* (1966), 78–86, 110–20.

'Capt Wms'. John Williams, un o gefnogwyr eiddgaraf Vavasor Powell byth oddi ar 1642. Gŵr, mae'n ymddangos, o Sir Faesyfed, ac yn un o gomisiynwyr y milisia yn y sir. Yr oedd yn un o gomisiynwyr Deddf y Taenu ac fel henuriad yn eglwys Vavasor Powell, llofnododd, gydag eraill, yr ail epistol at 'Y Darllenydd' yn yr apoleg dros Vavasor, *Vavasoris Examen, & Purgamen* (1654). Yr oedd yn ysgolfeistr yn Llanfair-ym-Muallt yn 1650 ac ar ôl yr Adferiad gwysiwyd ef am gadw ysgol heb drwydded yn 1664 ac ar ôl hynny am anghydffurfiaeth. Yr oedd yn Bumed Brenhiniwr selog. Bu'n aelod o Senedd y Saint a chynorthwyodd Vavasor yn y cyfarfod yn Llanddewibrefi, 10 Chwefror 1654, i lansio'r ymgyrch yn erbyn y Ddiffynwriaeth, a llofnododd y *Gair Dros Dduw*. Yn ei ewyllys (a brofwyd 3 Awst 1671) dymunodd Vavasor Powell i John Williams, ymhlith eraill, helpu ei weddw i'w gweinyddu. Mudodd i Langollen a thra oedd yng ngharchar o dan writ *de excommunicato capiendo,* clafychodd, a diolch i'r Esgob William Lloyd, cafodd ddychwelyd adref, ond bu farw yno. Bu ei gorff am ddeng niwrnod yn gorwedd yn y fynwent, gan nad oedd caniatâd i'w gladdu, ond gorchmynnwyd i'w gyfeillion ei gladdu yn ei ardd. Bu farw felly yn niwedd mis Awst 1681. (Ceir y stori gan Philip Henry yn ei ddyddiadur, M. H. Lee, (gol.), *Diaries and Letters of Philip Henry* (1882), 305; am y cefndir cyfreithiol, gw, T. Richards, *Wales under the Penal Code* (1925), 18–19; am fanylion gweddill ei hanes, gw., R. Tudur Jones, *Vavasor Powell* (1971), mynegai.)

56
Vavasor Powell at [Morgan Llwyd], 27 Mehefin 1659

(LLGC 11439D, f. 32)

My very deare friend & brother
The auncient affection is not extinguished, & I hope rather encreaseing & renueing than decaying, tho. I cannot iustifie my neglect in visitting you soe long, tho ther were divers things hindered as my owne frequent, & continued infirmities, my being from home, hearing of your Recovery wn I once intended to come, together wth some other Rea: better suprst than exprst I hope wtever fire was kindled (besides zeale for our owne Judgemts) god hath in some measure quenched it, & our Lord's visitat. hath cooled or spirits, that if we have ye happines to see one another againe 'twilbe without any animosity, preiudice, or evill surmise wch hath beene too long gendred in ye hearts of ye Sts. one agt another. I hope if I have given you any offence to heare, acknowledge & satisfie, I doubt not of ye like from you: my lines would have signified ye continuance of my love, had I suppos'd they would have beene welcome, however I can say in the sight of ye Ld. I never unsainted you in my opinion, nor unfriended you in my desires. You were never out of my heart, nor shut out of my poore prayers: & I finde an honest intention to doe wt in me lies to remove all ground of disaffection, & Spirit: comunion. If I know my self, you may commit as much trust in me as ever you could, or as in another St. of equall infirmities, & temptacōns. If I come to Wrex: shortly, iudge it is ptly (yea chieffely) to visit you & not to divide, as some have formerly (ye Lord lay it not to their chardge) thought & spoken. Brother I cannot adde, but that I am truly & I hope sencibly affected wth your manifold afflictions, wishing (as to my self in qualitie & degree) a sanctified issue thereof & wherein I may be & be ye Lord for you, or you in, for him very
Yor once credited, & still so be beleeved (brother) friend

27th of ye 4th Mon. 59 Va. Powell

My wife rem: her respects to you, & both of us to Mr, & Mrs Moston. Had not ye Bearer beene in great hast I would not have beene soe short.

'Mr. & Mrs Moston'. Ambrose Mostyn a'i briod. Ail wraig Mostyn oedd hon sef Elizabeth, merch Syr Edward Broughton, barwnig, o Farchwiail (1610?–1665). Bu Jane, gwraig gyntaf Mostyn, farw 26 Gorffennaf 1651, a'i chladdu yn Sweeney (*Bye-Gones* (Mai 1880), V, 57). Gw. hefyd *Cofiadur* (1962), 64–5.

57
Hugh Prichard at Morgan Llwyd, 1 Rhagfyr 1651

(LLGC 11439D, ff. 13–14)

These
ffor Mr Morgan Lloyd pastor
of the Church at
Wrixham
Present.
Capt. Hugh Prichart

Honored & beloved in the lord,

I did expecte to reseave sume few lince from you ere this time elce I had before, this, Comes to you written; few words to you, I have not (had) few thoughts, nor Commune wth my own heart, wth seekinge, to knowe, from ye dissernere of secreets who understands ye bottom of yr heart, wth my own, Concerninge the trueths, of what you Charge me, and as yet neither ye lord of ye spirits, nor my own heart Chargeth my conscience, in ye leest to bee guilty, of what you Charged me. I can bouldly appell to ye Allmighty aboute it, who knowes what delight it was & is to my soule to see and here of that sweet unione and peace wth love amongh ye saints in fellowshipe in the Church at Wrixham, and further I speeke ye trueth wthout dissimulacōne, that I have had as much, Care, yea, & feare, in my heart, leest I should either by speekinge, silence or Cariages, make fractiones, as to my best observationes I had in any thinge or place, since I knew ye lord or my selfe in any mesure, I must Confess I have Receaved through grace, good from what you Chargd me, all though yor words have layed, and yet doe more heavy one my spirit, then any thinge did (to my best Remembrance) these 13 yeares I am Jelous wheather you have not sume preiudous against me, and truly I feare it, and yt upon these grounds, yt what soever I say or doe, if it be not accordinge, to what you hould forth before, you questione my end in it, I wish you to Consider ye grounds of these expresions. I hope ye lord will Cleare to me, and soe to you our straingene in our Imaginacons as well, as axtiones. Sr. I would o that I could maintaine the honorable thoughts I have had of you, what ever thoughts you have of me. Truly I say wth grife I am not Cleare to sitt doune wth you, leest I should be unto you, that wch I should not be, and you to me that I wch expected not, if my wife should not Come I am Resolved, through gods providence to returne whence I came, but if shee Comes, I am in astraight what to doe. The lord whose I am, and knowes, better then I doe, the end of my stainge directe my way and helpe me, simply wth out any selfe and to seeke his Glory, what ever Comes, of the outward man.

Though it is Sd wth me yet I am glad it is Joyus wth you in regard god helps you to give better Contente to yors, and yors to see more love in you, my desire is yt sattan & Corruptions may neaver prevaile to make ye leest breache any more. ye lord Jesus ye fountaine of wisdome fill you wth ye wisdome of ye spirite, and in riche you in knowlege and spirituall understandinge in ye Revelatacone of the gospell of Jesus, ye love of my Spirit to your selfe wth yours, whom I love in ye lord wth all ye bretheren and sisters yt walk in ye spirit to ye praise of ye Glory of his grace,

wch is ye request of him,
Who is and would serve you
though unfitt to be termed
brother

London i, 10. 51.

Hugh Prichard

I have opened my heart unto you, and I hope, our father will helpe to receave it in love, and to teach you, Improve what is right and may Conserve you.

Yours
H.P.

I have no news wroth ye writinge Therefore I am silent; my pretious wife is not as yet come. I would not willingly *live* in this Citty no longer if providence made way to goe out of it.

all our welce freinds yt are here are in health, though a litle troubled aboute ye cariages of things. Ye lord will doe a stranegh thinge in ye earth, and wil befoole ye wisdom of ye wise poletitioners of these dayes. I am afraid there will be great Changes in Churches shortly, ye spirits and Cariages of professors is not Consonant to ye Gospell, as I here dailye, from ye mouths of such as the lord sends to declare his will to his people vale, in hast, hopinge ye lord will help by his spirit you to make aright Constructions of my letter beinge my request it may answere ye lord will what ever elce.

Yours H.P.

58

Hugh Prichard at Morgan Llwyd, 18 Rhagfyr 1651

(LLGC 11439D, f.9)

To his much honord freind
Mr Morgan Lloyd pastor
of the Church at
Wrixham these
wth trust
hast hast
Capt Hugh Prichard

London 18. 10. 51.

Honored & deer Brother,

Yors I have received by Mr Powell 17th of this Instant wch I longed to see and for that by Capt Ellis, I have not as yet received it, many times, I have bine Inquiringe at his quarters for him (att leste 10 or 12 times) but could not meet wth him. These lince of yors, is welcome to me, and I beleeve cordially written, as ye heart speeks, though sume things yt is farre beyonde my deserts there expressed, I must tell you (but not wth ye leest thought in my heart to ad greefe) that yor words lay hevier on my soule, then any Externall thinge (to my Remembrance) yt Ever befell mee, and truly I speeke wthout dissumilacone, I thinke it arised from the Great love worth and esteeme. I had in my heart of you, as david in another Case sd, so might I in this, if such expressiones fell from any or most of all ye Christiane freinds I have in Engl: I could (as I conseave) have borne them wth less trouble of Spirit then from you, truly Sr if you knew my heart, what feare, Care, unwillingness, ther is in my spirit to speeke, or do, ye leest thinge yt might preieduese, ye welfare, of ye spirit of any deer brother or sister wth you, or to here, much more to see, there distractiones, dissipationes, Confutiones, defillements, delutiones, or the leest evill yt may weeken and Coolle love betweene them selves, and to any trueth or way of Xt, you would say, as I desire now in ye presence of ye lord to speek, that I have you and them all, in my heart wth all yor Spirituall Inioyments, and externall mercyes, to Continue and maintaine, unto the death. There is still a bodye of bitter death wthin me, ye fruts & bublings of wch breeks & kills my soule daylye, & make mee to lye doune wth much sadness many anight, & to walke heavilye & pensively many aday, wch no mane knoweth of it, and truly I am looth to speeke of it, to any leest I should discourage, and sadden there hearts, when I should further there Joy:) as you expresse you have longe expected a earthquake of Churches, I beleeve ye riddelinge shiftinge and wynnowinge of all sorts of persons mingled now amongh saints in

Churches and in outward esteemes), is neer at hand, and ye lord who is Jelous of his name Glory Saints & truth, is unmaskinge and unbowelinge ye secret wayes Grounds roots. and ends, of all such whose Circumscitione is not of the heart, and unto whom the knowlege of Xt Crusifyed is not more pretiousser, then all painted masked, vexatious, profitts, honor, & deseavable Glorye, of this earth, beinge ye chiefest, and great while, yt made them move in ye seeminge way of the Gospell.

Our freinds here are in health & mery in ye lord however sum great once discountenance them, knowinge ye lord will make ye wisdome of ye wise in this world, folly, and that to appeere (shortly) to all in liftinge, honoringe, and fillinge, his, slighted envyed, and disesteemed people wth his own presence, Countenance and Eminent imployments, wherein he will trust them and Kashiere all selfe seeking, proud Earthy minded and close, secret haters of Xt people, and ye power of Godliness, beinge not willinge to trouble wth, no more at present, but wth ye Remembrance of Inwards and united Affectione to you, wth yours wch is deer, and Respected wth my soule, wth all the rest of my bretheren, and sisters whose hearts and minds, is keept close to Jesus, and whose Conversatione is (faine what) shutable to the Gospell of truth. Intretinge this request, of you (as if it weare ye last) that you would mind my soule wth ye various temptacone, yt often doth belegers me round, yt presseth me fore Even to the graves brinke, hopinge you will be mindfull of me, especially wth ye spirit raiseth faith to hould ye soule close to Xt in ye promises, and as opertunitye permits send a few lince unto me. I take leave, but shall remaine

Yors to love and serve through grace
Hugh Prichard

direct ye letter to one Mr P Perke at the three arrowes in Cannan Street wollen Draper, for there I quarter.

if I can be servitiable any way to you, use me in manifestinge love I am like to stay aleger here, 6 or 8 weeks yet if ye lord gives life.

H.P.

'Mr Powell' oedd Vavasor Powell.

'Capt Ellis' oedd Andrew Ellis (neu Ellice), un o gomisiynwyr Deddf y Taenu oedd yn byw yn Althrey, plwyf Bangor-Is-coed. Yr oedd yn Ustus Heddwch. Ef sy'n cael ei enwi gyntaf (fel 'Andrew Ellise of Hanmer gent') yn y rheithgor a benodwyd i setlo'r anghydfod ynglŷn â gwahanu Worthebury oddi wrth Bangor-Is-coed adeg ordeinio Philip Henry, Ebrill 1658, gw. M. H. Lee, *Diaries and Letters of Philip Henry* (1882), 24–5. Gw. hefyd, A. N. Palmer, *The Older Nonconformity of Wrexham* (1888), 7, a T. Richards, *History of the Puritan Movement*, 82, 91, 98, a *Religious Developments*, 130–2.

59

Hugh Prichard at Morgan Llwyd, 17 Ionawr 1651/2

(LLGC 11439D, ff. 11–12)

ffor Mr. Morgan Lloyd pastor of the Church of
Christ at Wrixham
these
Present
wth trust
Capt. Prichart

Dear Sr London ye 17. 11. 51

Here is, but smole newes of any Good Consequence, sturringe, as I here of, only, yt there is, a fiere kindled in France, wch I hope will neaver be quensht, till it hath devowred Antichrist both roote, and branch, ye Spirit of Xt in his people here that quickence them in a constant seekinge of his face, (wch is acceptable to him) is much Calumniate, envied, and censured by many, that weare not our proffesd Enemyes few dayes agoe they charge them to have, aleavelinge designe, in the bottome of it, and very many pass there Judgment, and yt not only, on there meetings, but likwis on there persons, and expressiones, and this Goeth from hand to hand, as ye Custome of Sattan was of old. Ye lord doth more incorage, his people to persevere, in seekinge after him, wth Confidence, ye lord will not longe delay, to supply yr wants, and fullfill ye longings of the Spirits of his Children. I am often wth severall of ye cittisonces where they mutually comunicate there thoughts and what they here one to another, and I perseave, they are very Jelous in there hearts, if not malitious against Honest. (as in my Conscience I beleeve hee is) M.G.H. and reports there is severall articles produest or to be exhibited against him for severall things, and say he is to be suddenly cast out of ye house, as well as out of the Councell of State. This I thought good to Certify you in Generall, for this end yt you would use your interest in heaven daily for him, for he hath more need of the helpe of ye prayers of saints, then any man I know this day, if wee love Xt, if wee respects ye Good of ye people of Xt, if wee desire ye removall of wickedness and wicked persons from supreame places, and ye Glorious prograce and Inlargments of ye high way of Xt Kingdome, lett us mind Constantly, for Good such, as (not only, wish well to Sione, but are stackes and pillares therein) if you wth sume of our Bretheren mett 2 or 3 aweek to spend a litle time in seekinge ye Lrd for him, yt hee would stand by him to support him against all ye waight of ye malice of men and Devill, and to wipe away the blake aspertions, ye wayters for his hottinge Cast upon him.

There is much to be done in ye nations, Especially in relatione to Xt raigninge amongh us, The maine busines of most (truly I allmost sd of all men,) is to seek ye inrichinge of them selves, and inlarginge, of there own honor, and posessiones, as if the Exaltatione of Xt and his Interest weare but a poore loe unprofitable, and unshutable thinge for them, well might ye spiritt of Xt say of us, all men seeke there own, advantage, and profitt, but no man seeke ye things of Jesus, att best as zelously, and naturally, as wee should. There is many things on my heart yt I can not well Express, much less at this time in few lince declare, I hope you are not Ignorant and unsensible of ye statt of things, if saints weare ever sturred up in an extraordinary manner to seek ye Lord. Now it is necessary, ye lord Jesus Crowne, is redy, to be pluckt of his hed, afore well it sett one in this poore natione. This is our Incoragment, yt he is alone our foundatione, and wee shall be built upon him, therefore men wills, polecye, selfishnes, shall not prevaile.

I am here yet waytinge on ye lord sweet providence, to bring my wife and children to me, I hope I shall see you and shall mutually Joy through ye spirit in ech other shortly.

Yor letter dated ye 21, 9, I receaved but ye last day of Capt. Ellis, I am glad to here of yor welfare wth dear Mrs lloyd all though I heard not by you alonge time, and yt ye rest of my bretheren & sisters are well in ye body much more in ye prosperity of ther Inward man, my hearty Affectione remembrd to you wth Mrs lloyd and all ye rest yt longs to see ye lord of Sion advanced, and Constantly wayts for, ye fullfillinge of ye Glorious promises made to us in Jesus. I shall ad no more att present but yt I am

Yors, if ye lord to serve in ye love of
ye Gospell
H. Prichard.

'M.G.H.' oedd Major-General Thomas Harrison (1606–60), un o'r rhai a ddienyddiwyd am eu rhan yn condemnio Siarl I i farwolaeth. Cafodd ei enwi fel aelod o Gyngor y Wladwriaeth pan ffurfiwyd y corff hwnnw yn Ionawr 1649 ond ni chafodd ei ethol yn ffurfiol iddo tan 10 Chwefror 1651 (*Commons' Journals,* VI, 532). Am ei yrfa, gw. *DNB.*

60
Hugh Prichard at Morgan Llwyd, heb ddyddiad

(LLGC 11439D, ff. 5–6)

ffor his Honored Ffreind
Mr Morgan Lloyd
Pastor of the
Church at
Wrixham
These dil
Capt. Prichard.

Honored in the Lord

The more Glorious and nearer, the presence of the Lord Jesus is to his people, the more will there one deformitie appeere to them and unsound hearts, be descouered, Xt as are finer fire is comminge not only to burne up briers, and thornes, beinge not shrubs of his own plaintinge; but to Consume, the Drose and Sinn, that remaines, in saints, The Lord will do strainge things in Righteousness, and ye spirits of his people, waites on him, yeai longes, for Inioyments of those times when Xt shall weare his Crowne in Engl, and all the nationes, when oness of saints in all relatione shall be pure, (as in glory, there are sume, blessed saints, that Can not rest, in all there Inioyments, untill, ye interest of Jesus be more purly Advanced amongh ourselves, flesh, earth, selfe, Antichrist, and Babilon, bratts and rages be no more. As for the Reason why Mr Cradock and Mr Powell went out of towne, I can not certenly tell, But severall times I perseaved that there hearts weare much saddened, att ye spirits of sume, in respecte of sume transaxtiones. I know not what you meane by the Elders beinge wth ye Generall, Except it be those few wch went to him, to make the professione of there dishowinge, and disafectinge, The meetinge of severall saints of (all) the Churches in London yt meet to seeke ye Lord, to perfecte his work, in settinge, his Sonne in his Throne, and makinge all, secrett, with open Enemyes of his Gospell, & people, his foot stoole. Mr Rice Vaughan I could not speeke wth for yors came to hand latt last night, & this day ye meetinge was att all halowes. Capt Strainge I spake wth him about ye moneys aweeke agoe and he tould me that he would returne ye moneys to one in Chester for you wch I think he hath done, however I purpose to speek wth him wthin 2 dayes, and you shall here sodenly from me. Jon Lilburne is Gone 5 dayes agoe wth about 40 or 50 Gentlemen rod wth him beinge unarmd through ye Citty many pretious soule think ye censuer to be very heavy (if not uniust) notise was taken of the names of those that rode wth him, I feare it was not for any good end, open warre is like to be betweene us and ye hollanders, I desire all such things may be on ye accounte of Xt. M. G. Lambert is voted for Ireland, I am afraid ye pettitione wch you hint of, come (I feare) to latt. Coll. Barrowe writts to me by way of renewinge a former motione, to come for Irland I must Confess it was longe in my heart, to attend to any Cleare Call of the lord to goe there, I am loth to Conclud either way. I would see my wife and returne for wrixham first, let me request you to mind my Conditione, especially, when yor spirit hath warme Communione wth Jesus, That hee will Guid me in his paths, and make my heart willinge to follow him, to his foot, not only walk forward, but wheele after him to the same hand, as hee Commaunds, my wife is not louded. I herd not any thinge from her since the last shipp. I am here waitinge on ye lord Good pleasure to fullfill, the Good will of his Eternall love in his unchangable purposse before ye world was.

The great funerall by Report is ye next 6 day of ye week. If ye pretious soule weare in ye body I am persuaded would loth, such foppery and vaine prid, wth amase of treasure, spent aboute it. Time is short our dayes is all most rune out. blessed is ye Soule who longs for the Glorious appeeringe of our lord and keeps up his watch and maintaines a wakfull and livelye Eyinge of the Glorious advancinge of ye name & Kingdome of Jesus Xt, and lives not to himselfe and men, but to him that hath bought us to be for his praise, the presence of our lord in ye spirit fill you wth light, power & life, I rest Salut all ye saints wth you who are ye Glory of Xt especially yor proud selfe.

Yor Brother H. Prichard.

When you send to me, direct yor letter Imediatly to my lodginge elce I may not have them in 8 or 10 dayes. I pay here no more for 3 or 4 letters if they be well pact yn for asingle letter.

'Mr Cradock and Mr Powell' yw Walter Cradoc a Vavasor Powell.

Rice Vaughan (bu farw c. 1672), ail fab Henry Vaughan, Gelli-goch, Machynlleth. Cyfreithiwr wrth ei alwedigaeth. Yr oedd yn un o gomisiynwyr Deddf y Taenu a gweithredai dros gomisiynwyr y Ddeddf yn Llundain, yn neilltuol ynglŷn ag apeliadau yn erbyn eu dyfarniadau (T. Richards, *History of the Puritan Movement,* 236). Ar 18 Awst 1653 penodwyd ef yn ddirprwy glerc y Sesiwn Fawr yn siroedd Dinbych a Maldwyn. Yr oedd hefyd yn awdur. Gw. *Bywg.* a *DNB.*

John Lilburne (1614–57). Yr oedd hyn yn union wedi i'r Senedd basio deddf, 30 Ionawr 1652, yn ei gosbi â dirwyon trymion a'i alltudio o'r wlad. Cyfeirir yma ato'n gadael am yr Iseldiroedd. Am yr hanes, gw. M. A. Gibb, *John Lilburne. The Leveller* (1947), 299–303.

'M. G. Lambert'. Major-General John Lambert (1619–83), un o gadfridogion Cromwell. Mae'r cyfeiriad yn y llythyr at waith y Senedd, 30 Ionawr 1652, yn ei benodi'n Arglwydd-ddirprwy Iwerddon ar ôl marwolaeth Henry Ireton. Fel y digwyddodd hi, bu i'r Senedd ddileu swydd yr Arglwydd-lifftenant (a oedd yn eiddo i Cromwell) a diflannodd swydd y dirprwy gyda hi, ar 19 Mai 1652. Am yrfa Lambert, gw. *DNB.*

'The great funerall by Report is ye next 6 day of ye week'. Cyfeiriad at yr angladd mawreddog a drefnwyd i Henry Ireton ar gost y cyhoedd ac ar orchymyn y Senedd, 9 Rhagfyr 1651. Bu'r claddu ar 6 Chwefror 1652 yng Nghapel Harri'r VII yn Abaty Westminster. Ar '6 day of ye week', sef dydd Sadwrn, oedd hwnnw, fel y dywed y llythyr. Ar 4 Rhagfyr 1660 gorchmynnodd y Senedd godi ei gorff a'i hongian yn ei arch yn Tyburn cyn ei gladdu o dan y grocbren.

Mae'r cyfeiriad hwn yn dangos mai tua'r ail neu'r trydydd o Chwefror 1652 y cyfansoddwyd y llythyr.

61

Hugh Prichard at Morgan Llwyd, 28 Rhagfyr 1652

(LLGC 11439D, f. 18)

Indeared Brother

All though I have litle or nothinge to writte, haveinge this opertunitie, I can not but salut you, wth a few words, in aparenthasis for news. I presume you have more fully then wee here, being out of ye rood quarteringe, what will ye lord do wth this prophaine unthankfull, superstitious natione These sinfull times, weare neaver so disorderly observd and keept to my remembrance, in walce, as it is here and in all ye places where wee quarter, free willers. and non sinners do abound in these Countrees; and have there meetings; but refuse to here ye most precious, Gospell preachers yt is. There is more, ranters over all the Countree, yt slight all ordinances, and abhores Godly Conversationes, then there is of sober minded saincts. I longe to here how Mr Browne doth, wth yor familye and ye rest of any dear freinds in ye spirit. Ye Lord Jesus fill you wth ye spirit of Knowledge and power, wch is ye request of

Yor
Hugh prichard

Newport pannell

28. 10. 52

62
Hugh Prichard at Morgan Llwyd, 1653

(LLGC 11439D, f. 8)

In Deared in Jesus,

I have nothinge to Impart to you but ye Generally (as I am Informed) the hearts, and eys of most thriuight, prosperous, heavenlinese, cleare, frequent, and Constant in Comunione and familiaritie wth ye father whose is from Eternitie, and loagh to scorne ye politicke, wisdome, and wayes, of all his, and his poore lambs sutch enemyes. They are lookinge, and resolvd to waite, wth Confidence to Inioye redress, of these severall Grevances, and ye Inioyment of those Glorious things, held out in severall prophesies and promises, wch shall be in due time made Good to ye uttermost tittle, to those yt wait, for ye vitionee of his Appeerance. It is no smole Incoragment to my dule soule to find ye same spirit revelinge the same light, way, and pleasure of the father, and workinge in same measure ye like Confidence yt our lord will bringe to Glorious spirituall Inioyments though it be through, trialls, stormes, and Temptationes all his people shortly. honest brother Powell, I conseave will aquainte you fully how things Goeth nothinge as yet is done about ye petitione, ye lord, our life fill you wth renewed power Daily, to do his will wth might.

Salut all yt are pretious and yrs wch is in my heart to love & serve who am through our lord,

Yors
Hugh Prichard

Strand 20d = 53
ffor his honored ffreind Mr
Morgan Lloyd at
Wrixham
these del

63

H[ugh] P[richard] at Morgan Llwyd, 23 Mehefin 1654

(LLGC 11439D, f. 7)

Indeared Brother,

I may say wth Job, ye Evill wch I feared, is Come (or is really Intended) by the Enemy, and his Instruments; to be brought upon us ye designe ye last day was Caried on by Mr. Porter who, in the Generall (as they use to say was prety honest, but had sume cleare, & close wipes) and one Mr Cooke, who was full & firce Could not hould, but wth fire & brimstone vent out against ye wayes of Xt and his people prophessinge his name in this place much presuinge wth Egerness yt they menige ye prisbeteriance & caueleers of whom there was a great Company that weere Gathered to here them would soodenly settle a minister [?] amongh them, I am Informed yt some of ye prisbeteriance weare not satisfyed wth his preachinge, but it was wth ye unseasonableness of his Expressione. They would not have had ther designe discended so soone Many if not all ye sheep of Xt here about are much troubled at it & ye more sadned, because yor partinge wth them at such a Juncture of time, as this I can not here of any upright & pretious heart Contended in yor Journey therfore. Cooke bake & more deeply consider ye will of God in it; what Comfort should you have at yor returne to see ye wolfe beinge full wth ye blood of severall sheepe & lambes and many (through ye crueltye, of ye foxces & wild beast yt is creept in) of ye pretious children of Sione scattered wee have need looke about us for there are many spirits sent out at this very day here is one I ffor him not, but D. LL. tould mee of him yt doth know yow & you him though you neaver so his face nor herd his name.

Ye Enemy is beesy & suttle & fits his Temptatione to ye humour wth most raignes in ye naturell spirits of people. I would have written ye heads of ye sermon to you, but yt our freinds for ye most part weere out of Towne, you may visite all ye parts in Merrionyth & Carnarvone shyres where ther be any Inquiringe after ye Lord but I expecte you returnd wthin 15 dayes at furthest. It Groes late Therefore no more at present but yt I am

Yors H. P.

Wrixham 23th 4: 54/

64

P[hillip] Rogers at Morgan Llwyd, 23 Chwefror 1653/4

(LLGC 11439D, f. 17)

These
for Mr Morgan Lloyd
att Wrexham
present

Endeared Brother

Your lines I receaved, wch were indeed very welcome to me, & soe much the more because I had not seene you nor heard from you this longe time (accordinge to naturall Computations) I have had many tryalls & stronge temptations A llawer *llwybr garw tywyll dierth y bûm* ei yn ei rhodio, since I saw your face, & I have been very much unsettled in my minde, wch were I wth you I should relate partickularly but now (through mercy) I doe apprehend the riches of grace and love made out (not onely unto me but allso) in me in ye beloved son & saviour, wch doth stay & settle me somewhat, since my Cominge hither I have beene very dead & much distempered in my minde, meetinge wth unusuall temptations, the Carnall unmortyfied part, stealinge away my thoughts & leadinge ym after the various vaine & confused noyses sights etc. that are in this Sodom, but now it begins to be otherwise wth me. I heard a voyce in me saying keepe the heart wth all diligence & I finde in measure A power inablinge thereunto and indeede this is my present Joy & Confidence that I shall have a heart to love him and to keepe his word & way, & so to be loved of him & to inioye him & manifestatns of him, as himself hath sayd.

I Cannot give you any perfect account of thinges here onely this that men (eminent proffessors (and for ought I Know really godly too) doe differ in their mindes & Judgments of present transactns more then their faces differ one from another, but this I observed amonge some that the question is not so much now who is Independnt Anababtist Seeker etc as who is for Ct & who for Crom. . . but the day of god will put an end to these things: W: Erbery is in the Cittie he hath put forth *some papers since I came hither*, some say he makes A trade of it havinge no other way to subsist. I have it in my thoughts to goe heare him shortly, here be some new bookes put *forth by the qua: but you have the summ* of them allready I shall not add, but my dear love to your wife, I hope you will not forgett me when you are speakinge to yr father, for indeed I have need of helpe, & in what ever I may serve you here I am ready.

Gorchmynwch
Ych brawyd ach gwasanaethwr
P. Rogers

23d. 12m 53.

'P. Rogers' oedd Phillip Rogers, y ceir ei enw gyda gwŷr eraill o Wrecsam ymhlith llofnodwyr y *Gair Dros Dduw*. Tueddai A. N. Palmer i uniaethu'r Philip Rogers a gafodd drwydded o dan y Declarasiwn, 22 Mai 1672, i gynnal oedfaon yn nhŷ Roger Kynaston ym mhlwyf Rhiwabon, â'r gŵr o'r un enw a oedd yn henuriad yn Eglwys Annibynnol Wrecsam yn 1675 (*Older Nonconformity of Wrexham*, 48). A chredai Thomas Richards mai'r un un ydoedd â'r Philip Rogers a gafodd drwydded, 22 Gorffennaf 1672, i bregethu yn ei dŷ ei hun yn St. Martin's, Amwythig (*Religious Developments*, 500). Yn sicr, nid ef oedd y gŵr o'r un enw a osodwyd gan y Profwyr yn Llanwyddelan yn 1658 oherwydd cydymffurfiodd ef pan ddaeth yr Adferiad.

Am William Erbery (1604–54), gw. *Bywg.*

65

Phill[ip] Rogers at Morgan Llwyd, 24 Mawrth 1653/4

(LLGC 11439D, f. 15)

Beumaris
the 24th of ye 1 month
1653

Deare Sr

Havinge such a Convenient opportunitie, I have made bold to present you wth these few lines, I am through providence brought into this darke Countrey where I meete wth many new & stronge temtations Dayly, & somtimes have much sadnes partly from the unclean conversation of the people and partly from a sense of mine owne darknes & vilenes for I *finde the motions of the* old man which is corrupt very stronge and ready to breake out upon every occasion, I am sensible of much Ignorance and Carnalitie in my selfe as when I thinke of that blessed *trinitie. I have not such high* and reverend thoughts as I am Convinced I should have, but my thoughts and apprehensions are low & meane & Carnall and when I speak to the people I canot doe it nor behave my selfe towards them wth *that plaines* & meeknes & love & tendernes as I ought to doe, I desire therefore that you wold remember me before the throne of grace & that you wold speake to our bretheren allso to minde me that the father wold fill me wth his spirit and Knowledge of himselfe that I may honour him in my place & not dishonour him. I have another request to you & yt is that (if your busines permit you) you wold write *A few lines Concerninge the thousand years* mentiond in revelations the 20 when & how it will be. My desire is that you wold give som hints that may lead me to the right understandinge of it, & if you will mention som scripturs that doe speake of the same thinges, it may be the lord will give me som light in them & revive my spirit there by to ask from him. I will not further trouble you at present,

but remaine
Yours to serve you
in what I may
Phill Rogers

66

P[hillip] Rogers at Morgan Llwyd, 4 Mawrth 1654/5

(LLGC 11439D, f. 16)

These
for
Mr Morgan Lloyd
at his house in Wrexham   Present
Books by Paine Carrier
per Chester post

Beloved ffreind.

I have (accordinge to your desire) sent you some bookes by James Payne: the Carier, he told me he wold be in wrexham the last day of the next weeke, here be some other bookes, wch I had thought to send you, namely the tryall of spiritts, put forthe by Will Dell, & the examination of Accademies treatinge of the nature of things put forth by Mr Webster, & some bookes put forth by the qua: (so called) but I did not know but that you might have them allready, therefore I did forbeare untill I heare from you, we have very little time to read or inquire of any thinge but what we are about, for we doe reade every sheete of ye bible 4 times before it is printed, and notwthstandinge, some faults escape us the printers being unacquainted wth the language, I suppose you have heard by this that Mrs Courtney is ffallen asleepe, he is accordinge sorrowfull, you would doe well to write to him. I have not time att present to write of my Condition, either past or present, onely this I finde in the bottome of my thoughts that I would Chuse to suffer rather than to inioy the pleasures of sin wth the wicked & this I find that the more I looke on or thinke off the vanishinge Gaudie gloryes of this world (wch are aboundinge in this place) the more my minde is alienated from them & the more my minde is wthdrawne from them the more I inioy of that sweete glorious & onely soule satisfyinge fellowship wth the father in the son, I desire you to write to me as frequently & as largely as you Conveniently may, for I finde good in those meanes especially now, I desire to be remembred to & by all my ffreinds I shall not trouble you further, beinge in some hast but remaine

Your Brother waytinge wth you for the
day of the lord

Millbank   P. Rogers
4th 1 mon *54*

The bookes I sent you are these, Divine Essayes, by Is. Pennington, the discovery of mans returne, newes cominge from the north, light out of darknes, the olive leaffe, the man of peace, & A voyce from heaven.

'William Dell', *The Tryal of Spirits Both in Teachers & Hearers* (Giles Calvert, Llundain, 1653). Am Dell (bu farw 1664), Meistr Coleg Gonville a Caius, Caergrawnt, gw. *DNB* ac A. G. Matthews, *Calamy Revised.*

'John Webster', *Academiarum Examen: or, the Examination of Academies . . .* (Llundain, 1654). Ar 12 Hydref 1653 yr oedd yn gweithredu fel gweinidog All Hallows, Lombard Street, Llundain, a chafodd ef a William Erbery ddadl gyhoeddus gynhyrfus gyda dau weinidog anhysbys. Yn y rhagair i'w lyfr y mae Webster yn mynegi edmygedd o waith Jakob Böhme, y gŵr yr oedd Llwyd hefyd yn ymddiddori ynddo. Am yrfa Webster (1610–82), gw. *DNB* ac A. G. Matthews, *Calamy Revised.*

Cyhoeddodd Isaac Penington ei gasgliad o ysgrifau, *Divine Essays* yn Llundain yn 1654. Yn 1657 yr ymunodd Penington a'i wraig yn gyhoeddus â'r Crynwyr er ei fod yn closio atynt cyn hynny. Am Penington (1616–79), gw. *DNB.*

'qua': yw 'Quakers'.

'we doe reade every sheete of ye Bible 4 times before it is printed'. Tybed ai cyfeiriad yw hwn at 'Feibl Cromwell', sef *Y Bibl Cyssegr-lan . . .* a argraffwyd gan James Flesher yn Llundain yn 1654 ac a werthid 'gan Thomas Brewster, tan lun y tri Bibl yn ymmyl Pauls'?

'Mrs Courtney is fallen asleep', cyfeiriad at wraig Hugh Courtney.

67

P[eter] Sterry at Morgan Llwyd, Mehefin 1651

(LLGC 11439D, f. 44)

Sr

I have saide nothing of Beaumont, nor of ye Ordinances, concerning wch you put mee in mind with so much true Love, & in so sweet a manner, wch makes you truely deare to mee. But I intend to trouble you againe very sodeynly, Pray let mee heare frequently from you. I rejoycing exceedingly in ye outgoings of our Lord Jesus in your Spirit; & in your ffellowship. My most affectionate Service to ye Major Generall, whom I desyre alwayes to remember in my prayers.

Your Brother in ye hope
of Christ. Peter Sterry.
June 1651

I hope no more to make so long an Intermission on my part.

Mr P Sterry
ffor my Honoured ffriend
Mr. Morgan Lloyd.

Leave this with Mr Walter at
Major Generall Harrisons
Lodgings in Whitehall.

Am Peter Sterry (bu farw 1672), pregethwr Cyngor y Wladwriaeth a chaplan Cromwell, gw. *DNB* ac A. G. Matthews, *Calamy Revised.*

Yn Whitehall yr oedd llety Sterry ac eto mae'n cyfeirio'r llythyr hwn at Thomas Harrison yn ei lety yntau yn Whitehall. Erbyn hyn yr oedd Harrison ar y ffordd i'r Alban i gyfarfod y perygl a ddilynai laniad Siarl II yn y wlad. Erbyn 5 Mehefin yr oedd Morgan Llwyd, gyda'i ffrindiau Edward Taylor a Hugh Prichard, gyda thrigain o gefnogwyr o ogledd Cymru wedi ymrestru i gefnogi'r ymgyrch. Ar 25 Gorffennaf 1651 yr oedd Walter Cradoc wedi pasio trwy Henffordd ac ychydig cyn hynny, Vavasor Powell, hwythau â gosgordd o filwyr yn eu canlyn. Mae'n bosibl felly fod Sterry wedi anfon ei lythyr i swyddfa Harrison er mwyn iddo fynd gyda llythyrau eraill y fyddin tua'r gogledd. A dyna pam y mae'n anfon ei gofion 'to ye Major Generall', Thomas Harrison.

Am ei ohebiaeth â Llwyd, gw. N. J. Matar, 'Peter Sterry and Morgan Llwyd', *Journal of the United Reformed Church History Society,* ii (1981) 275–9.

'Beaumont' oedd Jakob Böhme.

68

P[eter] S[terry] at Morgan Llwyd, 14 Ionawr 1651/2

(LLGC 11439D, ff. 42–3)

Deere & Beloved in our Lord Jesus

It is in part a Losse of Life, & Vailing of Heaven from mee yt I am so much interrupted by ye Shakings of this Tabernacle, where now I dwell, in my Communion with my Bridegroome in you, wt could make up this Losse, if I did not find a Living way of Enjoying you in Him, in whom All Saints doe not live, but are Life, have not a Beautifulnes, & Sweetnesses, but are themselves, ye Eternall Beauetys, & Sweetnesses, multiplying, & begetting themselves from ye ffather, upon ye Son, in One Spirits. Your Severall Letters, to wch I have returned no answer, were like Jacobs Rods, welcome Appearances of my God, forming other Appearances in mee, wch I would gladly have returned yt wee might thus have as Members by our mutuall Supplys built up one another to ye Increases of God in us. But it is ye good pleasure of Jesus Christ to suffer much of yt little Store of New Wine wch from himselfe, or any of his Bottels, Angels, or Saints, hee is pleased to poure into mee, to bee spilt, through ye Crazines of this old Bottle, this Crackt Body. Three things I have still carryed in minde, to returne you my Thoughts concerning them; ye Lord in you judge how farre my Thoughts come forth from ye Minde of Christ in mee.

1. There is nothing, wch is such Marrow, & ffatnes to my Soule, such a ffounetayne of Wine taken off ye Lees, such a Ground worke for such an Unvailing of all ye Mysterys of ye Gospell, such a Roote, Heade, Light to all Truths of all Sorts, as ye Godheade of Christ, & ye Trinity, wch is connext with it. Deere Sr Let not goe your Hold of this Truth for all ye ffayre or Sweet Appearances, yt can bee presented to you. It is it selfe ye ffayrest, & sweetest of All Appearances, ye Crowne, Substance, Life of all; All are Shadowes, wch have not this as theyr Beginning, theyr Ende, theyr Life. These three, ye ffather, ye Word, & ye Spirit; All Three but One; Each One, yt Same One Entyrely, Each One All Three; ô wt Volumes of Mystery, of Glory, of Ravishing Pleasures, doth this Truth of ye Trinity write upon those Hearts, to wch it is pleased to appeare in any Thing of its owne Lights How much Paper how much Time could I spend from my Empty Treasury in speaking Great, Glorious Things of This High, & Holy Place? But I doubt whether it bee Possible, or Lawfull to utter them any further than by Hints; ffor they are such Pearles, as cannot bee held forth, save by theyr owne Lustre in ye Spirit, & are sullyed by ye

Handling of our Expressions. Deere Sr, pray to ye ffather of Lights, yt hee would shed abroade from ye fface of Christ this Light, wch is inaccessible by Man, untill it selfe come into Man. Out of this Trinity ye Lord Jesus comes forth, ye Word, One of ye three, & All Three in yt One. Hee brings forth Himselfe into ye Mediatours Kingdome; from thence into this Creation, where hee disappeares, & is imprisoned by Sin under ye Powers of Darkenes, Then Hee comes up againe being made truely Man of ye Virgin Mary. By his Death, & Resurrection hee returnes out of this Creation unto ye ffather, meeting him first in ye Mediatours Kingdome, where God, & ye Lambe raigne together. After yt Hee rests with him in ye Kingdom of ye ffather, wch is yt Blessed Trinity, out of wch hee first came forth, where God is All in All. Thus Hee yt Ascends above All Heavens, is ye same, who first Descended, & Hee, who, while hee comes downe, & goes up, is ye very same still unchangeably There above All.

2. Concerning Beaumont [Bohme] whom I have much perused, I have this to offer to you. I have very much doubted in my selfe, whether our Lord Jesus, or some Angell of ye Rulers of ye Darkenes of this Creation, cloathing himselfe with yt Light, & Glory of this Creation, as God & Christ, appeared to him in his Visions, & directed his Pen. Those things, wch so farre, as I understand him, are unsavoury to my Spirit, are: 1. His Exaltation of ffree — Will after ye manner of ye Arminians. 2 ly, His making yt Blessednes wch Christ hath purchased for us to bee onely ye Restitution of ye ffirst Adam, ye ffirst Paradise, & ye Bringing of us to Angels Thrones. 3 ly. His Darke, Confused, Mistaken (as I humbly concejve) Discourses of ye Trinity. 4 His over-much affectate Mixtures, Heathenish Philosophy, & Chymistry. All these things, wch for ye present occurre in my memory have made mee jealous, yt hee saw ye Glory of this Creation, & not ye Difference betweene ye Two Creations, ye Two Adams, ye Two Images; One Earthly, Naturall; ye Other Heavenly, Spirituall. Wn I first saw him, I beleeved, & saide, yt wch I have seene since proove true by manifold experience, yt many by reading of him, have bin led aside from ye Mystery of ye Gospell, having lost themselves some in one maze of Darkenes, some in another not rising above this Creation, but running after One Part or another, as ffree Will Starre, Angels, Elements, set up in a false manner before ye eyes of theyr Minde.

Yet on ye other side; I cannot but confesse, yt ye Lord Jesus hath ministred, as much Heavenly Pleasurs, & Profite to mee by reading of him, as of any Discourses, besides those of ye Holy Scriptures. I have met with rich Depths, Sweet Heighths in him. Then ye Discouery of ye Spirit of AntiChrist is very cleare, ffull, & Powerfull in him. The Sweetnes, Meekenes, Humility, Holines, of Heavenlines of ye Spirit of Christ run along like Rivers of Milke, & Honey thorow his Writings, wch seeme to have an Authority, & Glory in them, beyong yt of ye Scribes, & Pharisees. Upon these Accounts I have againe bred in mee very Reverend Thoughts of yt Spirit, wch wrought in him, & so am apt to conclude; 1. The Lord gave him his Spirit by Measure, leaving much Darkenes mingled with his Light. 2. They yt reade him, had neede come to him well instructed in ye Mystery of Christ, with a Heavenly Newnes of Mind, by wch they may bee able to try, wt ye Good, & Acceptable Word of God is. Others will bee perverted by him, I desyre, yt wt I have written may bee understood as spoken with ye ffreedome of a ffriend, but ye Meekenes, ye Humility of a Christian, who is able to judge nothing so much, as this, yt it is not yet Day with him, a Day of Judgement, though Light bee sowen in Him, & thorow Grace come up in ye Herbe, & a Little in ye Blade. I thought to have saide something of Ordinances, but my Paper, & Strength are spent. Love mee in ye Spirit. Pray for mee always. Refresh mee often with your Letters. The Lord Himselfe build us up to His Kingdome in yt Spirit, & in yt Kingdome bee ever with our Spirits.

January 14, 1651.

P.S. (Peter Sterry).

69

[Peter Sterry] at Morgan Llwyd, 4 Gorffennaf 1652

(LLGC 11439D, ff. 40–1)

Most Deere in ye Unity of ye Spirit, & ye ffellowship of ye Mystery of ye ffather, & of Christ.

The Springings of my Love, & Glory in your Spirit, manifested to mee by your sweet-smelling Letters are not thorou ye same Jesus without ffruite of more Love, & Praise to our Beloved in my Spirit. How pleasant is it to my Eye to see you looking forth like ye Morning, & ye Heavenly Man, who is ye Quickning Spirit in ye ffirmament of Eternity, as a Sun, comming forth out of ye Chamber of your Heart, as a Bridegroome, revealing him selfe in you, as hee riseth, & forming himselfe upon you by those Revelations. Beleeve mee in ye Spirit of Christ, it is a ffeast of ye Wine, & Marrow of Divine Loves to mee, wn I recejve from you or write to you & Yet thorow ye naturall indisposition of my Body to labour, thorow frequent illnesses, & ye subtlety of ye Enemy; yt watcheth as much to hinder ye sowing of ye precious Corne, wch makes ye ffieldes of ye Spirit Greene, as to sow tares; I am kept from writing Dayes, Weekes, Moneths, wn I may with confidence say, no one Day lightly passeth over mee without Affectionate Remembrances of you, Longings after your Embraces in ye Everlasting Armes of yt Love wch is God Blessed for ever. How pleasant is this Countenance of yours, how sweet this Voyce, wch you make mee to see & heare from Mount Sion, yt cannot bee toucht, ye Hierusalem above, ye Deare, ye true Mother — Church of us all, I meane, yt Great Assembly of ye ffirst-borne, ye ffellowship of all ye Sons of God in ye Uncreated, & Eternall Spirit. A! let my Spirit, & yours bee ever found walking hand in hand, Spirit in Spirit, in this Garden of ye Spouses above ye third Heavens, Here it is, yt Christ, & His Church are Rose, & Lilly, invisible to every Created Eye, but all Eye to themselves, to see theyr owne Beauetys all Sent to smell theyr owne Sweetnesses, all Love, combining ye Rose, & ye Lilly in so perfect a Mixture, yt Both are Both, Rose & Lilly too, Both ioyntly grow up out of one Common-Roote; Both enterchangeably spring up out of each others Bosome. Here Christ ye Spirit, & all ye Saints in particular are ffellow-Roses, & ffellow-Lillys wch sang together flourished together in those Garden-beds. Thos Habitable-Worlds, ye Cheekes of ye Eternall Bridegroome, before they were yet in ye Earth, & sprung up out of ye Earth. Here God, & ye Lambe are Sun, Moone, & Temple; Life Order, & Ordinances; Light, & Manifestations; Power & Wisdome; All in All; ye Power of an Endless Life, a ffountayne of Living Waters flowing freely forth. I have reade in ye Bookes of ye Wise men of ye East, yt ye Naturall Spirit of this Visible World being unmooveably intent upon Intellectual Glorys, according to yt copy brings forth, & governes this vast fframe, without any Sense of it, as wee carry our shadowes along with us, or moove our ffeet by our eye. This is to mee ye greate Ordinance for ye Governing of my outward Man, to abide in a Close Unison with ye Inward Man, yt from him, ye Beames of Spirituall Glory may passe thorow to my Shadow also to cover that, & to forme it, as it is with a Man, yt walkes with his fface towardes ye Sun. The Dispensation, wch Moses brought in was, a Visible Image of Christ to ye Senses of ye Naturall Man, imposed from without, as by a Schoole Master, while ye Lord from Heaven lay hid, as a Seede onely in ye Hearts of his Elect. Wn Our God ascended from ye Grave to ye Throne, then hee tooke away yt Bondage of Pedagogy, hee shooke ye Earth. The Heavenly Man was revealed in ye saints: Hee formed upon ye Naturall Soule a Glorious Image of Himselfe: This Image freely governed ye Body, & ye Outward Part of ye Naturall Man. So yt now insteade of Visible fformes, here is an Invisible Temple, or Image. Insteade of Moses comming downe with ye Platformes of a Tabernacle, & Worship from Mount Sinai; you have Jesus Christ shining from Mount Sion, & forming upon ye Inward Waters of your Earthly Man, upon your Angelicall Part ye Bright & Beautifull Reflection of his owne Immediate Beames! Insteade of a Letter, & a Law you have Light, & Love as Two Raines by wch Christ from within governes, & manages your fflesh. As for those Outward fformes, wch ye Scripture mentions they seeme to mee to bee so farre from ye proper Dispensation of ye Gospell, ye Minde, & Command of Christ, yt they were at most Conniuencys, Condescentions to ye present Weakenes of Christians, to bee out-growne, & cast off, wn they should bee able to walke in ye Spirit. Insteade of this, those Tables became snares very sodeynly, Mens backes were bowed downe to beare those burthens alwayes, & never were they able to lift up themselves into ye Liberty of ye Spirit by ye Crosse of Christ, on which hee tryumphed over all Wordly Rudiments. Thus ye Mystery of Antichrist tooke its Like, wch is a Revivall of Judaicall Dispensation, yt ye Evangelicall Ministery may bee by it throwne into ye Grave, out of wch it selfe is brought forth. A Created Principle is againe set up in place of ye Last Adam: A letter is made our Law in ye Roome of ye Divine Glory shining in ye fface of Christ from within: In place of ye ffree, Living Streames from ye Spirit in our Inward Parts, flowing forth thorow our Senses, & Bodyes; Set fformes, Imposed Rites are made our Glory. Thus ye Earth, wch God hath shaken, & remooved is reestablished, wn wee should bee waiting for ye Last Appearance of our God, & Saviour, wch is ye Third Dispensation, wn our Heaven also shall bee shaken, even this Spirit of Gifts, & Graces, this Inward Temple, this Invisible Image framed upon our

Intellectuall, & Angelicall Part by ye Naked fface of ye Eternall Sunne shedding his Beames upon it shall bee remooved; yt so wee may bee gathered up into ye Substance of yt Sun it selfe, as into a Tabernacle descending upon us to take us up into its Bosome, wch is our Everlasting Mansion in ye house of our owne ffather, above all Heavens.

Deere Sr, beware of Dogs, wch barke at Pearles cast before them, as stones throwne at them. The Worlde cannot Know a Saint, or Christ, or ye Church, because it hath not Knowne ye ffather. I speake not this to reproach, or riject any Person, yt waites for ye coming up of ye Heavenly Seede under any fforme of Outward Worship; but to yt seede onely, wch being borne after ye flesh, persecutes yt, wch is borne after ye Spirit. Hee yt Keepeth a day; & Keepeth it, to Superstition, to Antichrist: Hee, yt Keepeth not a Day, & Keepeth it not, to Profanenes, to Beelzebub; both are an Abomination. Hee, yt Keepeth it, to ye Lord, & hee, yt Keepeth it not, to ye Lord, both ought to receive each other into ye Glory of God, as they are both alike received of Jesus Christ Pray for mee.

I am
your affectionate Brother
in our Deare Saviour Jesus Christ

July 4 1652. (Peter Sterry)

I have entreated
Captayne Ellis to send
you one of my last sermons.
Ffor my Deerely esteemed
ffriende Mr Morgan
ffloyde of
Wrexham.
Give this to Captayne Ellis.

'Capt Ellis' oedd Andrew Ellis.

70

Peter Sterry at Morgan Llwyd, 23 Gorffennaf 1654

(LLGC 11439D, f. 25)

July 23. 54. Whitehall

Deere Sr

I intreate you, according to ye manner of God your ffather to measure my love, not by its Effects, but Principle. ffirst looke on mee in Christ, where wee are as Light in ye Sun of Love: then looke on Christ in mee, where hee is alwayes ye same Sun, though often under ye Shadow of this Cloud, this Earth, ye Body. I thinke, I may say with modesty, yt I have not wanted a Heate of affections, & yt from heaven: but I have wanted straw, & chips, ye fuell of naturall Spirits, to draw forth this Heate into a Fflame, wch might be Visible to you, & Tangible. I remember in generall, yt you desyred my Sense on Ffive Subjects. I remember at present onely three, ffree will, ye Shakers, this Power. A ffree-will in man undetermined by ye ultimate, Dictates of ye understanding, whose illuminations flow indispensably from its proper Obiect, seemes to mee to carry with it these Evills. It makes too great a division betweene Truth, & Goodnes, wch seeme as inseparable, as Harmony, & Sound in Musicke; as Beauety, & ye shine of yt Beauety in Light. It makes too great a Division betweene ye spirit, Understanding, Will in ye Soule, wch in this represent ye ffather, Word, Holy Ghost in Trinity, yt All are One, & each One in All: The Spirit, as ye Ffather; ye Understanding as ye Word; ye Will as ye Holy Ghost, by whom ye Ffather & Word dwell, & delight mutually one in another, from wch Union all sts in ye Trinity, all Affections in ye Soule spring, as children from ye Marriage-bed. The ffreewill, of wch wee speake in Man, is plainely contradictory to ye ffreedome of ye Eternall Wisedome, & Will in ye Divine Nature: consequentially, to ye Whole Beauety, & Sweetnes of ye Evangelicall Mystery.

Where are ye Ravishing pleasures of an Undeserved, Unexpected, Irresistible Love, if this Love bee subiect to ye Indifferent Receptions, or Refusalls of my Will? Where is ye Glorious Tryumph of a Deepe & Rich Designe comprehending yr whole Creation, carrying Eternity thorough Time like a River under Ground, till Time breake up into Eternity againe, till yt, wch was ye ffirst, bee ye Last, & ye Ende proove ye Beginning awakened, & returning to it selfe againe; if ye Will of Man bee not as a Linke fastened in this Chaine, but bee a compleate Circle having its Beginning & its Ende in it selfe; if ye Will of Man depend not in its

Workinge upon ye Designe of God, but yt Designe upon ye undetermined Licentiousnes of these Workings? If Christ bee ye Universall Image of Things, sure ffree will is in ye face of this Image, as a skarre, a Wound, wch Physitians define to bee, Solutio continui. If God bee ye Ffirst cause of things, either ye Will of Man is in all things determined by a Cause above it selfe, or hath a Godheade in it selfe.

(2) Ffor ye Shakers I have onely this to say: ye Christ, as hee growes in us, will not judge by ye Hearing off ye Eare, or ye Sight of ye Eye. How then? ye Jewes say; by ye Spirit tanquam odore, discerning not ye Word, but ye Savour, ye Power. The Kingdome of God comes not with observation, in multitudes, in outward Noyse. These are all like ye Net in ye Gospell, wch brings up ffish, & Trash together. The Day of ye Lord is as a Theefe in ye Night, cleeres it selfe up without Noyse. Wee neede not goe forth this way, or yt Way after ye Cry in ye Streets; where ye Carkasse of Christs body is, ye Eagles ye 7 Spirits of God will alight in theyr Season & become theyr owne Witnes. As to ye present Power, if wee bee ruled by man after ye fformes of Men, wee are of all nations ye most wretched. But if by ye Spirit & Annoyntings of ye most high, then is ye Kingdome of God come downe into ye midst of us, & as fflatterers have saide, yt ye Crowne covers all Defects, ye Divine Annoyntings will much more, though they should bee, as Davids or Samsons,
Pray, Love, Live, for mee, with mee, in mee, in ye Spirit.

Peter Sterry.

Ffor Mr Morgan ffloyde
of Wrexham in
Wales poast paid.

71

Peter Sterry at Morgan Llwyd, 27 Medi 1656

(LLGC 11439D, f. 46)

Deere, & Beloved in ye ffounetayne of ye seven flaming Spirits of ye Eternall & Innumerable Company of Loves.

While a bubling Sweetnes from ye naked Heart of ye Godheade, our Deepe, & Common Center, ariseth up immediately, into a Pure Spirit in mee, wch is alone my True, & Waking Selfe, in wch my Jesus, & I flourish like Twin-Lillys on ye same stocke, bearing all Invisible Spirits, & Visible fformes of things, as ye leaves of these Lillys, & ye shining Colours upon these Leaves; while I feele you, are ye same Sweetnes springing up in ye same Spirit, & Bright Image of Eternity, & Time within my Spirit;

Ô wt Joy have I in my Delicious ffellowship with you! wt auntient, & new ffloods of pleasure flow from within us, & betweene us, in wch wee melt one into another in Spirituall Waters, wch are Lustre, Life, & Love? How is our Communion at once in each exchange of Spirit, both with ye Ffather & ye Son; ye Son every moment being borne anew out of ye Bosome of ye ffather, as a Bridegroome ready trim'd, or a fresh Day of Eternity; & ye ffather every where in all ye Glorious Varietys of ye Son opening himselfe to give to each a Satisfying ffulnes in ye Unity, & a Ravishing Newnes by Endles Births — it! But how have I lost my selfe in ye Ma (trix of) these Loves; & wandred in yr Labyrinth of ye — of this Heavenly Virgin, ye Divine Wisedome? O Sr this alone is Life, & ffruitfulnes, to bee planted by these Rivers, these Divisions of Waters, where all Varietye of fformes breake forth Immediately from theyr Unfathomable Heade to water all things Invisible, and Visible.

This is ye Glorious Wheele of Immortality, by ye property of ye Son, to bee ever issuing forth into all pleasant Births, by wch wee ride upon ye Circuits of ye Heavens, ye High places of ye Earth, ye floods of ye great deepe, like ye pleasant Light of ye Sun; & then by ye property of ye ffather to bee ever returning into yt Blessed Wombe, yt Greene Bed of Loves out of wch wee came forth. Blessed is hee, who in every Day, & Night, in every Creature beholds this Wheele & each Day, each Night, each Creature, ye Revolutions of this Wheele within it selfe; & this Wheele his Eye, his Spirit, wch is also ye Holy, & Immortall Spirit; in wch God ye ffather, & our Lord Jesus everlastingly sport themselves mutually in one another. Sr, I shall say 2 words to those Two Hints in yours: 1 The Blessed Trinity is ye fflourishing Roote, & Patterne of ye State of Things in it Selfe; ye Standing of Things out of it selfe; ye Turning of things againe into it selfe. But as Reflections of ye Sun multiply from a glasse to ye Wall, from ye Wall to my Eye, or as ye steps of ye Ladder in Jacobs Vision so Images from yt first flourishing Trinity bee propagated! Who can tell ye Generations of Him, ... Descent & Ascent fills all, no where leaving any Gap? Againe, who can discover ye severall Scenes, those Unsearchable Riches of Christ ye Wisdome, & Glory of ye ffather, those Diversitys of fformes, & Progresses, by wch Things rise up out of Eternity, & returne thither againe; except hee have first seene yt Incomprehensible ffulnes with wch they stand in ye House of theyr ffather Originally? But 2 ly your sweet Word about Courage in our Witnes is ye Savour of precious Oyntment. All yt I have to say is; I humbly desyre, yt ye Voyce of my Spirit may bee alwayes, as ye Voyce of a Trumpet, & yt ye Eternall Spirit may bee ye Breath, wch sounds this Trumpet. I feare making a Trumpet of Brasse for ye house of ye Lord in steade of ye Silver one. I would never bee single in my Testimony, but have it a Musicke in Consort, yt Spirit, & my Spirit witnessing in One. Besides my Musicke now, with wch ye Lord makes Melody to mee, & I to him in my heart, is rather still than Louder, yt of ye Golden Harpe, than of ye Silver Trumpets, fitted for ye Chamber of ye Bridegroome, rather than ye ffields of Battell. I beseech you ye Saints with you in ye Bowells of our Jesus, Love, Live, pray in One Spirit, each wth, each for other, with & for.

Your fellow Lilly of ye Valley
Peter Sterry

ffor Mr Morgan ffloyde my

Septem. 27. 1656. Poast paid.

Honoured ffriend in
Wrexham in
Wales.

72

[Peter Sterry] at Morgan Llwyd, heb ddyddiad

(LLGC 11439D, f. 19)

Honoured, & Beloved in our Lord Jesus,

Wt Joy have I like unto this to stand & heare ye voyce of ye Bridegroome in ye Chambers of ye Spirit of his Spouse? In a long & darke night, wn all things are husht up in ye sleepe of death round about mee, I watch, & waite for ye Morning, & Day-spring of thy ffface, ô my God. This is my Repast, if I see some few streakes of Immortall Light, some Lineaments, some Glymmerings of my Husbands beauety upon ye Top of my owne Spirit. Then my Heart leapes within mee, testifying to it selfe in the Evidence of this Light yt ye Night is farre spent, & ye day is at hand. But if my Jesus, shew mee ye Blessed Dawnings of His Brightnesses in other Spirits, like Scatterings of Light in severall parts of ye Sky; ô then I fall downe upon my Knees, & blesse ye ffather of Lights, & pray him not to mocke his poore Children, but to make good these Manifestations of Christ even at ye doore, & ready to enter in. Sr. ye Lord Jesus makes this Spirituall Communion betweene us very sweet to mee, & precious. My Canaan, my Land of Life, my Lord powres forth thorow mee his rivers of milke & honey with all increases of pleasures, where there is a Neighbouring Channell, as himselfe in your Spirit, so loving, so enlarging it selfe to receive them. As pleasant is it to mee to bee led by your Heaven-breathing Letters into ye Garden of Christ in your Soule, there to feede upon his Spices. I have seene a Glasse wch will make a poore dust looke with large parts & glorious colours: you to looke upon my poore Dust, both Letters & Person, thorow ye Spirit of Christ in your Heart, wch is pleased to shew you ye Reflections of its owne Wisdome, & Glory from them, ô Sr. I am nothing. I know a man in Jesus Christ all Glorious within, & Garments of beaten Gold. But as for this Man in fflesh, its onely portion is of Death, & Crosse of its now-tryumphant Heade. Seriously I beg your prayers for mee, yt ye Heavenly Man, wch is One Spirit with Christ may live, & I dy. Hee is a God to mee already, a Spirit of Revelation in some weake manner from ye Riches of his Grace to his most worthless servant. But hee is not pleased to bee a Mouth, a Spirit of Utterance. I still speake ye language of my Native Countrey with a Strange & Stammering tongue. Sr, Blessed is yt Heart wch feeles ye Lamb as ye Center of ye whole Creation, wch is a Seede bringing forth, bearing up bringing forth Himselfe thorow; all. Blessed are those Eyes, wch see Him, as ye Circle, ye Heade of ye whole Creation, comprehending, crowning, filling, ye whole Spheare of things. They yt so see him, see ye Ladder, & Angells, both in One, both together, Ascending, & Descending upon Him. While wee speake with ye Tongue of Men, or Angells wee can speake ye High Mysterys of Christ, wch are Mysterys even to Angells themselves longing to pry into them, onely in Parables. ffor wt is ye Whole Creation, but a Darke Parable, a shadow, of God, & Christ. Wn wee thinke to speake after ye most Heavenly manner, wee speake but earthly things concerning Heavenly, as our Saviour saith of Himselfe to Nicodemus. The ffleshly Seede will speake Evill of yt wch they know not in the Parable, ye Heavenly Pearle, ye Spirit, & Life, in yt of it, wch they know as bruite beasts, but sensuall, carnall, created Principles, ye outside of fflesh ye ffielde of ye Letter, in wch ye Pearle lyes, they pollute themselves. But one of ye Spirituall Seede there springs up a Light, wch leades them into ye Depths of ye Godheade, & opens to them all Darke Sayings. I blesse our Heade for ye Descent of yt Annoynting upon you my ffellow-Member. I intreate you to let mee know by your Next, wt you meane by our Blessed Saviour distinguisht into ye Wisdome, & ye Word. I have seene Him at ye Right Hand of God, wn Heaven hath bin opened to mee as Hee stands in ye Trinity, yt Originall ffountayne, & Utmost Sea of all Mysterys, all Treasures; 2 as Hee stands in ye Mediatory Kingdome betweene ye ffather & this Creation. 3 as Hee stands at ye Heade of this Creation, being Himselfe ye ffirstborne of every Creature. 4 as Hee takes fflesh of ye Virgin Mary, & stands on Mount Golgotha, by ye Crosse returning thithir, where Hee was at first, & ascending according to ye same degrees, by wch hee descended Sr you are pleased to desyre from mee, according to ye Measure of Christ in mee. 1. Wt yt Philosophy is, wch st. Paul condemnes, Colos: 2 8. Truely, Sr., it is yt Mystery of Satan, wch now workes, to cast a Mist before our Eyes, by setting up Naturall Images, heightned, & inspired by ye God of this world, to spoil us of ye true, & Eternall Image our Lord Jesus. This Creation is a Shadowy Image of God, & of Christ ye Substantiall, Essentiall Image. This Shadowy Image is threefold. I. ye Angelicall. 2. ye Celestiall. 3. ye Elementary. Each of these rightly seene according to its proper Principles, & fforme, is a most pleasant, wonderfull ravishing Image of ye other, & of Christ, At ye beginning these stood in Christ, as in theyr Heade. No one of them, no one Lineament in them was without him. As an Image in ye Apple of ye Eye, so was Christ in every one of them, & in all parts of them. Hee was ye Life, & yt Life was ye Light of Man, ye Light of this whole Shadowy Image, ye Image appearing in ye Light, & this Light holding forth it selfe in yt Image. Wn Sin came, ye Devill, & Adam stept up into this Image, they set up themselves in it, exalt, & rejoyce themselves with it, as ye Rich man cloathed himselfe with Purple, & ffine Linnen, faring deliciously every day; while Jesus Christ is a poorer Lazar, layde wounded, & begging at ye Gate of this rich man. Jesus Christ renewes himselfe, as a

Heavenly Seede, by wch hee holds up this Image, as raised from ye Dead, & set upon a Supernaturall Roote, but so, as yt hee drawes in his owne to live below this Creation, in yt Seede, in wch hee shewes them, as in a Prospect, as a Land affare of, ye Uncreated Glory, ye Crucifying of this Created beauety, by yt, as by ffire, then ye Resurrection of ye Creature, into ye One Spirit with ye Creatour, wn ye Shadowy Image shall bee passed away for ever, & like ye Tabernacle in ye Temple, stand drawne up into ye Heavenly Image itselfe, being made One Spirit, One Life, One Substance with ye Life, & Substance it selfe, yet not losing its Distinctions in Confusion but like innumerable Lillys of a most rich, & delicate variety standing in ye same stalke of an Eternall Unity. Accordingly ye Seed came, Christ hath accomplished this in his owne Person, being by ye Crosse ascended farre above all Heavens & having gathered all things backe into theyr Heade, & ffirst Originall, in Himselfe. Now, Sr, doth our Husband call us with a sweet, & lowde voyce from Heaven, to come up to Him, to set our Eye, & Heart on things wch are there where hee is, to have our Conversation with all things onely in yt Heaven of His Person, to bee in ye Creature, onely as Deade among ye Deade, as in ye Grave, waiting for ye Resurrection from ye Deade in our owne Persons; looking upon yt Life, wch sets up ye Creature againe, & sets up it selfe in, & by ye Creature, as ye Earthly, Sensuall, Devillish Life. Now Sr, in enmity to this are many Antichrists busy at Worke. Some Magicall, wch hold forth ye Naturall Image of God in Angells insteade of Christ, to worke wonders by Some Astrologicall bringing forth in all its Powers, & Beauetys ye Heavenly Image, of Sun, Moone, & Starres, to bee a Booke of Life, & ye Wisdome of God unto us. A third are a Chymicall who Blow ye Dust of from ye Elementary Image, refining it by ffire, & propounding to men ye Philophers stone for ye true Pearle, & ye Rosie-Crucians Castle in ye ffyre for ye Heavenly Hierusalem. A Last sort are those, who magnifie ye Naturall Image of God in Man, His Reason, as ye Light of Life, by wch alone they search ye Creatures, & ye Scriptures, thinking by this Light in these to finde Eternall Life. But thou ô man of God, avoide all these fables of yt olde wise Dame Nature, wch are not according to ye oeconomy or dispensation of God in Christ wch makes voyde his Crosse, & spoyle us of our Brabêum, ye Marke of yt High calling of God in Christ, as hee is risen from ye Deade. Sr, Philosophy is a Bringing forth, & setting up of ye Naturall Image by ye Light of Nature. The Deceit & ye Emptynes lyes here. 1 This Naturall Image at best was but a shadow not intended for our Continuance, or Rest in it, but to point out, & bee drunke up into, ye Essentiall Image. 2 The Shadowy Image hath lost its Heade now, wch is Christ, who stands no more in a Naturall Appearance. Hee is not here, hee is risen. The Light of Nature burnes blew at ye presence of ye Devill in it. Christ being gone up out of it into ye Light of ye Spirit onely, in wch Light Nature stands, as a Candle burning in ye Sun-shine.

The Naturall Image, where it stands not in a Supernaturall, Spirituall Principle, having its Roote in ye Resurrection of Christ from ye Deade, stands in ye Devill, & hath its Roote in Hell. 3 Even there, where ye Naturall Image stands in ye Roote of ye Resurrection from ye Deade, it lyes also under ye Power of ye Death of Christ. The Crosse of Christ is mortifying it, emptying it every day more of yt Vertue, Life, Beauety, wch formerly it seemed to have, & it is to a Saint either ye Moone under his ffeete, ye olde thing passed away, while he wraps himselfe up in ye Heavenly Person of Christ, as his onely Sun, & delights to see all things new round about him, or else it is as his ffeete, wch are Burning in a ffurnace, till they bee quite consumed, & changed to ye Brightnes of his fface, shining life ye Sun Jesus.

(Peter Sterry)

73

W[illiam] Rider a Walter Thimelton at Morgan Llwyd, 1 Chwefror 1652/3

(LLGC 11439D, f. 35)

Much respected in the lord

We are here listening to severall voices, & behoulding various obiects: that wth the lord (as we Judge) layes to our hearts to consider, is to observe what resemblance there is betweene that wch we see & heare wthout us, & that wch is wthin us; that soe we may diserne whether our spirits doe sucke in that wch is presented to our eyes & sounded in our eares; soe as to be one wth that we & heare or see; for we doe Conceive, that the Children of men: doe hear of & see many things wch abide not in or wth them; because, their spirits have not drunke them up: therefore doe we dayly more & more expect the lord: who is that spirit of unsearchable wisdome by his inhabbiting in us: to teach us; of all things in all Conditions, soe far as may concerne us to make a right use of them: we are desirous to sit still & be silently quiet: that the lord may act & bring forth the pleasure of owne will in us: for we are in some measure convinced how ready the fleshly will, is to rebell & raise tumults wthin us, yea & many times, under the pretence of high discoveries, of the cleerest brightnes of the most excelent glory: this proud flesh would set up it selfe above the highest glory & greatest dignities: this is some of the deceit of that great whore, or misticall babilon wch we find wthin us: & allsoe apprehend in others, to cry downe all Carnall outward excelencies, under pretence of being taken up to enioy god, in the purity of his owne being: when alas many times the poore creture would faine set up it selfe, to be lord & soverauigine King: & insteed of trampling flesh under foot, doth endevor to treade downe the lord of glory; we have heard the voices of severall men since we came hither, but truly our spirits can close but wth litle of that wch we have heard: we suppose you have heard of Mr Erberyes talke, by those that can give you a better account than we can, we found yr name mentioned by him in a booke as we conceive, wherein he writes of you as a man goeing into the internall world: we could not relish the booke: though there were many things that may be right in it, for we judge it to consist most of rayling slite speeches against all the churches: but we suppose you have seene the bishop of London ere this time: & the Welsh curate at his heeles (for soe Mr Erberyes booke is intitulated) there is another booke of his come forth, wch is intitulated a Call to the Churches, or a packet of letters to the pastors in Wales; wherein there is inserted a letter of yrs bearing date the 29 of the 4th mth 1652, wth an answer unto it, this booke we doe Conceive to be soberer then the other; but what is it to us to judge men or their bookes, (though we have tender thoughts of Mr Erbery for all this) for the lord shall passe by to try all, the sons of men wth their workes; we have heard that Mr Erbery hath bin Called before a Commitee on the 6th day of the last weeke; concerning some words wch he hath spoken, & we heare that he is Confined to a house, & that he is to come before them againe the 3th day of this weeke; we shall Conclude supposeing you may receive the bookes, & heare of this busines by some who can give a more exact account; we present our dearest Christian respects to Mrs Lloyd; we Commit you, & the Church of god wth you, to the protection of that allmighty unchangable eternall glorious power; who is in & about all his saints, to be their stay & comfort, amidst all the distractions & confusions that are amongst adams children,

& remaine
Your bretheren waiting for the arme of
god to setle things in their right order
Will: Rider
Wal: Thimelton

from our qrs at the george in hollborne neere Kings gate the first day of the 12 mth 1652.

We question not but you will diserne the faults; & Judge favorly of them we would gladly receive a line or two from you, if you have leasure to write to us.

One Mr Tracy a gentleman
of herefordshire, who knowes you
saide, that he hearde some one
say, that you were of the same way.
wth Mr Erbery.

Wm. Rider Walter Thimblt

To our respected friend
in the Lord, Mr Mor
Lloyd preacher of Jesus
in Wrexham.

Fel y gwelir, dyddiwyd y llythyr hwn 1 Chwefror 1653, yn ôl ein trefn ni heddiw. Yn ôl y *Clarke Papers*, ii, 233, gwysiwyd Erbery o flaen Pwyllgor y Gweinidogion Llwm ar 8 Chwefror 1653. Mae'r llythyr hwn yn sôn amdano'n ymddangos o flaen y pwyllgor ar 29 Ionawr, ddydd Gwener, ac ychwanega ei fod i ymddangos eto ar ddydd Mawrth, 2 Chwefror. Dichon felly mai'r olaf o sawl cyfweliad oedd yr un a groniclir yn y *Clarke Papers*. Gweler hefyd y llythyr nesaf.

Yr oedd 'Will Ridor' wedi llofnodi'r llythyr a ysgrifennwyd gan Llwyd ac eraill yn Wrecsam yn 1651 i ohebydd anhysbys (*Gweithiau Morgan Llwyd II*, 247) a cheir 'William Rider' ymhlith llofnodwyr y *Gair Dros Dduw*.

Ceir enw Thimbleton ar yr anerchiad a anfonwyd gan Biwritaniaid Sir Ddinbych i Cromwell (*Gweithiau Morgan Llwyd II*, 263–6). Llofnododd hefyd y *Gair Dros Dduw*.

74
Wal[ter] Thimelton a Will[iam] Rider at Morgan Llwyd, 16 Chwefror 1652/3

(LLGC 11439D, f. 37)

George neere Kings gatte in hole burne
ye 16th 12th *m 52.*

Beloved in the Lord Jesus,

Wee have once more put penn to paper to scrible a few linese to you as to one wch will not make a badd construction of what wee may speake or writte; Knowinge wee are but children that dwell in a darke lande yett; but are in hope to be lede out by the shipard in or laste to you, wee gave you a hinte of proseedinge against Mr Erberey and how that they in authority had appointed the third day of this weeke for the further triall of him, by the Committee for plundered m: wee wente to the place of meetinge, and wee heard a multitude of worde, but wth abundance of confution some speakeinge to this efect, that the Just was Judged by the unjust, many things they laid to his charge about Bap: churches ordenances, and when all was done made nothinge of it, but have appointed another meetinge that day forttnight; what a strange generation are wee in; and how doth the flesh vante it selfe; and will Judge of thinges wherein at length it proves a foole & comes to be jeered and scofed by its owne Brother; this honest man was (and is) moved not by an ordinary Spirrit to speake to all flesh; & this wee muste say (though his maner of speakinge did not relish wth us) the matter was noteable Speakinge plainely, & bouldly, to the corruptions of Parliament, Councell, M: A: and alsorte of Profesors; and also of their Ruen; who were nothinge but changeinge glory; it is probable his accusation; and answer wilbe forth shortly in Prient, and if soe you may Expect to have them; wee were at a meeteinge in blacke friers the laste 2d day wee saw a littell glory of Jehovah there: 4: M: (so called) did P: the next 2d day they have appointed to humble themselves in Fasting & praier wee would be humbled under the mighty hand of god for newes wee have littell the fleet is abroad and what or Lord will doe by them wee are dayly waitinge to heare Surely when Judah is made into abow, and Epharim into an arrow the lord will shute amonge the Sonnes of greece; but as yett the arrow is not fully polished, nor the bow framed and what can wee doe untill then; this wee would begg of or lord that wee may be fitted for him to act by.

There is a thinge called a Councell of officers heare, and seeme to be as a womane in travaile, if they bringe forth a child, wee (if in flesh) shall see its jmage, if but winde it will vanish, & none shall see it, onely heare the woman did travaill; wee would waite on the lord in to regardinge his works and the operations of his hande; wee have sent you 5 pamphletts 3 by a bro: & 2 by Lt. Weld, wee hope you have receaved them; now god himselfe & our Lord J: Ch: fill you wth life amen

Wal. Thimelton
Will. Rider

Yr Brethren waiteinge for the day of full freedom & perfection.

To the respected in the Lord
Mr Morgan Lloyde, Minister
of the church of christ
in Wrexham
these.

75

Wal[ter] Thimelton a W[illiam] R[ider] at Morgan Llwyd, 9 Mawrth 1653/4

(LLGC 11439D, f. 38)

Much Hon.rd (and deare) in or Lord.

Wee have not much to truble you with at this time; all things (as to visible appearance) beinge at reste, though its probable goeinge on in obscurity, Mr C. is heare Called Chaplin to the G. and usually preacheth at Jameses, where wee have heard him, Some Judicious Christians say the mattr of his P. is equall with Mr Erbereys; wee have heard him say some such thinge though in another forme; *Mr P. speaks highly,* thunderinge against all manner of people; he speakes of a higher dispensation then the A: was: for M. G. wee know not how he doth nor what he doth, but wee hear he is one of the Councell of State &c. Strange and Spencer wee have not seene lately, *there is a booke of Lan: Se:* if you have it not lett us know & wee will send it, There *is 2 books comeing fourth* of Bhemans: Mitteria Magnum, & Considerations on Isaiah Stivels booke, it may be a Levelinge Principill may arise out of the dust shortely; then lett nimerod looke to his Kingdom; wee hope the eternall father will bringe us wth Joy amonge you shortely, desireinge the Lord to fill ye heart wth Joy and peace wee remaine

Calverts shopp 9th 1°
M: 1653

Yrs to the uttermost extent of
all or power, in the Lord
and for the Lord,
Wal. Thimelton W.R.

Haggar is (as wee heare) one that houlds and P. generall redemtion accordinge to the letter, and to denieinge the power of or lord.

We have beene wth Mr Erbery
wee finde him loveinge and
sober

To or respected friend
Mr Morgan Lloyd at
Wrexham.
these
p Chester post.

'Mr C. is heare Called Chaplin to the G.' Caplan i'r Cadfridog Oliver Cromwell a olygir. Pwy tybed oedd 'Mr C'? Yr oedd Joseph Caryl (1602–73) wedi ei benodi ar 23 Mehefin 1651, ac mae'n ymddangos iddo roi'r gorau i weithredu yn Rhagfyr 1653 er iddo dderbyn cydnabyddiaeth gan Gyngor y Wladwriaeth ar ôl hynny. Ond prin y gall y cyfeiriad yn y llythyr hwn fod ato ef. Am gaplaniaid Cromwell, gw. Roy Sherwood, *The Court of Oliver Cromwell* (1977), 105–10.

Mae'n bur bosibl mai Vavasor Powell oedd 'Mr P.'

Ystyr 'his P' yw 'his preaching'.

'M. G.' yw Thomas Harrison.

Y ddau lyfr o eiddo 'Bheman' (h.y. Böhme) a oedd ar fin ymddangos oedd *Mysterium Magnum . . . By M. Simmons for H. Blunden* (1654) a gyfieithwyd gan J. Ellistone a John Sparrow, ac *A consideration upon the book of Esaias Stiefel of the Threefold State of Man . . . by John Macock,* 1653.

'Haggar' yn yr ôl-nodyn oedd Henry Haggar, awdur *No King but Jesus . . . For Giles Calvert* (1652) a *The Foundation of the Font . . . For Giles Calvert* (1653).

76

W.T. o Chapellizard at Morgan Llwyd, 5 Hydref 1653

(LLGC 11439D, f. 36)

To Morgan lloyd

Truely Hon.ble in the Eternall father,

The blessed father of life, hath safely brought us to Ireland, where wee are behoulding or Selves in a Strange place, and maners, wee landed heare on the first day about tenn, & the after noone wee went to heare one patience and also to see them breake bread, he spooke about the resurrection at the last day, but I may say according to the light in me, it was a peece of confused art, very out ward and dead, in ye evineing majr Jones began to discourse with us, who is exceeding zealous for the writting on the sands, & Johnes Baptizime of which thinge he first began to Speak, Shewing the danger of neglecting such a Command, and how such obedience did commend us to god, wth many like Sayings; Then Coll Jones enquired whether it were true of the Saints of Wrexham as was reported, for it is reported you have given over praying, breaking bread, & all meetings, &c. you may Judge what maner of Spiritt is amonge them, the day of the Lord is neere, to distory selfe, my heart is boyleing. I cannot writt unmixed language, I pray you lett me heare from you, I purpose if god will to retarne shortly, oh how sweet is to be in a corner groneing amonge the poore Saints. I Salute in the lord yr Companion; Just now this paper came to us, wee are Silent, not Speaking much for words are vaine, I trust the father will keepe us from vanity, and every evill worke, now the god of all grace make you perfect in every good word & worke amen:

Chappellizard 5th 8th mth 53

Yrs in all love
W. T.

'W. T.' oedd Walter Thimbleton
Yn Iwerddon, wrth gwrs, y mae Chapelizod, ar gyffiniau gorllewinol Dulyn.
Nid yw'n eglur pwy oedd y pregethwr 'Patience' na 'majr Jones'.
'Coll Jones' oedd John Jones, Maesygarnedd.

77

Morgan Llwyd at H[enry] Jessey, Gorffennaf 1656

(LLGC 11438D, f. 4)

friend & Brother
H. Jessey
honoured endeared eyed in the watchfullnesse of Christ. Its desired wee may converse mutually together (for this minute of our life) Neglect it not, when God mooves on your part as I hope I shall not do on mine when I shall heare from you in the lord. You sayd here that wee might plead (by Christs righteousnesse) at the very barre of Justice, & yet here you prayed, enter not into iudgment o lord. Both right. But how do you reconcile these, lett mee know. I am not I hope entangled in notions without formes nor in forms below notions, though you may peruse Jac. Behmens threefold life, & especially his booke of Baptisme & lords supper. And if it be putt in you lett mee heare what you learne or observe therefrom.

Humble hearts must soberly trye all things but swallow no poyson. I desire you to speake to John Goodwin for an answere of what I sent him. & I would know how to have converse wth Mr Hartlib.

Send mee one of your storehouses & an yearly thing which they call your Almanack. I shall gladly pay for them.

My wife mentioned to you the apprehendship of some of oure children. If it be putt in your mind, send word.

Yours lines & letters of love have oft refreshed mee, & if you will do so still it will increase that warmth & spirit of love which is the life betweene us in that sweet lord Jesus who is the fathers love (the mystery whereof is knowen in the spirit but unknowen to our flesh).

I am thinking you will have occasion to send word to mee about many things, trueths, soules, churches & revolutions in nations. The time is quicke. A faithfull & loving friend is precious, One that runneth not before nor stayeth behind the lambe of God.

lett me heare (at least) of the receipt of this. Farewell

One wth you is your
fellow branch
Morlloyd
Wrexham. 5m. 56.

Y ddau lyfr o eiddo Böhme y mae Llwyd yn cyfeirio atynt yma oedd *The Third Booke of the Authour being the high and deepe Searching out of the Threefold Life of Man . . . Englished by J. Sparrow* (1650) ac *Of Christ's Testaments, viz:- Baptisme and the Lord's Supper . . . Englished by John Sparrow* (1652)

Am John Goodwin (1594?–1665), Annibynnwr ac Arminydd, gw. *DNB*.

Mae Llwyd yn gofyn am ddau lyfr gan Jessey. Yn 1645 cyhoeddodd *The Scripture Kalendar* ac ymddangosodd bob blwyddyn tan 1664. Ei amcan oedd disodli gwyliau'r saint a'r enwau 'paganaidd' ar y misoedd a dyddiau'r wythnos. Yn 1650 cyhoeddodd *The Store-house of Provision for . . . Cases of Conscience.*

Am Samuel Hartlib (bu farw 1670?), addysgwr, gw. *DNB*.

78

Mor(gan) Lloyd (Llwyd) at Samuel Hartlib, 30? Hydref-Rhagfyr 1652

(Archifau Prifysgol Sheffield, Papurau Hartlib 65/8/1–2)

Wrexham in Denbighshire
1652. 10m. 30d.

Sr

Prouidence hath made you so publique in England that you must expect to heare from strangers whom you neuer saw in the flesh. A friend of mine that lately spake with you gaue mee ground enough to thinke you will please to comunicate the trueth of what I request. I am knowen to some in London that waite for the kingdome of God & the saluation of Israel (whom I shall not now name) but your owne Epistle to that (much to bee considered booke) clauis Apocalyptica hath most emboldened mee so to aime as to meet with trueth from you in the same center (as your Expression there is) & to enioy a reciprocation of loue in the gifts of the spirit betweene the members in whose minds (you say) the walls of Ierusalem should bee built.

your Epistle to my L[ord] St Iohn doth make mee promise my selfe refreshment concerning the new heauen dropping vpon the new earth

They that waite for the bridegroome in these parts would know the trueth of that rumor of the appearing of the signe of the son of man in Germany or Poland in the clouds. And for my part I haue grounds (which for present I shall not trouble you with) to expect that in that region there shall bee shortly an emminent—which the world shall note. If the son of man (who respecteth not persons) will honour you so farre as to make you a teller of such great things (explaining the manner & particular circumstances) [*left margin:*] as all the Prophets & Apostles & saincts in all ages waited for, It will much oblige you in spirit to him who is Alpha & Omega & much engage my heart to you in loue. Sr I would haue foreborne this but that I presume the bearer Mr. H. Iesse is acquainted with you. so I cease but intreating an answeare of so great a matter as that of the appearance of Iesus

Sr I am yours to serue you, waiting for the hope of Israel. Mor. lloyd.

[*65/2B*]

[*top right, another hand:* Mor[gan] Lloyd of Wrexham
about the day of Iudgment]

To the Honoured Mr
Samuel Hartlib
these
present
I pray

Samuel Hartlib (—1670?), yn enedigol o Wlad Pwyl, ymsefydlodd yn Llundain yn 1628, gan ymdroi mewn cylchoedd Piwritanaidd. Gw. *DNB* a Charles Webster, *Samuel Hartlib and the Advancement of Learning* (Caergrawnt, 1970), lle ceir rhagymadrodd rhagorol i'r detholiadau o waith Hartlib.

79

[Morgan Llwyd] at ohebydd dienw, heb ddyddiad

(LLGC 11438D, f. 5)

Deare Brother,

I send this paper for your advice. My wife being weary of 9 l a yeare rent for this house, desired some lands in the countrey. A few friends advised & so we agreed on these few articles inclosed. Now I doubt we shall loose many opportunityes especially in winter if we reside there. And if the landlord after 3 years be rigorous, we Know no house in towne fitts my wife as this wee are in. To Keepe both some would advise for one yeare. What say you? Women (& men also) are apt to thinke another place & condition better than the present. We would live honestly & not turne to earthinesse & loose the relish of heaven, as I feare many, that have taken burdens of clay on their shoulders have done in these dayes. The countrey place is pleasant so it obstruct not better pleasantnesse.

80

[Morgan Llwyd] at gyfaill dienw, Chwefror 1658–9

(LLGC 11438D, f. 1)

12th m, 58

Dear Friend,

You write no Hebrew to mee (as you say you do) nor shall this bee Arabick to you. You writt lately to mee when I was not able to crawle in the streets for many weeks nor go a bow shoot off my bed (I shall not now tell the cause of that bodily weaknesse lest some canot beare it) I say then you writt to mee that it was a venerable thing for mee to come to South Wales, where I would have come (had I beene able) to visitt that my one owne friend, as if my other alien friends had all mett in one. But though you (it seems) & others bee not satisfyed, every one shall have praise of God when all is cleared up. In the while, If any bite behind ones back its seasonable to thinke that our lord is no blind or deafe lord. Hee Knoweth all. Our consciences know a litle, & I doubt, my great old friend Knowes litle of my present condition. for you list to looke on mee through a false glasse. If it were otherwise, you would send mee one line at least of some particular unsoundnesse in my doctrine or books which you call volumes, though they all will not amount to the bulke of an ordinary booke. & so they may be accounted of: And if no particulars be mentioned but generalls (& dolus in universalibus) it may proove Gospell grace to leave off the backbiting in letters to others, or otherwise in discourses to traduce any. I will as willingly recant an error as publikuely as ever I delivered it, if first it bee an errour indeed & so prooved to mee. I could but note your change of Doctrine. One while (the first blessed while to mee & many more, for which I ever praise God & honour you in him) the doctrine of the new birth from phill 2.12. Joh. 3. 3. Another while to Antinomy in your house which relieved sinkers out of Deut 8. And for my changes in opinion.

I lately read a letter of yours to my wife wherein you say. That it was the Devill Himself that you or shee had a hard thought of mee, though (as you write) I was of another temper. But now not hard thoughts only but hard words also seeme very warrantable & lightsome to some. I leave it to him that iudgeth his people mercifully in righteousnesse without partiality.

You order my neighbour to tell mee from you such a thing, & why could you not tell it your selfe in writing, at least in consideration of what I of late (though very sicke) have sent to you. I wish also, hee that saith that I deny or dispute principles, proove not a sclanderer before the true Judge. If your sorrowes have driven out lightnesse, why then do you call mee my Pure etc. If your soule (as you say) were aflicted for mee & mine, you would surely expresse it otherwise then you do, or lately have done to mee. You needed not to have written to mee that you were an alien & yet could pitty. I had cause & a heart also to pitty much more than aliens, though I could not helpe as I would in that offensive matter. I beleeve if you knew all you would be more tender, as once you promised to bee when you had but a hint (in a garden you may remember) many years agoe of my family affaires.

I hope you will (when I am in dust) extend kindnesse out of your aboundance to D D. Hughes son, as I have maintained him here out of my poverty. (The lord) (& possibly you in him) may then pitty mine).

This is a remem. for hereafter I hope in vaine that you would a litle have refreshed my condition. I much want your helpe, you afford it not at all (as I see) I boast not of my love to you. The dissemblers of these dayes exceed in that vanity, & hyperbolically expresse it, which is too much the fashion of that countrey. Fe ddiangodd pawb (ymron) oi calon iw tafodau.

You mention my ankle (where you may remember that your hands (in your care & love) here cutt an issue in the very ioynt (but I thanke my Maker it did not runne) but my ankle is not in & out (as you say) nor my soule tossed about opinions (seing the end of them) though you may possibly take pleasure to iest wth others about mee. I hope my deare late wife hath told you (if you visitted her often) of many of your things, as shee had done mee which I could not creditt from her, nor from any against you my dearest of all men, though I bee nothing & would so bee:

81

Morgan Llwyd at dderbynnydd dienw, heb ddyddiad

(LLGC 11438D, f. 3)

What you have written (Deare and Honoured) hath stirred up in mee more endeared affections to you then I had before, though the expressions are rough hewen, which are all one when they have waight in them. And I hoped I had writt nothing to you but what might effect the same in you. I would rather lye downe in dust & ashes then (in the least) *grieve the Spirit of Jesus* by word writing or practice. The intent of what I writt (I thought plainly) to you (who is much taught in the mysteryes of God, to whom a hint is more plaine, then many words to others) was to offer a brotherly caution in things that concerne the best of saincts in these dawning dayes. You have acted according to your light in Tho. Tilliams & I according to mine in breaking bread at Chester, for 1. I have knowen & examined divers of them & found them seekers of God, not daring to speake against the Godhead of Jesus (whereof I hinted to you what did satisfye mee in that point, when some mens methods were short) 2. There was care that none but the approoved should partake. 3. To him that told mee of some disatisfaction I spake before (I meane T. Rawlinson) at whose carriage wee were here grieved & are desirous to deale further wth him as with a friend. 4. I was very indifferent to that matter untill divers there & some of that society helped to sett it on. Not that I love wranglings in the Darke (which have filled the earth to this day), neither do you yet charge mee that I did write any thing therein, but only that I did doubt your controversyes were carnall. But I say plainly, it was carnall on your part as far as the mixed spiritts (as liquors) came out of you (though you bee in the right as Job was in that one thing) & on his part it was ignorant, hee answered not to questions that touched the root, but for his spirit the lord is Judge thereof. I shall have no time now to coment upon the will pleasure & power you take notice of (which I beleeve you will find to bee the root of this & other matters, most thought of now) but yee are blessed in part & ancient & I am a child & a foole. You have followed God (& I know it also) you have stood long in the gap, & reioyced many, you have beene a stake in the hedge & a flower in the garden also. I may not yet expresse the mixtures of heart in that kind. But I am perswaded you will become dayly as a litle child more & more (which is the present lesson of the teachers of this age) I M. LL. that writes this is as dung & durt but a spirit of trueth & love in this time is speaking to you. & I am distinguishing (& do but begin to discerne) betweene my owne selfe & the spiritt that inhabitteth in mee. My heart beleeveth better things of you & that you have better learnt to untye this knott in yourselfe. And for my manner of expressions in my letter I intended no quibs but love (though it seems mistaken). I hope I shall not mistake that blessed spirit inhabiteth in you which also is knowen in yours, Mor. lloyd.

82

Cyrnol John Jones, Dulyn, at Mrs Lloyd, 24 Mawrth 1652/3

(LLGC 11441D, ff. 1–2)

Most deare Mrs Lloyd

Your lr̃e wch was beyond ordinary measure freindly and Cordiall was by mee very joyfullie received, and with some Reluctancy (as coming from you) parted with in ye way you Commaunded, which may occasion some imperfection in the Account I shall give you of yt matter. As touching the Person you menconed, I can with much Comfort beare this Wittnes and many Christians in this Place can doe the like, that shee is (soe farr as wee Cann iudge of one another) a Cincere humble sober discreete Christian faithfull to her Trust, painefull, and free from Sloth, and in her person every way worthy of a more Comfortable Condition than That wch Report Convayed unto you. But when I consider that there is not a live any Creature yt can affirme with trueth that ever my thought was that way your lre mencōns. It makes mee question by what meanes, and to what end, such a Report should bee raised and brought to you, and I am inclined to beleeve yt God is pleased hereby to minde mee of the temptacōns I am more apt to bee ledd by; to avoyd them. (That is) greate Beauty, greate Birth, greate Riches, to satisfie lust, Pride, and Covetousnese; and (since your kinde lines brought my Thoughts to this subject), I am taught thus to reason, That Grace is not allwayes Concomitant to such Endowments, corrupt Nature prompting such, to imbrace the vices they feede That greate Endowmints, will and iustly may chalenge greate Dowryes, wch in mee would bee injurious to graunte, and thereby deprive my poore boy of that Patrimony or portion wch his precious Mothers Care & industry preserved for him; that the fittest object for my Thoughts should bee an humble meeke spirited Kinde hearted Sainct, that could love my sonne as her owne first borne; and reckon her owne children, as the Children of his Mother, and thereby harmelessly supply the absence of that blessed sainct, as her faithfull Deputy, I Confess this may bee thought but an Utopian fancie, a thing more to bee desired than hoped for; yet it is possible yt such a one may bee found, & if found, it will most probably bee amongst those saincts that have the least portion of the said three outward Endowments, and have some helpe by allyaned Consanguinity or some other extraordinary obligemt to dispose them to see much selfe dingingnesse seeing you have beene pleased, to send mee with such gracious & wholesome advise in a matter of such import. unto mee, I shall desire to knowe what your Thoughts are upon this discourse. I confesse the present Condition I am in is subject to snare, and perhaps more to mee than to another. But hitherto the Lord hath hedged mee about by his preventing and restrayning Graces, a Wise Phisitian will not discouradge his Patient by discoursing the daungerousnesse of his malady before hee hath his plasters and lenitives to apply to the same which you have performed by yor sober Christian advice as to the inner man but the Plaister of ffiggs you have forgotten, ffreindly & Christian negative advisis are wholesome but incompleate.

I desire you not to iudge that my affections are bound up to the way of my present reasonings. I am hithreto thorough mercy free to imbrace what my God by my Christian freinds shall propound in this matter. Present my love to my precious freind Mr Lloyd to whom if you please you may Comunicate these my Extravagancies, and then that this paper may receive a due reward for troubling you, committ to ye ffire.

Deare freind I am exceedinglie obliged to you for yor Kindnesse to and Care of that litle peice of ffamily I have with you, God in his due time will reward you for your Bowells of love and Compassion to ye Motherlesse I find by my deare freind your husbands lres that hee is sometimes inclinable to melancholines, which may much impaire his health if not prevented, And therefore I presume to advise you to improve & act out the sweetnes and placidity of your Nature constantly to dispose him to harmles mirth & Contentiones. This is phisically the best meanes for such distempers And if you give him trace to come to Ireland this Spring, or come yor selfe with him, I am perswaded hee wold bee much refreshed.

I shall not presume to inlarge further but rest
Your most affectionatly to love
and serve your
J Jones

Dublin 24 March *1652*

Am y Cyrnol Philip Jones (1618–74), un o brif gynheiliaid achos Cromwell yng Nghymru, *gw. Bywg.*

83

Cyrnol John Jones, Llundain, at [Mrs Lloyd], 28 Mai 1656

(LLGC 11441D, f. 9)

Deare freind [Mrs Lloyd]

It is upon the minds of some freinds here to indeavor the obtaining of some settlement in a certaine way without Trouble upon our deare freind yor Husband, for the mayntenance of himselfe and ffamily. And therefore I desire you to procure for mee a Coppie of the last settlement upon him, and how long that is in arrears unpaid, all wch you may I conceave have out of Mr Dan lloyds Booke, and likewise some advise upon what or out of what particular it may best issue for the future. Let your letter to mee bee directed to my brother Hen. Jones wth directions to him (If I bee not in Towne) to deliver it to Coll Phill Jones, with whom directions will bee left to move in it, and who is very desireous to bee instrumentall in the doing of yt service for owr Countrey. I shall not trouble you further at present but rest,

Yor most affectionat
freind to serve you

London 28 May 1656 Jo. Jones

84

E. Herbert at [Mrs Morgan Lloyd?] 5 Mawrth 1658/9

(LLGC 11439D, f. 4)

Deare Sister,

Wee were in much heaueines at the receauing of your Letter but wee would not detayne your messenger but dispatch him and wee are takeing advice here as to you and you shall wth what speed may here from us in the meane tyme I pray Lay on your selfe noe burthen but what the Lord Layes one you the tyme of our departure hence the Lord knowes it and it is our duty to wach for it that wee may be found doing his will but I and your sister bege of you that you would not burthen your sperit but that you would bege for power to put your selfe into the Armes of your deare father doeing his will in your thoughts & actiones come Life or death but this power cometh from our deare father for wch and for all other supplyes for you as to your condition I hope wee shalbe sutors wth you to him in whose hands wee Leave you remembering deare Love to you from my selfe and wife and the like to my brother and frind wth you wch is all at prsent but that I am

Your Affectionate brother
E. Herbert.

5, Mr.
58.

Atodiad A
Manion Barddonol a Nodiadau

Pan oedd Thomas E. Ellis yn paratoi ei gyfrol *Gweithiau Morgan Llwyd o Wynedd* (1899), cododd y farddoniaeth o gyfrol fechan yn llaw Morgan Llwyd a oedd i'w chael erbyn hynny yn Llyfrgell Rydd Caerdydd. Y mae'n cyfeirio ati fel Llawysgrif Phillipps 2954. Ond gadawyd amryw fân bethau allan o'r gyfrol brintiedig a chyhoeddodd E. Lewis Evans y rheini yn ei gyfrol, *Morgan Llwyd* (1930). Y mae ef yn cyfeirio at y llawysgrif fel 'Welsh Poems, Vol.2, MS.24'. Erbyn heddiw ei rhif yw Llawysgrif 1.6. Rhoddir isod y darnau hyn wedi eu cywiro oddi wrth y llawysgrif. Cyfeiria'r rhifau ar ddechrau'r darnau at y dalennau yn y llawysgrif.

Doth Satan cry DD's riding
Psalms were short stalework
wring & wrong spirit long
art strong that bears mee

Daw'r uchod ar ddarn bach o bapur rhwng dalennau gwynion a heb ddim byd arall arno.

* * *

8v
As is the fruitfulle apple tree Among the other trees
So Christ excells all other men, By thousands of degrees

under his shaddow we sitt downe in safety with delight
his fruits are sweet unto our tast, his words are good & right.

stay me with flagons of thy loue. wth appls comfort mee
for I am fainty still & weake, and sicke of loue to thee.

My Christ vnto my soule thus spake Rise up & follow mee
The winter rain & storms are gone the summer visitts thee.

The flowers appear, the birds they sing the fig tree doth reioyce
the vines putt foorth their tender grapes. Rise love obey my voice.

As is the pleasant Sharon rose & lillyes of the fields
So is our lord among his Saincts & great refreshing yeelds.

As is the lilly faire & tall compared with the thorne
So is the earth the Churchof Christ that from aboue is borne.

Under my head is his left hand, his right hand me embrace
He cometh skipping over hills to show my soul his face.
The foxes take, the foxes small that spoyle the fruitfull vine
the vines putt forth their tender grapes that yield most pleasant wine.
O lord beloued of my soule turn now about to mee
Come like a roe, come that so my soule may ever be in thee.

(Sylw E. Lewis Evans (*Morgan Llwyd*, 176) ar y rhain yw, 'gadawyd allan o Gân IV ar Ganiad Solomon'.) Ceir Cân IV yn *Gweithiau Morgan Llwyd I*, 10–11. Gall hyn fod, ond y mae arwyddion yn y llawysgrif eu bod yn ddwy gân wahanol. Ynddi hi y mae penillion Cân IV wedi eu rhifo — er bod T. E. Ellis wedi hepgor y rhifau wrth ei hargraffu. Nid yw'r penillion uchod yn y llawysgrif wedi eu rhifo. Mae Cân IV mewn penillion pedair llinell; fel y gwelir, mae'r uchod mewn cwpledi. Ac nid yw'r ddwy gân ar yr un tudalen. Mae Cân IV ar dudalen 8; rhaid ei throi i'r ochr chwith i gael y penillion uchod. Er hynny i gyd, Caniad Solomon yw sylfaen y ddwy. Dilyniant y cyfeiriadau yn Cân IV at Ganiad Solomon yw 1.2; 1.3; 1.4; 5.16; 6.3; 2.16–17 a 4.16. Mae'r penillion uchod yn mydryddu 2.2–6, 10; 2.12, 13; 2.1–2; 2.6; 2.16–17, yn y drefn yma.)

* * *

11–11v

A hymne vpon Esay 53.

The father of light loue and life, his only son sent downe
That arme of God, that root of sts that plant of great renowne.
A man despised in this world A man of sorrows deepe
A man acquainted with our griefs, that doth us loue & keepe.

Our woes & griefs and burdens all, upon himselfe he tooke
our peace to make our sores to heale, he freely undertoke

Our trespasses mett all, on him, to prison he was cast
and being God as well as man, he conquered all at last.

He doth delight to see his seed for whom he travailed sore
who with his father do ascend to raigne for evermore.

His love exceeds, his might is great his kingd. shall remaine
our souls to pitty he hath learnt he'le visitt us againe.

Our hearts lord quicken thee to love & pleasing praise to sing
our sins destroy our souls embrace & rule us as our king.

Bring downe high things the meeke exalt thy face let Sion see
Make way through for thy renowne & ever with us bee.

Proximat
estas. 1648

---

(4) Felly mae mwy (ôs credi'r rhain)
 na chant a thrugain myrddiwn—160000000
or ddayar hon ir drydedd nef
 Ei fawredd ef rhyfeddwn.

ond y mae gair y ffydd yn agos
attat. Rhuf. 10.8.

Vn mil a rhugain a chwechant
 sydd (meddant) o filldiroedd
ir dyn segurllyd sy'n ei fryd
 Amgylchu'r byd ar moroedd.

Tri chant a thrugain a phum dydd
 a chwe awr sydd mewn blwyddyn.
Ter centum, ter viginti cum quinque diebus
sex horas, neque plus integer annus habet.

Cyfieithiad Lladin o'r cwpled blaenorol yw'r ddwy linell olaf.

* * *

52
Ni wŷr (*sic*) ni weles ffordd oedd well
Di ei ymmhell ir siglen

Ceir y llinellau uchod ar ddiwedd Cân XLV yn *Gweithiau Morgan Llwyd I,* 86.
Fe ddylai'r penillion gael eu rhifo yno, ond gan ddechrau gyda'r rhif '2'. Ceir '7' o flaen y cwpled uchod, sy'n dangos mai pennill anorffenedig ydyw. Nid oes pennill rhif '1' yn y gyfres.

* * *

55
The inheritance of the eldest son. The second shall have leave to copy it from the first & the third of the second &&. 4 intrusted to print it, verbatim gair yngair, that my bird sing not your tune but its owne.
One thousand books printed

Hymne booke 12 sheets octauo.
One Great Booke in folio. As the latin Anatomy.
A 1000 leave, 500 sheets, one Rheame.

Catechise of the deepe things.

Ceir y geiriau uchod ochr-yn-ochr â Chân VIII *Gweithiau Morgan Llwyd I,* 18.

Ystyr y gair Groeg cyntaf yw 'agos' a'r ail, 'yr haf', a phosibl mai dyna yw ystyr y ddau air Lladin — os cymerwn mai llithriad am 'aestas', hynny yw, 'haf', yw 'estas'. Ffurf òd yw 'proximat'.)

* * *

18v

A hidden part, a broken heart, a heavenly art I find
A passage steepe a secrett deepe, I loose I weepe I find

Yn y llawysgrif mae'r cwpled hwn yn dod yn union ar ôl y pennill, 'Come wisdome sweet . . .' (*Gweithiau Morgan Llwyd I,* 37). A dyna'r cwbl o'r gân sydd ar y dudalen hon ac y mae'r ddau bennill ar yr un dudalen â'r ddau englyn sydd yn *Gweithiau Morgan Llwyd I,* 32. Ond ceir fersiwn llawn y gân yn y llawysgrif, tudalen 21.

* * *

24v

Gwagair a drygchwant a phruddder a sorriant
In soule in family in Wales & england & ever shall be & therefore

---

Ceir ffurf orffenedig y cwpled hwn yn *Gweithiau Morgan Llwyd I,* 36.

* * *

26v

Yn y llawysgrif teitl Cân XXVI (*Gweithiau Morgan Llwyd I,* 55) yw'r uchod De Charolo Ultimo rege Britt.

(1) O Gant a deugain rhan (medd rhai)
nar haul mae'n llai'r ddayaren
Dwywaith a deugain llai no hon
iw'r lleuad gron yn'r wybren

(2) Tair mil o eitha'r ddayar gron—3000 milldir
sydd i wynebion hollfyd.
or ddayar isod ir haul crwn
Mae Pedwar myrddiwn hefyd—4000000

(3) Mae pedwar vgain myrddiwn da—80000000
or haul i eitha'r wybren
Ir nef oddiyno mae ffordd hir
Un wedd ag ir ddayaren.

Books to be written by M.Ll si vult Dom.
The written sermons copied verbat by Davy in one of the prayr books.
2. Abstract of all serm.
1 Abreviat. history of his life 10 verses in each chapter. this large, 5 mounts, pembrook.
3. of prov. similes
4. of songs, hymnes
5. of the golden ball, tossed dialogu wise
6. a warning piece for the last dayes
The root & top of all
last will & testam.
Gods great oath. As I live hereaft. Turn back to Welsh hanes Cymro

---

Argraffwyd y nodiadau hyn gan E. Lewis Evans yn *Morgan Llwyd,* 4–5; mae'r mân gywiriadau yn dilyn y llawysgrif.

'Davy' oedd David, mab hynaf Llwyd. Bu farw Awst 1678.

Y tri mab arall y cyfeirir atynt oedd Samuel, a fu farw yn 1718, Caleb a oedd ar dir y byw yn 1683, a Joshua, yntau hefyd yn fyw yn 1683. Am fanylion pellach, gw., Gweithiau Morgan Llwyd II, 314–15.

Tebyg mai cyfeiriad at Jeremeia 44.26 yw 'Gods great oath'.

* * *

58

The gospell trueth the liberty the oneness of it too
which once we had, Away doth fly
At length mount Sinai undermines

* * *

59

The church that once on sinai was
came on to sion hill
It went from Christ to Moses glasse
This cup all men do fill.

Y pennill hwn yn unig sydd ar y dudalen hon.

60

The best of saincts have but their time
the strongest churches fall
because their hearts are full of slime
& pride & selfe withall.

The pilotts waite. The ships do sinke
for sinners are therein
Sinai & churches now bethinke
how all may strive for sin.

Dim ond y ddau bennill yma sydd ar y dudalen hon.

* * *

61

The saincts lye low. The trying wind
will tumble many downe
Haue loue in heart & light in mind
else loose the blessed crowne.

64

An verum est dicunt patoribus.
Yee must doe no work for your family, but preach
const. & give yourself to it, &&
Heb. 13.5 I Tim. 6. 5.6. Math. 6
heart made heavy with cares of this world
Wilt thou care for 3 or 3 score years not for
forever for Childr.

(Argraffwyd, ond yn anghyflawn, yn E. Lewis Evans, *Morgan Llwyd,* 182.)

* * *

65v

Pα ywvi ζ e cum mat. pro exigu *nulla* habitatio tam
claus ut mea.
16 Annes vixi in teneb. varijs.
16 postea in lucibus varijs
null: egrot. & nisi in Pot nulluam asthma
but sciat in crux. then in gen. part dead,
& the oyle not melt on it.
Tunc electu vanus misinform Wm.J.DD
null. palt. betweene in
Pec a welsoch chwi Mr Ow yn ebrius mewn tafarn.

Mae mwy o ddefnydd yn y bachgen yma nag a
wyddost ti a minnau

O when shall I
Be gone
a way
depart
go to rest
lye down
fall asleep

escape
go in

be at home
returne
wthdraw

after the Tune of
Psalm 100

ascend
putt to show

73

DD. fill
first Eng B I writt
with serm. notes

1. A booke of speeches (all in Welsh)
2. *A booke of proverbs small*
   MS. patience golden ball. Dialogues.
3. A booke of Questions hard & plaine
   Henwr Plentyn
4. A booke of Hymnes withall.
5. A History of all m. life last will
6. A booke of letters minister to Jes Christ
7. A booke of script. songs & psalms

The root & top of all.

75

The day doth grow, the cocks do crow
new men shall go
Sts rise & go & walke
beasts run away larks loue the day
the stars still may

79

Note this outw. provision & doubt not.
provid. brought thee to bromffield beyond thy thoughts.
provided at llanvair. Then at Monm: then Bristoll.
Portsm. lond. Carlisle. *leave Dec. Cant. Nou.*
de cupidit Trust God. He took childr. from thee. 5.
To lighten thy care that thou mayest run better.
10 argum Math.6
care not for to morrow
Cantic. Nou. de vita fidei
supply all your needs in Xt sth Paul. phil.4

Atodiad B
Cerddi Dienw

Y mae llawysgrif Chirk A4 yn Llyfrgell Genedlaethol Cymru, a ysgrifennwyd gan mwyaf gan ŵr o'r enw John Wynne yn lled fuan wedi 1665, yn cynnwys amryw gerddi o waith Morgan Llwyd a gyhoeddwyd eisoes, a'r cwbl ond un yn ddienw yn y llawysgrif. Y mae'n cynnwys hefyd un gerdd nas cyhoeddwyd o'r blaen sydd ac enw Morgan Llwyd wrthi: fe welir honno uchod ar dudalen 20. Yn ogystal fe geir yn y llawysgrif ddeg cerdd ddienw a all yn hawdd fod yn waith Morgan Llwyd ac fe gynhwysir y rheini yma. Dylid nodi fod yn fersiynau'r llawysgrif hon o'r cerddi a gyhoeddwyd yn barod rai darlleniadau amrywiol diddorol.

A4, 5

Si Christum discis, satis est si caetera nescis
Si Christum nescis, nihil est si caetera discis

1 Cais gadw ffydd bob dydd ar waith
Cei gyssûr maith a chryfder
Ag wedi ymgynfino ar jâu
Cei lawenhau mewn amser

2 Yr un iw yr arglwydd ymhôb gwlad
ai gariad sydd heb dreio
iw fonwes towallt dy holl fron
dy galon agor iddo

3 Dy amser pryn nag ymdrymhâ
a gwilia bob ymffoli
Am Grhist hiraetha ymhob lle
hwn iw/r/ câr gore a feddi

A4, 31

Habbakukes walke hab: 3.17.18.19

1 Although the fig tree blossome not
although the vine bee drye
Although the fieldes yeeld not a jotte
although the oliue lye
2 Although the flocke bee cut off now
although the head bee gone
Yet for all this my soule knowes how
In god to joy alone
3 I will rejoyce in god my strength
and moue away the sighing
My Saviour sweet hee will at length
giue strength vnto my going

4 My feet shall bee as quicke as hindes
and I shall walke on high
Aboue sinne griues grones and windes
all this is verie nigh

A4, 41

1 Cais gadw ffydd bob dydd ar waith
Cei gyssur maith a chryfder
Ag wedi ymgynfino ar jau
Cei lawenhau mewn amser
2 Yn ŷn iw/r/ Arglwydd ymhob gwlad
ai gariad sydd heb dreio
yw fonwes towallt dy holl frôn [*sic*]
Dy galon agor iddo
3 Dy amser pryn nag ymdrymha
a gwilia bob ymffoli
Am Grist hiraetha ym hob lle
hwn iw/r/ câr goreu a feddi.

A4, t. 41
Cyfyng iw porth Paradwys/ nid â iddo ond y cwymwys
Llawer o bob math sy'n ceisio, ag ychydig yn mynd trwyddo

Prin y cedwir y rhai gorau rhag echryslon vphern boeneu
beth wrth hymy [*sic*] a ddaw or amhûr, ple yr ymddengys y pechadur

A4, t 43

1 Thy patience Lord is wounderfull
Thy kindnes verie great
Thou dost us spare, thou hast us heard
when wee did thee intreate

2 Thy anger bussied [*sic*] round about
Thy wrath swept manie away
to us whose sinnes doe much abound
thou giuest a joyfull day

3 Blessed bee Christ our great high Priest
who for our liues did plead
Stood in the gape, turn'd off great wrath
hee liues to intercead

4 In Christ, God lou'd us in our blood
Through Christ hee doth us call
ffrom Christ hee often sent us light
By Christ hee woo=s vs all

5 When wee were scattered far and neere
our god went with us still
hee sham'd our foes and brought us backe
to prayse his loue and will

6 Now for his patience loue and care
for all his kindnes free
ffor his great wounders in our Land
ô lett us thankefull bee

7 ffor mercies formerly receaved
for treasures yett in store
lett us with all sainctes blesse and blesse
and blesse evermore

8 Yett who can give him as he ought
all his deserved prayse
or comprehend his glorious Loue
his wise and wondrous wayse

9 Grant us o lord to liue in loue
and trueth & voyed of blame
o make us such as wee should bee
a people for thy ñame

10 Thou wilt us with thy counsell gu[ide]
and rule us with thy word
and soe receive us to thy selfe
to glory with our Lord

A4, 47–8

1 Sing vnto the lord withall yor hearts
with reverence, with praise
o lett our soules melodiously
his name exalt and prayse

2 How glorious art thou in thy selfe
abounding still in grace
Thy councells who can comprehende
or who thy steps can trace

3 How faithfull to thy selfe and saincts
how excellently wise
how dreadfull to thy stubborne [foes]
that durst ag[st] thee rise

4 To them thou giuest blood to drinke
whereof they worthy bee
for they haue sucked the hearts blood
of such as loued thee

5 The teares and bloode of all thy saincts
thou dost in bottles lay
ever before thy Jealous eye
ag[st] the wrathfull day

6 Thy saincts thou makest as lions stout
as vnicorns they bee
ô happie Israel in thy kinge
he—l not relinquish thee

[t.48] [7] Thy voyce o lord a thunder is
thy wheeles a fiery flame
viols of wrath are in thy handes
how dreadfull is thy name

8 Who shall not feare this Lord of might
A lion fierce and stout
Whose judgm[t]s now are manifest
whose hand is stretched out

9 Before whom Islands are as dust
what men or might can stand
before thy wrathfull burning fire
or who can stay thy hand

10 Thy iron rod The sickle sharpe
The wine presse of thy wrath
who can indure or yett find out
what force thy anger hath

11 Thine arrowes are made drunke with blood
Stronge is thy arme and bow
Thy swords [*sic*] devoures the flesh of men
That sinners may thee Know.

A4, 48

Cei gystudd beynydd drwy boenau/n dy byd
o'r bedydd hyd angau
ond yn hyf cais ymgryfhau
yn helw Christ yn olau

A4, 49

1 The best men haue but their time
The strongest churches fall
because theire hearts are full of slime
and pride and selfe with all

2 The pilots waite the ships doe sincke
ffor sinners are therein
Sinai and churches now bethincke
how all may striue for sinne

3 O saincts lye low the tryinge winde
will tumble manie downe
haue loue in heart, and loue in minde
so gaine the blessed Crowne

4 When I am gone out of this life
I wishe yor striffe may dye with mee
but this I know it will not bee soe
in trueth you are not fully I see

A4, 49

Let all the world forsake poore mee
I never shall forsaken bee
Let friends and foes withdraw away
I shall haue comfort in Christ day
The day doth grow, the cockes do crow
now rise and goe and walke in light
Beasts runne awy, Larkes loue the day
now come away to Salem bright

A4, 49

The Turke and pope are out of hope
their plotts and scope are kild with dearth
The day is neare that costs them deare
and burnes them cleare out of the earth.

Mynegai

Abertawe 90, 125
Aylesford 36–7

Baker, Elizabeth 133
Baker, Thomas 133
Bangor-is-coed 152
Baxter, Richard 98–105
Bayly, Lewis 26
Biwmares 106, 163
Böhme, Jakob 99–100, 165–6, 168, 186–7, 189
Bowen, Rein 90
Brookman, George 95
Broughton, *Syr* Edward 148
Browne, John 78–9
Brynffynon 121–2
Burrough, Edward 121–2
Butler, James 106–7

Caer 47–52
Caerwrangon 30, 130
Caryll, Joseph 34–5, 187
Catherine ferch Edward 145
Chute, Chaloner 123
Clynnog 106
Courtney, Hugh 106, 164–5
Cradoc, Walter 56, 78–9, 106–7, 125, 155–6, 166
Crees, William 126–7
Cromwell, Oliver 30, 38, 53–7, 69, 123, 130, 147, 156, 161, 166, 183, 187, 199

Davies, *Dr* John, *Mallwyd* 26
Day, Cornet 78–9
Deddf y Taenu 46
Dell, William 164–5
Dent, Arthur 26

Edeyrnion 92
Ellis, Andrew 151–2, 172
Erbery, William 108–20, 161–2, 165, 181–2
Eyton, Kenrick 122
Eyton, Philip 121–2

Fairfax, *Y Cadfridog* Thomas 36–7

Glyn, William, *Lleuar* 106
Glynn, John 34
Goodwin, John 127–8, 189–90
Gwersyllt 125

Haggar, Henry 186–7
Harrison, *Major-General* Thomas 153–4, 166, 186–7

Hartlib, Samuel 189–92
Henry, Philip 46, 147, 152
Herbert, E. 201
Herbert, Henry 34
Herbert, William 84–5
Holland, Robert 26
Holt 125
Hubberthome, Richard 121–2
Hughes, Ellis 140
Hughes, Robert 123
Hughes, Samuel 124–5
Hughes, Stephen 26

Inchiquin, *Iarll a Barwn* 106–7
Ireton, Henry 156–7

Jessey, Henry 126–8, 189–91
Jewel, John 26
John ap John 145
Jones, Esther 140–3
Jones, Henry 129, 200
Jones, *Cyrnol* John, *Maesygarnedd* 30, 106–7, 129, 131–40, 188, 198–200
Jones, *Cyrnol* Philip 198–200
Jones, Samuel 92

Kenrick, Edward John 124–5
Kynaston, Roger 162

Lambert, *Major-General* John 155–6
Lilburne, John 106–7, 155–6
Lloyd, Daniel 29–30, 129–30, 160, 200
Lloyd, *yr Esgob* William 147
Long, *Syr* Lislebone 123

Llandegla 92
Llanfaches 128
Llanwyddelan 162
Llwyd, Anne 198–201
Llwyd, David 207
Llwyd, Morgan *passim*
Llwyd, Robert 26
Llwydiarth 46

Mackworth, Humphrey 133
Maidstone, brwydr 36–7
Marshall, Stephen 34–5
Meredith, John 78–9, 145
Mostyn, Ambrose 34–5, 45–6, 124–5, 148
Myddelton, *Syr* Thomas 34, 125, 128

Nicholls, Thomas 46

O'Brien, Murrough 106–7

O'Neill, *Syr* Phelim 137

Ormonde, *Iarll a Dug* 106–7
Overton, Robert 123
Owen, Robert 135

Parke, James 144–5
Parsons, Robert 26
Penington, Isaac 164–5
Powell, Vavasor 26, 35, 45–6, 56, 65–6, 78–9, 106, 125, 132–3, 135, 146–8, 151, 155–6, 159, 166, 186–7
Prichard, Benjamin 91–2
'Pride's Purge' 46
Pritchard, Hugh 78–9, 91–2, 129–30, 149–60, 166
Prys, Edmwnd 14
Pwyllgor y Gweinidogion Llwm 35, 182

Richards, Benjamin 91–2
Rider, William 181–7
Robert, John 124
Roberts, John 78–9
Roberts, Richard 78–9
Roger ap John 145
Rogers, Phillip 161–5

Salmau Cân 14
Saltonstall, Hester 128
Saltonstall, Richard 127–8
Sixsmith, Bryan 145
Sontley, Robert 129–30
Sontley, Roger 129–30
Stalham, John 121–2
Sterry, Peter 100, 166–80
Sympson, John 78–9

Taylor, Edward 166
Thelwall, Simon 34–5
Theobald, Thomas 126–7
Thimbleton, Walter 91, 181–8
Thomas, Howell 91–2
Thomas, Oliver 26
Trevor, *Syr* John 34
Twistleton, George 106
Tyrone, *Iarll* 137

Vane, *Syr* Henry 99–100
Vaughan, Edward 45–6
Vaughan, Henry 156
Vaughan, Rice 155–6
Vaughan, *Syr* Robert 46
Vaughan, Rowland 26
Venner, Thomas 147

Webster, John 164–5
Williams, John 45–6, 146–7
Williams, Philip 125
Wittell, John 52
Wrecsam 30, 122, 125, 130, 143–5